GLOBAL
SHAKEOUT

GLOBAL SHAKEOUT

WORLD MARKET COMPETITION –
THE CHALLENGES FOR
BUSINESS AND GOVERNMENT

LOUIS TURNER
&
MICHAEL HODGES

CENTURY
BUSINESS

Copyright © Louis Turner & Michael Hodges 1992

First published in 1992 in Great Britain by
Century Business
An imprint of Random House UK Limited
20 Vauxhall Bridge Road, London SW1V 2SA

Random House Australia (Pty) Limited
20 Alfred Street, Milsons Point, Sydney
New South Wales 2061, Australia

Random House New Zealand Limited
18 Poland Road, Glenfield
Auckland 10, New Zealand

Random House South Africa (Pty) Limited
PO Box 337, Bergvlei, South Africa

Set in 10½pt Garamond, by Deltatype Ltd, Ellesmere Port

Printed and bound in Great Britain by
Mackays of Chatham PLC, Chatham, Kent

British Library Cataloguing in Publication Data
A catalogue record for this book is available from
the British Library

ISBN 0–09–174809–7

Companies, institutions and other organizations wishing to make
bulk purchases of this title or any other Century Business
publication should contact:

Direct Sales Manager
Century Business
Random House
20 Vauxhall Bridge Road
London SW1V 2SA
Fax: 071–828 6681

Contents

_____

Acknowledgements

The old cliché about the merits of a book being due to many, and its faults to the authors alone, has never been more apt than in the case of this enterprise. Our book is the product of over twenty years of discussion and debate between us since we first met in the library of the Royal Institute of International Affairs in 1970, when multinational corporations were little understood and widely mistrusted. Since that time we have written, singly and jointly, several books and reports about the relations between governments and international business – though none of them with such an ambitious scope.

A succession of very bright postgraduate students from many countries in our course 'International Business in the International System' at the London School of Economics has forced us to re-examine our ideas continuously in order to make some sense of the rapid globalization of business competition. Such a demanding clientele has mercifully prevented us from suffering brain-death in middle age and we thank them for it.

We also owe a debt to colleagues at our respective institutions, for their ideas that we have shamelessly purloined and their tolerance of distracted authors, red-eyed from nocturnal word processing and pursuit of the half-remembered fact. Louis Turner will now be able to look his cheerful but overworked colleagues in the Conference Unit at Chatham House straight in the eye again, while students in International Relations at LSE may find their essays get speedier attention from Michael Hodges until he finds another excuse.

Less generic thanks are due to Amy Frizell, Owen Sloman, Amy Charles and Gyongi Patocskai who were of immense help with our research, and to Judith van Walsum who not only researched but also drew up most of the tables and charts in this book with great dispatch and unflagging cheerfulness.

The book would not have appeared as quickly as it has done without the indispensible assistance of our agent Michael Sissons, whose sixth sense about when to spur authors on and when to leave them alone continues to amaze us. He also takes credit for bringing us to Martin Liu and Elizabeth Hennessy of Century Business, who have been endlessly helpful and awesomely efficient in transforming our words into this book. Our thanks to all three, and their colleagues.

Finally, we want to thank our wives (our favourite pair of Jeans) for not only tolerating our anti-social behaviour but also providing encouragement and support through many lost weekends and evenings. This book is dedicated to them.

1

GLOBAL SHAKEOUT: THE SUPER-COMPETITIVE ERA

THE WORLD OF Big Macs, Sony Walkmans, Teenage Mutant Ninja Turtles and Marlboro cigarettes may not seem worthy of serious analysis. Surely these are ephemeral products? They may amuse tomorrow's cultural historians, but do they really need to concern us today?

Admittedly, on the surface, they indicate that we have entered an age in which products compete on a world stage – an age in which the tastes of consumers in Japan, North America and Europe increasingly converge. However, it is easy to claim that this world is best left to companies such as Sony, Philip Morris and Unilever. The competition between them may seem of little import to the rest of us.

However, such products are the symbols of a new world of 'super-competition' – in which companies and national economies compete between continents, and in which technology challenges the very way that executives and politicians do business. The products of this super-competitive world may seem trivial, but in fact they reflect forces which influence us all, as consumers, wage-earners and citizens. Technological change (and in particular the shrinking of the globe through the increased speed and diminishing cost of international transportation, telecommunications and data processing) has created world markets that override national frontiers with increasing ease. Faced with demands from their populations for sustained economic growth and access to a wider choice of the latest goods and services, national governments have sought to tap into the networks of international business, even if this reduces their control over their national economies.

Super-competition may well produce a world which will be a richer and happier place. However, it also challenges our certainties. To enjoy the benefits of the global market-place, we will all – wherever we come from – be faced with a series of psycho-economic challenges.

Whatever the material benefits from global super-competition, they will be gained at the expense of long-established companies going bust, the passing of national symbols into foreign hands and the dilution of national cultures within a mongrel culture, which increasingly rests on the near universal acceptance of English as the language of commerce and a widespread admiration of American popular culture by the world's youth.

Super-competition is thus inaugurating an era of Global Shakeout, which will see the demise of all but the strongest corporations. In a number of key industries – airlines, telecommunications, computers, car manufacturing, among others – we will enter the twenty-first century with less than a dozen companies in dominant positions. These global companies will reign at the expense of weaker national or regional competitors, who will get brutally shaken out of the world system in the coming decade. There will still be a place for small and medium-sized companies, able to adapt quickly, to adjust to local or niche markets, but increasingly the largest firms will be those with a global presence, strong brand identification and heavy investment in future-oriented research and development.

For the others, hitherto reliant on regional or national markets sheltered from the winds of global competition, the message is: 'You can run, but you can't hide.'

The reason we talk of 'super-competition' is because the world is faced with an intensity of competition which is completely unprecedented. The globalization of competition is forcing companies all round the world to reassess their strategies and restructure their operations. Citicorp has modified its ambition to be a full-service bank worldwide by withdrawing from certain financial sectors and consolidating some of its overseas offices; Philips has withdrawn from the large home appliance sector; Federal Express has abandoned its attempt to establish an intra-European delivery network. At the plant level, company after company is having to make drastic employment cutbacks. Today, we are seeing cases where companies even rid themselves of 100,000 employees, as British Steel was forced to do during the 1980s. Even IBM, which long prided itself on never making an employee redundant, has had to resort to personnel reduction policies that come very close to enforced layoffs.

At the level of company ownership, trans-national solutions are increasingly being found. Japanese companies, having initially concentrated on 'transplants' (that is overseas plants primarily replicating Japanese-based operations) have moved into an era of corporate acquisitions, of which Sony's acquisition of CBS and Matsushita's of MCA are the most visible. In Europe the British (who have long been aggressive corporate raiders) are being joined by the French and other continental Europeans who are starting to flex their muscles by investing in other European companies.

Within certain industries such as airlines, financial services, telecommunications, automobiles and defence industries the global shakeout is taking place on a global basis. Whatever their nationality, the companies concerned now accept that a purely national strategy is no longer defensible in the super-competitive world. The talk is of 'strategic alliances', which increasingly straddle continents, bringing together combinations of European, Japanese or American companies in alliances which will have varying fortunes, but which will, in many cases, lead to permanent merging of corporate identities.

At a deeper level, countries (even continents) are having to learn that they cannot do everything. The UK has been the first major industrial power to accept that it does not have a single entirely British-owned company in the automotive sector, while it has virtually accepted the same position in computing. On a wider front, the Europeans are desperately resisting the possibility that the whole continent may be left without a viable semiconductor, computer or consumer electronics industry. In each case, Europe is down to at most two serious potential players in the world economy. In no case is it certain that these players will last the course against the might of Japan.

Some governments are actually increasing the pressures for global shakeouts by conscious decisions to liberalize or deregulate hitherto protected sectors such as financial services, airlines or telecommunications. Led by the Americans, with the British closely behind, such governments have become convinced that their economies will gain competitive advantage if they take the lead in such liberalization. The gain will come partly from the benefits offered to consumers: partly from the increased competitiveness which will result from being forced into global competition relatively faster than competitors in other nations.

Super-competition not only involves products, brands and firms. It is also a contest between views of the world and frameworks for organizing economic life. The sudden collapse of communism was one product of such competition. But within the victorious capitalist camp there still remains a considerable diversity of approaches.

The Anglo-Americans have a strong belief in the virtues of market discipline imposed by reliance on equity financing, and find governmental intervention suspect (this approach was particularly strong in the 1980s, when the Thatcher-Reagan revolution was at its peak). The Japanese believe that competition should be tempered by the need to develop consensus and have certainly believed in the past that it should be guided by targeted governmental intervention. The Germans profess a faith in the 'Social Market' whereby managers and the workforce are given much stronger protection against the ravages of unrestricted competition than is true of the more financially-oriented Anglo-Americans, and engage in an ongoing dialogue with government aimed at promoting efficiency and competitiveness.

Then, in the Third World and the former Soviet bloc, there is a spectrum of views ranging from the Chinese who are still trying to reconcile socialism with market forces, to the ardent professional free-market economists who are currently driving policy in a surprising number of countries – including such important economies as Mexico and Russia.

Up to now, these differences in industrial culture could be preserved because competitive pressures between continents were weak. Today, though, the pace and the intensity of global competition is such that there is no hiding place if the wrong policies are adopted (or the right ones are applied too slowly). Just as failures in product development are punished almost instantaneously, so are policy failures at the national level. Those policy approaches which fail to react adequately and promptly to global competition will be shaken out of the system, just as permanently as communism was shaken out in the late 1980s.

The Global Shakeout will thus not just affect products and companies. It will also affect industrial cultures and policy approaches which are badly suited to today's competitive world. The Global Shakeout will be increasingly unrelenting.

THE TWIN REVOLUTIONS

There are two prime forces at work.

Most obviously there was the political revolution of the 1980s which included both the triumph of capitalism over the communist system and, within capitalism, the Thatcher-Reagan revolution with its major shift towards an unquestioning acceptance of the virtues of the free-market economy. A new emphasis on privatization and deregulation of hitherto-regulated industries such as telecommunications, aerospace and much of financial services injected a major competitive thrust into the world economy. If one adds developments in Europe (the whole '1992' phenomenon) and a major lurch toward free-market approaches in key Third World countries, it is clear that the world economy entered the 1990s massively more open to global competition than it had been ten years earlier.

Beneath these important ideological shifts, though, there is a deeper, more fundamental revolution at work: the electronic revolution which has been gathering pace since the 1950s. The miniaturization and cheapening of electronic components has had an impact right across the industrial spectrum – particularly in the speeding of information flows.

Ultimately, the world of super-competition is driven by this electronic revolution. On the one hand, this has resulted in developments such as the emergence of 24-hour financial markets, in which events in Tokyo, Wall Street, London and Chicago instantaneously react with each other. In a world of increasingly rapid information flows, significant competitive breakthroughs in one country will almost without fail be replicated everywhere else in world markets over the course of some three to four years. This is a speed of competitive reaction unparalleled in economic history.

At the same time, this electronic revolution is adding to the intensity of the Global Shakeout, because companies are discovering how to use electronics to miniaturize products, to build flexibility into production

4

lines, to increase quality and to speed product development. As boundaries between many industrial sectors become blurred (say, between computers and telecommunications) so the varieties of ways in which electronics can help companies improve their competitiveness increase. The end result of this technological ferment is that the pace of technological change is quickening, while the effort needed to remain at the forefront is intensifying. In these circumstances, innovative companies need world markets to reward them for their efforts. They thus increasingly challenge technologically sleepy competitors wherever they are found. The Shakeout gathers pace.

This new world of near instantaneous global competition is starting to produce its own fossil record of companies which failed to stand the pace. In the consumer electronics sector for instance, both the American and the West European industries have come close to extinction. Once proud names such as Admiral, Magnavox, Philco, GTE-Sylvania, Warwick, Zenith, RCA, Grundig, Thorn-EMI, AEG-Telefunken, Decca and Rank have all lost their leadership positions – several of them losing their independence, others going bust and still others withdrawing from the sector altogether. Effectively only the Dutch giant, Philips, and the French company, Thomson, remain to compete with the Japanese. Japanese latecomers such as Sony, Matsushita, Toshiba and Hitachi have virtually swept the world before them in a 20-year campaign of nearly continuous success. What has happened in consumer electronics has to a lesser extent been paralleled in industries such as automobiles, semiconductors and machine tools. The speed with which Japanese competition has emerged, and the competitive havoc it has wrought, are unprecedented in economic history.

SUPER-COMPETITION: THE WIDER CHALLENGES

We are thus dealing with intensification of world competition. On one level, this competition works in the way that Japanese consumer electronic companies have smothered most of their world-wide competitors. On another level, it manifests itself through developments like the rolling, global panics which periodically sweep world financial markets. On an apparently more trivial level, this is also the world of global fads such as Teenage Mutant Ninja Turtles which, though masterminded from the USA (where the comic strip characters were developed), were popularized by two feature films produced in the UK and promoted toys supplied by a Hong Kong company made in mainland Chinese factories. What are the wider implications?

First, very few industries are now exempt from such competition. We are not likely to see a knock-down competitive global battle between, say, European, American and Japanese cement producers, since there's not much technology involved and transport economics do not encourage long-distance competition. On the other hand, whether the competition comes from Japan, leading Third World countries such as South Korea or Singapore, or from elsewhere in the industrialized world, it is increasingly with companies beyond one's immediate national boundaries. Competition is no longer something which occurs within single nations.

Global Shakeout is now taking place across whole continents. In the automotive industry, for example, it is no longer possible to build up 'national champions' as a strategy for improving national competitiveness. Admittedly there is over-capacity in the world automotive industry, but in the age of super-competition the cutbacks will have to be made across whole continents, and not just within single nations.

Second, no country in the world is immune from global competition. During the 1980s, it was the turn of the hitherto unchallenged industrial super-power, the USA, to discover this – and it has been a thoroughly unpleasant discovery. To the Europeans who experienced the wave of American multinational investment in the 1950s and the 1960s which triggered the famous book by Jean-Jacques Servan-Schreiber, *Le Défi Américain*, there has been a degree of wry satisfaction in watching how ungraciously the Americans have responded to having the tables turned on them. However, the virulence of some of the 'Japan-bashing' which has taken place in the USA (including the literal bashing of Japanese cars by unemployed car workers in the Midwest and the smashing of a Toshiba radio on the steps of the Capitol in Washington) can only be explained in terms of the psychic shock triggered by the unexpected speed of America's comparative industrial decline.

Although the current beneficiary of most of these developments, not even Japan is impervious to global pressures – though signs of Japanese vulnerability did not show up significantly until the early 1990s. Interestingly, the financial system which was so effective in financing the country's post-1945 recovery has self-destructed. The cosy, club-like world of Tokyo property and financial markets has just not proved effective in the 1990s. As world financial markets were liberalized during the previous decades, Tokyo was forced to go along as well. This triggered a speculative boom which, when it collapsed in early 1990, could no longer be handled by traditional Japanese methods.

In addition, Japanese companies are slowly discovering that many of the management practices which helped produce the post-1945 boom are no longer adequate now that they have caught up with the West, and are having to respond to competitive changes ever faster. In particular, lifetime employment practices and promotion by seniority are ineffective when the success or failure of key overseas investment depends critically on the personality of top appointments. When pace of response did not matter as much, the collegial Japanese system could work, but there are now real questions as to whether there is a need to move to a system which is less democratic and relies more on appointments made on talent.

All countries are experiencing challenges to the autonomy of the nation. When considering a new plant, a global company can often choose between locations on a continental scale. This means they can choose between nations, which must therefore compete on the kind of investment climate which is on offer.

Part of the challenge to the nation state is ideological. When companies have this freedom of choice, they will steer away from countries with anti-business ambitions. High taxation rates or a tendency toward nationalization or heavy regulation will frighten off the global company, which will arbitrage business environments as readily as it does interest rates or foreign exchange. In the Global Shakeout, there will be a bias against relatively left-wing governments.

The challenge of the super-competitive world is also cultural. At the forefront of the global challengers are firms like Coca-Cola and McDonalds which embody something more than just global competition. They are, also, offering archetypal American culture, and can be seen as part of what one might call the Californianization of the world. It is not just that American companies push this culture as they go overseas, but that non-American competitors look to the USA as a model of how life-styles and, even, political developments (particularly on the environment) may evolve.

Although competition is becoming increasing global, and liberalization has been embraced by most governments as a means of promoting the welfare of their citizens, the world is also becoming a more complex and demanding place in which to do business. The emerging global agenda contains a number of new challenges to which companies must respond. A prime example is the movement to protect the environment, which places new pressures and constraints on international business. These pressures will grow as politicians grapple with the problems of climate change and other less catastrophic environmental issues. At the level of the individual company, the vulnerability to hostile global publicity campaigns is ever-growing. From the backlash against ITT for its attempted malign involvement in Chilean politics in the late 1960s, through world reaction to the disastrous explosion at Union Carbide's Bhopal plant and Exxon's Alaskan oil-spill, to the global publicity accorded Toshiba's evasion of strategic export controls when selling to the Soviet defence effort, it has become clear that hostility towards companies caught in such events is growing in intensity as each decade goes by. A world of near-perfect information may make global strategies easier to plan, but this transparent world can be a double-edged sword in terms of hostile publicity.

At the cultural level, changes are also afoot. An increasing number of global companies use English as their working managerial language; this challenges nations with proud linguistic traditions like France or Japan at a deeper level than mere product competition. Asea-Brown Boveri (ABB), the Swedish-Swiss electrical engineering multinational noted for its adaptability to local business environments, conducts all its high-level discussions in English. As the Global Shakeout knocks out each national champion, attempts to maintain distinctive national cultures are subject to a series of defeats.

During the heyday of the Reagan-Thatcher revolution in the 1980s, it became fashionable to argue that a distinctive 'Anglo-American' (preferred to the implicitly racist 'Anglo-Saxon') business culture was moving to the fore. We argue in this book that it is unclear whether one model will end up dominant within capitalism, but there can be no doubt that some homogenization of industrial cultures is occurring. Not all of this will be in the direction of Darwinian market capitalism, red in tooth and claw; markets may now increasingly ignore frontiers but they abhor disorder. The liberalization and globalization of markets will therefore be accompanied by convergence of national systems of market regulation and – in some cases – the emergence of limited but global regulatory arrangements. This is particularly noticeable in areas of financial market regulation, where countries such as Switzerland have been forced to modify their adherence to banking secrecy under pressure from other governments concerned about the abuse of such confidentiality. Ironically, it was in Basel in Switzerland, home of the Bank for International Settlements, that an agreement was signed in 1988 to establish minimum international requirements for bank capital reserves – an essential stage in international regulation of banks. Pressures will grow from countries which take regulatory issues more seriously. In a world of mobile investments, governments which take regulation as seriously as the USA does cannot allow countries like Switzerland to maintain unregulated corporate bolt-holes. The pressures on small countries to conform to the emerging global norms will be severe.

The creation of regional economic blocs will intensify cross-border competition – not only the European Community's single market programme which will facilitate competition across Europe, but also the extension of the Canada-US North American Free Trade Area to embrace Mexico and the deepening ties between Japan and the industrializing economies of the Pacific Rim. These regional groupings will exert a magnetic attraction for neighbouring states, as evidenced by the lengthening queue of states seeking to join the EC. The gradual re-emergence of the former Soviet republics and the countries of Eastern Europe into the global economy is a further indication that economic isolation is no longer an option – and that adaption to the chill wind of international competition is a prerequisite.

In this new world, no country can stand on one side. Competition will push progress whether a country wants to take part or not. To stand on one side for the sake of national autonomy will be in almost all cases to fall behind the global competition. Autarchic policies are unlikely to prove effective.

At the societal level, it is still difficult to demonstrate what ultimate constraints are imposed by this new era of competition. Certainly in the past one could point to countries like Argentina and Uruguay which, though once among the richest in the world, threw it all away by following policies which paid too little attention to international competitive realities. The economic backwardness of the Soviet and East European economies are further examples of the perils of economic isolation: Czechoslovakia was in 1939 among the most productive countries in Europe. Forty years of central planning has undoubtedly taken its toll.

What is less clear at the moment is the degree of freedom which today's advanced industrial countries have in coming to terms with this new world. Some countries such as the UK have come as close as can be to running non-nationalist economic policies, where a British company with a weak management is of less attraction than the same company under strong foreign (even Japanese) management. Others are still hesitant about going such a radical route. The jury will remain out for a while about which is the best strategy.

One potential model for survival (the Marxist one) has clearly been demonstrated as a model for extinction. What has yet to be demonstrated is whether any of the East European and Soviet economies are going to be able to evolve in any way which gives them a non-dependent role in the next two or three decades.

The question for the rest of us is how deeply our societies will have to evolve to guarantee us survival among the world's leading economies. It goes without saying that all companies within the industrialized world will have to develop increasingly flexible and globally focused strategies if they are to survive as independent entities. Some will find defensible niches in this global economy. Some will seek alliances to guarantee survival, even though most will inevitably be short-run affairs. What is certain is that fewer and fewer companies will be able to sustain a strategy based on a single national economy. For most sizeable companies, such a strategy will be a one-way ticket to the fossil beds.

We also have to examine how societies as a whole will evolve in the super-competitive world. Will governments feel obliged to support their companies with forms of industrial policy? Does national survival at the global level require not just an undemanding fiscal policy, but modifications to labour relations and educational policies designed to upgrade the attractiveness of the country's labour force?

And what is the future for legislation and regulation designed to control corporate behaviour? In whatever future we can imagine, governments are not going to fade away, even though global companies will play increasingly sophisticated games to avoid control and regulation. How will national governments respond to this global challenge? Will forms of international regulation emerge to supplement the national regulations which companies should be able to avoid? . . . and if such international regulation does come about, whose regulatory culture will be dominant? Observers are already talking glibly about the 'triumph of capitalism' or 'victory of the Anglo-Saxon regulatory culture'. Does it make sense to speculate along these lines? Or will international regulation evolve in unexpected ways to respond to the new challenges thrown up by global competition?

The Global Shakeout will not necessarily result in a bland homogenized global market. Distinctive differences will remain – between continents and within them – but the forces for convergence are forces that companies and governments alike ignore at their peril. This book will trace the continuities, and the differences, in the way in which the dynamic of super-competition is affecting the major regions of the world economy, and what maps of the future the survivors must create – be they managers, policy-makers or interested bystanders. Like most maps, they will be subject to compression, distortion and rapid revision – but they will provide a point of reference in an unstable and ever-changing world.

2

TECHNOLOGY: THE FRONTIER TO END ALL FRONTIERS

'Praise be to information technology!' Eduard Shevardnadze, former Soviet Foreign Minister, commenting on the role that CNN's satellite-transmitted news coverage played in keeping information flowing during the failed coup of August 1991.[1]

THE INCOMPETENT AUGUST 1991 coup attempt in the old USSR was a dramatic example of the political impact of new communication technologies. The plotters failed to appreciate how satellite broadcasting techniques had started to undercut their control over traditional terrestrial transmission networks. They similarly failed to come to terms with an automated telephone system in which operators could no longer effectively supervise telephone calls, because of subscribers' direct-dialling. Nor could they stifle the flow of fax messages between centres of resistance, or the use of the computer bulletin-board networks linked by phone and modem with others in the Soviet Union and with some in Europe and North America. The coup failed on several levels, but the failure of its leaders to control information flows within the liberal establishment played a particularly crucial role.

Within the military sphere, the 1991 war against Iraq showed the impact which communication technologies could play. Laser-guided smart bombs could hit targets with an accuracy of within 20 feet, even when launched from 50 miles away. This compares with the Vietnam war where bombs were getting within 200 feet of their target, but had to be launched from within three miles of it; while in World War 2, accuracy was no better than one mile around the target from planes within three miles.[2] This increase in military precision graphically demonstrates the impact of electronic command and control in the field of death and destruction. It was not accidental that the first bomb in the war against Iraq was a 2,000 pounder dropped squarely into the AT&T building in central Baghdad by a Stealth fighter. This was the key building for the communications of the Iraqi military.[3]

Information technology and communications are clearly key factors in determining military success, but they are equally influential in the business sphere. It is only by understanding the technology that one can begin to understand why the forces of global competition are biting so deeply. It is a revolution in information technology which has produced a coherent global economy.

It was during the 1950s that this revolution became widely significant. With the mass-production of transistors and the resultant impact on the fledgling computer industry, the cost-performance of information technology started to improve at between 20–30 per cent per annum.[4] So, at a time when the cost of technology inputs into manufactured goods (automobiles, cameras et al) was rising in proportion to labour costs, the computer industry was delivering sharply increased price/performance ratios. A mainframe computer, which, in 1980, cost the equivalent of the annual wages of 210 skilled workers, fell in price over the decade to the equivalent cost of two such workers, and could even, by the year 2000, fall to no more than a tenth of that.[5]

Looking back on economic history, it is difficult to come up with any technology which has consistently improved its cost-performance ratio so significantly over such a long period – and the IT industry is still a long way from maturity. Because this technology deals with information flows, we are actually talking of a revolution in the cost-structure of all aspects of handling information. This is a genuine revolution which is pervading all aspects of contemporary society. It is the business sector which is now driving this revolution, both as the provider of relevant technology, and as the innovative user of the ever-cheaper information flows which are the result.

THE TRIPLE CONQUEST

The IT revolution has primarily been a liberating force, making it easier for companies to view the global economy as a single unit. It has reduced the importance of national boundaries. It is allowing companies to manage increasingly sophisticated systems. It is encouraging a steady miniaturization of products.

In effect, technology has conquered three problems which have traditionally held companies back. We are seeing a triple conquest – of distance, complexity and size.

DISTANCE

Obviously the conquest of distance is not just about the use of information technology – after all there has, over the last seventy years or so, been a dramatic progression from steamship, to propellor-driven planes, to the earlier jet planes, and then the current generation of jumbo jets, which are able to fly non-stop half-way round the globe.

Although the cost-performance improvements in long-distance travel have been nowhere near so dramatic as those within the IT sphere, one should certainly not discount the impact of the spread of cheap, reliable air transport. The conquest of the oceans by commercial airlines has been largely a post-1945 development. Flights from London to New York initially took almost a day, with fuel stops in Gander or Bangor; now Concorde can transport executives from London to New York in a little over three hours, at a cost that in real terms is less than it was forty years ago.

In the last thirty years, travel time has been slashed by the introduction of jet aircraft, the steady extension of their range, and the increase in their size (the jumbo revolution). In real terms the cost of air transport has fallen and, even today, simple things like the introduction of new, longer haul jumbos can still produce significant effects such as shortening the Tokyo-to-London or Tokyo-to-Washington flights by up to seven hours.

The impact on managerial mobility has been immense. Before World War 2, the coordination of subsidiaries on another continent could only be achieved through lengthy secondments and the occasional stately progress of an emissary from corporate headquarters. Today it is not unusual for executives to visit subsidiaries in other countries monthly or even weekly, with constant telephone, fax and electronic mail contact between visits.

And we are not just chronicling the speeding of people. Of equal importance is the speeding of freight by the development of air freight and containerization. Once again, this has been primarily a post-1945 phenomenon, with freight increasingly being carried in planes dedicated to freight and nothing else. In addition to the development of the relevant aircraft, the standardization of freight containers in the 1960s sharply reduced the amount of cargo handling.

The impact of these developments means that we can see even bulky products such as auto bodies being air-freighted across the Atlantic, as Cadillac was doing in the late 1980s, when it had its Allante bodies built in Turin, flying them daily to Detroit for attachment to their chassis.[6] Fashion-sensitive industries can be located in geographically remote locations such as Hong Kong, without companies losing any of their ability to respond rapidly to demand changes in other continents; electronic point-of-sale terminals in retail establishments make it per-fectly possible for store chains to reorder fast-moving lines every day, and for clothing manufacturers to relay orders (and even design changes) electronically to their subcontractors thousands of miles away.

But the conquest of distance is not just about the transport of people and products, it is also about the transport of information and ideas. Here we are dealing with a number of technology paths which, greatly facilitated by the information technology revolution, are converging on each other. The first path has been wire-based, starting with the telegraph which took off in the 1850s (the first trans-Atlantic cable was laid in 1866)[7] and developing into the telephone. The second path has been a broadcast path, which started with radio and then added television. The IT revolution has hastened a convergence between these once mutually exclusive communications paths, to produce a world in which intensive computer data traffic, telephone conversations and multiple television channels can be transmitted in a digital form allowing them all to share the same channels – be that via a satellite or a fibre optic cable.

It was the telegraph (and Morse code) which was electricity's first major contribution to a shrinking globe – but, since then, progress has been overwhelming. In 1850, using the telegraph, a dollar would get a standard one-page business letter transmitted at an average 1,400 miles per hour. By the 1960s, using analogue technologies, a dollar would get a thousand times more information sent over that distance (1.4 million miles per hour per dollar). By the 1980s, using digital infrastructure, a dollar would get a further 27-fold increase in traffic (38 million miles per hour per dollar).[8]

What this kind of crude calculation does not do is give a sense of how the quality – as well as quantity – of transmitted information has changed for executives. In the 1850s, the telegraph was used for Morse code messages about information such as the price of wheat or meat in different parts of the USA. Today, we might be talking of a videoconference between executives in, say, New York and Tokyo. With some slight picture degradation, each set of executives will see a television picture of their opposite numbers; they will be able to talk with each other perfectly naturally (with the slight delay due to distance); they will be able to fax documents to each other as they talk; they can refer to computer terminals which are linked in real time.

Videoconferencing across widely separated time-zones is still not very satisfactory (there are very few hours when people in New York and Tokyo actually feel like talking to each other), and the television pictures still suffer a bit in quality. However, in a world where executive time is precious and days lost travelling (and suffering from jet lag) are expensive, videoconferencing is coming into its own and is an excellent example of the richness of the information flows which can now take place across the globe. During the Gulf crisis of 1990–91, the reluctance of companies to expose their executives to possible terrorist attacks against airliners gave a significant boost to videoconferencing. Telecommunications have come a long way from Samuel Morse.

A different example is the development of round-the-clock financial markets. Reuters, the leading provider of instant financial information had, by late 1990, got a system of 200,000 terminals in 129 countries, allowing currency specialists to watch financial developments in all the main markets of the world on an instantaneous basis. In times of financial crisis, it is systems provided by firms such as Reuters which allow the trading community to continue transactions as the markets in different time-zones open and close. Other global networks – such as airline reservations systems (Amadeus, Apollo, Sabre and others) – play a crucial role in linking markets across national frontiers, though the scale of

Figure 1

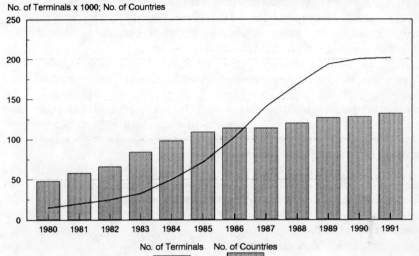

REUTERS HOLDINGS PLC
Growth in No. of Terminals and Countries Served

No. of Terminals x 1000; No. of Countries

No. of Terminals   No. of Countries

Sources: Annual Reports Reuters 1987-1991

business put through them is considerably less than for the financial trading networks.

One need only point to the television coverage of the collapse of the Soviet Empire and the Iraqi war to illustrate the strides which global broadcasting technology has made. One of the authors remembers watching the breaching of the Berlin Wall live in a Tokyo hotel room, with Germany's Willi Brandt being interviewed on a French television channel with Japanese sub-titles. During the Gulf War, the President of Turkey, Mr Ozal, watched President Bush live on CNN as he put through a call from the White House to President Ozal in Ankara. Many people think of the Iraqi war as being almost CNN's war – from the initial live transmissions from Baghdad as the first bombs and missiles went in, through the interplay of continued live transmissions from Baghdad, London, Washington, New York, Tokyo and so on which meant that the world's diplomats came to rely on CNN both as a vital information source and, increasingly, as a conduit, in its own right, for diplomatic initiatives. And then there was the attempted Moscow coup, after which Shevardnadze went on record, not just to praise information technology, but to single out CNN: 'Praise be to information technology! Praise be to the reporters and announcers of CNN! Those who had parabolic antennae and could receive this station's broadcast were getting a full picture of developments, while the obedient TV of Leonid Kravchenko was pouring forth the murky waves of disinformation and lies.'[9]

Such pictures are filmed on miniaturized video cameras, and transmitted back to studios using portable satellite dishes of 1.9 metres in diameter. During the Gulf War, there were some 120 satellites available for commercial use around the globe. Alternatively, as when the Chinese blocked satellite transmissions after the Tiananmen Square massacre, fledgling camera technology produces electronic pictures which can then be sent via modem over conventional telephone lines.[10]

THE CONQUEST OF COMPLEXITY

Such conquests of distance would be of little importance if management had not also been given the power to manage geographical complexity. Once again, technology has come to the rescue through steady, but massive improvements in computing power.

In the early days of computers, it was major national undertakings such as the Manhattan Project which produced the first atom bombs in World War 2, or the Apollo Programme which put the first man on the moon, which benefited from the application of the most powerful computers of the day.

By the late 1950s, though, emerging multinationals such as Ford were starting to apply computers to the task of coordinating their activities across whole continents. It was at this point that it became worth their while to create regional or international divisions with the task of rationalizing the activities of competing subsidiaries within the same continent. In the case of a pioneer like Ford, the first faltering steps toward such coordination came over thirty years ago when Ford Europe was created to bring together the then semi-independent subsidiaries in the UK, West Germany and Belgium and create integrated production networks on a pan-European basis. Attempts to tighten transatlantic coordination came later.

Today, the picture is very different. Firms such as Ford and General Motors have a world-wide network of assembly plants, component supplying plants, joint ventures and other strategic relationships with a variety of different companies throughout the globe resulting in a complex, ever-shifting pattern of component flows within and between continents. Thus the US-assembled 1991 Ford Crown Victoria was 73 per cent US made, but also included a fuel tank, seats, and instrument panels from Mexico, shock absorbers from Japan, front wheel spindles from the UK, electronic engine control from Spain, and an electronic control for the anti-lock brake system from Germany.[11]

Now this is just one model assembled in the United States. However, each Ford model produced anywhere in the world will have a similarly complex flow of components, though not necessarily as many flowing across the Atlantic or Pacific. Even at the assembly level, plants will tend to specialize in the production of just one or two models, but these will generally be for sale across a whole continent and, sometimes, for export elsewhere.

Quite simply, coordinating this cobweb of component and product flows is something which could only be achieved in a computer age. The apparent complexity of the flows results from the fact that each plant is supposedly producing at its optimal scale economies.

FLEXIBLE MANUFACTURING

The impact of computing power has a different, more subtle significance, because it has changed the way in which factories themselves are organized. Without computers, factories had to be kept as simple as possible. Henry Ford's approach to mass assembly was the dominant one – where possible, lines would be dedicated to one product with limited or, if the great Henry could have his way, no variations. ('You can have any colour you want, as long as it's black.')

Today, assembly lines are very different. If you visit one of the Toyota plants in Toyota City, you will see partly assembled cars following each other down the line, each distinct in body style, colour, types of wheels, size of engine and so on. They are being produced to the precise specification of customers, and production technology can now handle the coordination of flows of parts needed to support this customization of the assembly process.

As the seminal work of an MIT-led team, *The Machine that Changed the World*,[12] has shown, we are living through a revolution in factory automation and product design. Factories are becoming more flexible, allowing much more customizing of products to the personal needs of consumers. The customer is being given an attention which is unprecedented since 'Fordism' replaced the craft-based manufacturing processes aimed at privileged elites (*The Machine that Changed the World* reminds us that it was possible in the 1890s to dictate where one wanted things like the brake and engine controls to be located – a luxury which mass assembly took away).

However, today's assembly companies are not just producing a greater variety of models, but producing them at an ever-increasing rate. Again, as the MIT book demonstrates, the Japanese are leading this process. Some of their gains in speed are the result of 'parallel engineering' – i.e. getting different specialists to work in parallel on the design, prototyping, production engineering, and final assembly cycle. Computers, when used in the design process, can cut whole stages in the development process. The battle is on to integrate manufacturing directly with computer-aided design so that, ideally, as designs are finalized on the computer screen, specifications and orders for the relevant components are automatically fed to suppliers, factory layouts are determined, and marketing plans set in train.

Once again, computing power, which is still bounding ahead at an undiminished rate, is allowing companies to manage complex processes which used to be totally separate activities.

THE CONQUEST OF SIZE

One of the drives in the electronic underpinnings of the IT revolution has been the need to apply technology right down to the workings of individual atoms. By so doing, the micro-electronic engineers are gaining yet more speed, at lower power consumption, and with less heat emissions. As they get down to this level, they are able to cram more and more functions into any given space. A miniaturization revolution is therefore at work as well.

Its impact works in a number of ways. Firstly, it has allowed the revitalization of apparently mature products. The radio market, for instance, was transformed when fragile, bulky valves were replaced by the solid-state transistor to produce a smaller, portable product which was one of Sony's first global successes. Today, companies use the power of miniaturization both to increase the range of functions a product can offer and to decrease its size. This is very much what is happening with computers which were first offered in a 'luggable' form, then became genuinely portable and now are being offered in 'notebook' or even 'palm-top' size.

Secondly, it has helped develop new consumer products by miniaturizing and cheapening what were hitherto large and expensive specialist products. This is what happened with the video recorder, which before miniaturization was a bulky product selling to broadcasting studios and not widely used elsewhere. The application of microelectronics produced something which was both affordable and could sit at home under the domestic television set. By mastering this process (originally developed by the American firm, Ampex) and beating off the competition from Philips, the Japanese produced a consumer product which went on to overtake colour televisions in export volume.

This process of downsizing and cost reduction also occurred in the case of the personal computer, a massively successful attempt to get professional computing power onto an individual's desk at an affordable price; the pioneers of this desktop revolution were Apple and IBM of the US, although later Japan and other countries became key suppliers of both personal computers and their components. Downsizing created new company giants: by 1991 the market value of the firm that developed the operating system software for the IBM personal computer, Microsoft, was as great as the market value ($22 billion) of General Motors, the largest manufacturing company in the world.[13]

This miniaturization also allows product designers to cram a steadily increasing range of functions into a given product. Sometimes the results are obvious: for example, radios combined with tape recorders, then compact disk players and so on. Often it is less obvious; when, for instance, the electronics under the bonnet of the automobile are incrementally improved, this allows the provision of functions such as anti-lock braking devices, sophisticated fuel-injection control devices, electronic window controls etc. – and as the cost of the electronic components drop, these functions move from the luxury ranges to the more basic models. None of these refinements are revolutionizing the automobile as the transistor did the radio, but the functions built into luxury cars like Cadillacs and Porsches are more and more being built into standard middle-of-the-range models.

Moving to a deeper level of impact, the miniaturization process has created a number of further effects. For instance it is at the heart of the growing capacity of satellites used in international telecommunications, thus lowering the cost of telephone calls, video transmissions and so on. Similarly, it helped to produce the drastically improved effectiveness of electronic warfare shown in the Gulf War.

Ultimately, though, there is a dark side to this miniaturization process. It is not just the consumer electronic giants which value the ability to decrease the size of their products. Equally interested are terrorists and other potential challengers to the global status quo.

What the electronics revolution has effectively produced is a wealth of 'dual use' technology – technology which is overwhelmingly produced for consumers, but which can also be used for military purposes or by terrorists and criminals. A simple example is the increasingly sophisti-cated timer circuits built into products like a video-recorder. No longer does a terrorist bomb-maker have to construct a timer out of an alarm clock; electronic timers which allow times to be set precisely for weeks or months in advance can now be bought commercially. Access to such technology is very difficult or even impossible for governments or firms to control, and transfer of 'dual use' technology will remain a politically sensitive and sometimes fractious issue.

TECHNOLOGY PUSH AND THE PACE OF CHANGE

So far, we have been describing the liberating impact of technology. However, the IT revolution is also a tyrant, because it has accelerated the pace of technology change. At the same time, it has been a factor in increasing the cost of staying at the forefront of any particular technology. This has raised the stakes for any company which sees itself as a technological leader. To stay in the race, firms are increasingly forced to treat the world as a single unit. A company which tries to pay for its growing research and development budget from the income of one national market, or even one continent, is nearly always going to be outstripped by competitors which sell world-wide. This technology push is one of the prime forces making companies think globally.

In more and more industries, a new venture will require a minimum of $1 billion investment. This is true of automobiles where each generation of models requires at least this amount of expenditure. In telecommunica-tions switching equipment, the cost of developing a new range of digital telephone network exchange equipment is at least $1 billion – more than any single European country's telecommunications market could sustain. In semi-conductors, the industry is looking to a future where each new semiconductor factory will cost between $1.5–2 billion, and by the year 2000 it is probable that only ten such plants will be needed to supply world needs. In aero-engines, the stakes are similar. General Electric's revolutionary GE90 engine will need between $1–1.5 billion to develop.

At the same time, the production cycle is often drastically shortening. The parallel engineering described in *The Machine that Changed the World* is forcing western auto companies to cut development times per model by over a year just to catch up with where the Japanese companies have already got to (from roughly five years in the mid-1980s to under four years). In practice, the Japanese auto producers continue to progress, and some Japanese models are now being developed in under three years. In computing, the cycle is even faster, with production cycles for computer ranges having come down from four years to between 12–15 months. Although there are now clear signs that in some industries such as semi-conductors, the life-cycle of products gives very little chance for anyone to make adequate profits, there is a reason why the product cycle continues to shorten. Being first with a product gives a company a major competitive advantage over rivals, if only because it gets them on to the learning curve early, and thus allows them to keep a continued cost advantage over late imitators.

The impact of all of this on research and development is considerable. The proportional effort which has to be put into research and development is growing. In semiconductors, about 15 per cent of sales have to be ploughed back into research – which is, by historical standards, a very high proportion. Within an industry such as automobiles, one can show a steady annual rise in expenditure on research going back decades.[14] In industry after industry, there really is a sense of 'research or die.'

All these developments are forcing drastic choices on companies. First, they are increasingly being forced to 'bet the company'[15] with the risk that the failure of a particular product will bring the company down. Boeing had a crisis of this sort in the late 1960s when it developed the 747 Jumbo jet; in the 1990s the successor aircraft to the 747 was too expensive even for Boeing to develop on its own, so it formed a partnership with a Japanese consortium. The Rolls-Royce aero-engine company was driven to the point of bankruptcy and into the arms of the state in the 1970s when it underestimated the development costs of the RB 211 engine.

Faced with this kind of technological intensification, companies are being forced out of their national or continental habitats. However large or well protected a national market may be, it is not going to give the financial return needed to support an ever-shortening product life cycle. In capital intensive industries, companies are being forced to go global to recover their research, development and manufacturing costs.

What is happening at the company level to the likes of Boeing, Siemens, and Toyota can also be seen in relations between states. Through the SDI initiative, the USA escalated the financial cost of staying in the super-power league in the development of defence systems. Although the Soviet authorities had managed to match the American pace in the development of space systems, nuclear missiles, and conventional armaments, they finally had to capitulate. Under a fundamentally flawed economic system, the Soviets could not sustain the cost of developing yet another technologically sophisticated defence system.

CONCLUSION

We make no excuse for putting technology at the heart of this book, because there is no way that one can understand the spread of global competition, without understanding the underlying technological forces at work.

Some of these forces are working toward global decentralization. Telecommuters working at home with personal computers linked to their employers by phone line, factories retooling their production lines with software developed thousands of miles away, foreign exchange dealers concluding huge transactions by screen or phone with their counterparts on another continent: these are obvious examples of the vanquishing of the tyranny of distance. What works for individuals or firms also applies to entire countries. The breaking down of national boundaries through the steady improvement of international communications is making it easier and easier for new players like South Korea, Malaysia or Mexico to become significant global competitors.

On the other hand, the impact of technological intensification should not be discounted. Technology is changing faster and faster, and is becoming more and more expensive to develop – outstripping the resources of all but the largest companies. In key industries such as computing, telecommunications, aerospace, pharmaceuticals and automobiles there is a trend toward corporate concentration on a global basis. Corporate giants are having to run ever faster, to spend more, and to recoup their research and development costs from wider markets, just in order to stay competitive and survive.

3

LIBERALIZATION, DEREGULATION AND THE ATTACK ON ECONOMIC NATIONALISM

WHILE THE IT revolution was starting to erode the economic relevance of national boundaries, there were still many man-made barriers to the creation of global markets and the internationalization of business. Dismantling the laws and regulations that inhibited cross-border competition required political leadership – not from idealistic 'one-worlders' but from politicians who were by no means devoid of nationalist sentiment, but who saw that international competitiveness (and thus economic growth and prosperity for their respective countries) could only be attained through liberalization.

With Mrs Thatcher becoming British Prime Minister in 1979, President Reagan assuming office in the USA in 1981, and Prime Minister Nakasone taking power in Japan in 1982, a formidable trio of market-oriented political leaders came to hold power simultaneously in the three poles of the triad world. Between them, they oversaw a major advance in economic liberalization in their countries. To some extent they reinforced each other's views. Premier Nakasone dropped out of the scene in 1987, and Reagan a year later, leaving only Mrs Thatcher to serve out the decade. However, not only had they swung the industrialized world toward a more aggressively market-oriented stance, but they had prepared the world for perestroika, the collapse of the Soviet Empire, and (China excepted) the ultimate destruction of the command economy on which it rested. The ideology of the free market entered the 1990s in a much stronger position than it had left the 1970s.

Of course the forces behind this upsurge in economic liberalism are more complex than this. The Thatcher-Reagan revolution (and, to a lesser extent, the Nakasone era in Japan) was not just the result of politicians acting in a vacuum. There were other independent forces at work which encouraged them in their mutual determination to sweep away regulatory boundaries and to increase the amount of international competition.

If one adds to this the fundamental liberalization of the European Community, which started with the passing of the Single European Act in 1986 (the so-called '1992' process to create a single market in the EC), along with the collapse of the Soviet system of economic management, then the 1980s were truly a revolutionary decade in which the free-market philosophy ended up a significant winner.

This triumph of capitalism was no foregone conclusion. After all, in the late 1950s, Nikita Khruschev could still promise that Marxist economic management would bury the West. In the 1970s, it was still common for newly independent Third World states to adopt variants of the Marxist model of economic management, sometimes (as in Chile) through the electoral process rather than an authoritarian regime. In the same period, it was still necessary to take the communist movement seriously in OECD countries such as France and Italy, where communism remained a powerful political force until the early 1980s. By the end of 1991, however, communist parties everywhere were in eclipse (the Italian party even dropped 'Communist' from its name), the Soviet Union and its system of economic and political satellites had disintegrated, and Fidel Castro in Cuba was making speeches designed to attract inward foreign investment as a means of promoting economic growth.

However, by concentrating on the collapse of Marxism, one only picks up part of the story. Within the western 'capitalist' system, there were important developments which increased the intensity of competition in key industrial sectors – and it is this 'deregulatory' phenomenon we will focus on in this chapter. Originally, it was narrowly based in the US and (somewhat later) in the UK, with developments within a narrow range of hitherto highly regulated industries, including telecommunications, airlines and financial services. Gradually, as the 1980s unrolled, it became possible to talk of a wider liberal-market revolution within the capitalist world. The fact that Japan joined this liberalization process was significant, while the European Community's adoption of the 1992 programme can be seen as a further major commitment to liberalization within West Europe.

Deregulation has been one of the ways these economies have moved forward. In country after country, governments have retreated from the tight regulation of core industries. In some cases, governments have allowed companies to move into sectors hitherto blocked off from them (banks into securities and so on); in others, governments have given companies a freedom to compete on prices (as has happened in airlines in some countries).

During the 1980s, deregulation was accompanied by the privatization of key state companies, which were sold off to private shareholders. This was Mrs Thatcher's particular contribution to the liberalization phenomenon, and the British experience influenced thinking in Eastern Europe, where privatization is now seen as a generally desirable goal – though there are serious questions about how easily it can be implemented.

A number of measures were aimed at increasing the competitive pressures on protected industries. Thus key companies such as AT&T in the US have been broken up to provide a new set of competitors. Domestic competitors have been deliberately brought into existence in other situations; in Britain the British Telecom monopoly of telephone service was to be challenged by Mercury, a new entrant to the UK domestic telecommunications market. In still another approach, foreign competitors have been allowed to enter industries once treated as national preserves. One way or another, the number of competitors in key industries has been increased.

WHY REGULATION? WHY STATE ENTERPRISES?

There are a number of reasons why governments have in the past seen fit to get deeply involved in the running of industrial sectors.

National security, followed by safety considerations, have been the prime reasons why governments have taken an active role in supporting national airlines. Prior to World War 2, the strategic interests behind the international spread of 'national champions' in the airline industry – of Pan Am (for the USA), Imperial Airways (British), KLM (Dutch) and Deutsche Lufthansa (German) – were very clear. After the war, governments kept firm control over who could or could not fly into their territory. Governments saw a strong economic case for protecting airlines as a form of national champion.

In Europe and other regions with a socialist history there has been a belief in the importance of the state actually owning the commanding heights of the economy. Even where states have not been socialist, there has been a general understanding that some activities such as postal services were too important to run under private enterprise. Telephone systems were viewed as just such a community service. The USA was rare in having its phone system in private hands – but it ensured that AT&T was heavily regulated to protect the consumer and safeguard the quality and integrity of the nation's telecommunications network.

This kind of prudential regulation has been an extremely important force behind industries such as financial services. Clearly governments must always ensure that bank collapses do not wipe out the savings of large numbers of unlucky citizens and bring about the failure of the monetary system itself. Hence the insistence on things like capital-adequacy ratios to ensure banks do not become financially over-exposed, or barriers like that of the Glass-Steagall Act in the USA which stops banks getting involved in securities trading, or vice versa (the philosophy being that banks should stick with what they know, and should not embark on risky diversifications). Similarly in airlines, regulatory structures emerged to control safety and pricing policies (whose effect was more to protect the airlines than the consumers). In telecommunications, there has always been a network of regulation both to protect the integrity of the system and to ensure that the average citizen got fair value for money.

Finally, industries like telephones, electricity and gas supply have been seen as natural monopolies. Historically, few people have seriously considered having two or three phone companies all trying to provide networks to the same street or neighbourhood. In so far as the phone business was a monopoly, it needed regulating to protect the consumer from price gouging and other exploitative behaviour, and to ensure that all parts of the country received adequate service on equitable terms.

Many of the motives behind regulation are entirely laudable ones. However, in many cases the regulator steadily became an important force for restraining potential competitors and protecting vested interests – known as 'regulatory capture' in the literature on the economics of regulation. Quite often the regulator has also been a chauvinist, fighting the national cause strongly in any international negotiations.

Slowly, a consensus grew that old-style inward-looking regulation was no longer good enough – that it increasingly involved significant economic cost associated with whatever benefits it delivered.

UNLEASHING THE BEHEMOTHS

So far, we have looked at a variety of deregulatory moves. By themselves, each of these measures may seem minor, but, in their entirety, they have produced a major increase in the competitive pressures within a set of industries such as airlines, financial services and telecommunications, and have thus helped set the competitive tone on wider national economies.

The results have been startling. It has, in fact, been a little like unlocking the cages of a group of somewhat sleepy behemoths. Faced with increased competition in home markets, giants such as AT&T, Nomura, Delta Airlines, British Telecom, NTT, British Airways, American Express, Deutsche Bank et al have been forced to join the global competitive battlefield, further intensifying the pressures on those other companies already out there in the international arena.

At the same time, the technology push described in the last chapter has also been an important force behind the start of their global drive. The giant telecoms players such as AT&T, BT and NTT are being forced to think globally because of the massive development needs of their particular industry and the potential erosion of their domestic market share. The breaking down of the cosy regulatory environment in which they had long been sheltered has given them an increased freedom to roam the world looking for the scale economies needed to stay competitive in their industry. They are mostly satisfying themselves for the moment with strategic alliances with other related companies, but competition is beginning to stir.

In financial services, technology has worked primarily as a liberator. Initially, improvements in technology helped erode the ability of regulators to put a ring fence round national economies. As international communications improved through the decades, it has become increasingly easy to carry out financial transactions in less regulated parts of the world, thus leaving regulators with the dilemma of trying to maintain tight restrictions on a national industry which has perforce to compete in global markets. Tight regulation can thus be a significant competitive disadvantage, especially when financial institutions are under pressure to globalize their operations in order to serve their existing customers as they internationalize their own operations.

In airlines, the impact of technology has worked in a number of directions – all away from the once cosy world of national regulation. In the first place, the ease of entering the industry through the lease or purchase of a few planes undercut attempts to maintain a system of regulated prices – witness the initial successes of Laker Airways in the 1970s and People Express in the early 1980s. However, once authorities gave ground on pricing, then the scale economies to do with running airline networks started to take over – once again forcing a global strategy on airlines which used to view themselves purely in national or continental terms, and presenting strong pressures for concentration in the industry.

Figure 2

Examples of Deregulation

Year	Sector	Country	Comments
1975	Finance	USA	Elimination of fixed commissions (New York Stock Exchange)
1978	Aviation	USA	Deregulation of domestic aviation market
1979	Finance	UK	Elimination of exchange controls
1984	Telecommunications	USA	Deregulation of AT&T: break-up of monopoly and creation of seven regional companies
1985	Finance	Japan	Starts deregulation of financial markets
1986	Finance	UK	Elimination of fixed commissions and new option to create financial conglomerates
1989	Automotives	Mexico	Elimination and reduction of production and import restrictions and local content requirements
1989	Foreign investment	Hungary	Liberalization of foreign investment laws, allowing foreign companies 100% ownership
1990	Finance	Poland	Introduction of internal convertibility for currency; capital controls remain
1990	Aviation	Australia	Deregulation of domestic aviation market
1990	Finance	Germany	Elimination of capital controls
1992	Finance	Canada	Liberalization of financial services (Bank Act)

Source: Financial Times

THE PRE-HISTORY OF LIBERALIZATION

The first signs of the pressures that would build on national regulators came in financial services with the creation of the Eurodollar market in the 1950s. Bankers – initially the Soviets, ironically enough, because they were expected to pay hard currency on demand for their imports and thus had dollars standing idle – sought to keep dollars outside the jurisdiction of the American authorities, who limited interest rates and required certain reserves to be maintained by the banks they regulated. Their experience in short-term lending of dollars made it clear to other, more commercially-oriented bankers that they could get higher returns by keeping their 'Eurodollars' outside US jurisdiction.

The key to the success of this initial attempt to escape tight American regulation was the reaction of the British authorities. Only too aware of the relative decline of the City of London since its halcyon days in the nineteenth century, they realized that by providing a lightly regulated alternative to the USA they could pick up a significant amount of footloose financial activity which would be attracted by the market rates on offer in London.

London was brilliantly successful with this strategy of creating a financial regime that was largely unregulated for offshore transactions – the equivalent of the Bahamas with an inferior climate but better theatres and golf courses. Thirty years later it is still the leading financial centre in the European time-zone.

As a result, national regulatory authorities need to be aware that they are potential competitors. Competitive deregulation is a powerful tool in their lockers. Where an industry is as footloose as financial services, strict regulation will be undercut by other centres offering a more relaxed environment – a process of regulatory arbitrage. As we will see in later chapters, Wall Street was deregulated in 1975, mostly because of the pressures put on brokers by the largest financial players. This triggered a defensive response from the City of London in 1986, which led to reactions in other financial centres on the continent of Europe.

US LEADERSHIP IN AIRLINES AND TELECOMS

If the British took the original lead in liberalizing financial services, the USA very much took the political lead in deregulation from the mid-1970s, starting with the Wall Street Big Bang of 1975 which abolished fixed commissions on share dealing. This was followed in 1978 by the very different case of airline deregulation, where a steady stream of new entrants into the US industry was showing that there were a slew of potential competitors like People Express willing to come into the market offering prices well below the current regulated prices. The motivation for airline deregulation under President Carter was partly populism, but also a strong economic sense of the benefits which would come to consumers from deregulation.

Other countries reacted slowly to this American initiative, which has not been without its controversial aspects. What is increasingly clear is that early deregulation in the USA has produced drastic shakeout of players in the sector, leaving a small survivor group of financially strong US airlines which are going to be very difficult for the Europeans and the Japanese to deal with. **Lesson 1: early deregulation can bring important competitive advantages.**

In telecommunications, liberalization came about in a very different way. In this case, as in airlines, there were new competitors coming to the fore – in this case based on new technologies like microwave transmission. In 1982, the US regulator (Judge Greene) decided that competitive diversity would best be achieved by breaking the overly dominant AT&T up into a number of regional phone companies with AT&T remaining a provider of long-distance service and a manufacturer of equipment. 'Ma Bell' and the regional phone companies were to be prevented from entering related fields, such as broadcasting and information services, which allowed powerful competitors like IBM into the field.

This particular decision was very much driven by the IT revolution, which had begun to produce an increasing variety of commercially relevant technologies, in areas such as fibre optics, space satellites, voice- and data-handling networks and cellular telephony. What had been a natural monopoly – a wire-based telephone network – was now challenged by alternative transmission technologies and a diversification of the services that would be carried by them.

By this time, other countries were getting interested in the virtues of deregulation-to-gain-competitive-advantage. Both Japan and the UK soon followed the USA with their versions of telecommunications deregulation. This was another form of competitive deregulation aimed not so much at attracting footloose investment from round the world (as in financial services) but to encourage the development of a vibrant telecommunications infrastructure. The aim was both to stimulate technological creativity at the supply end, and to establish a competitively priced telecoms market which might benefit telecoms users. **Lesson 2: a competitive, innovative telecommunications service was seen to be as much an important part of a country's infrastructure as a decent road system.**

BRITAIN TAKES UP THE LEAD

Britain responded directly to all three of these American deregulatory initiatives. In so doing, it became the first European country to liberalize its telecommunications sector and – in establishing a duopoly for basic telephone service (with Mercury competing against British Telecom) – in some respects went beyond the American precedent.

The driving force behind this quick response was Prime Minister Mrs

Thatcher who added her own footnote to history by pioneering a wave of privatizations of the state sector as the foundation of her approach to economic liberalization. Starting in 1981 with the sale of a 51.6 per cent stake in British Aerospace, the British government had found buyers for £25 billion of assets by the end of 1986.[1]

The Thatcher Revolution showed up most distinctively through her privatization programme, which was to have an important demonstration effect throughout the industrialized, developing worlds and emerging ex-Soviet bloc countries. **Lesson 3: there were other ways to liberalize an economy than by sticking entirely to deregulation.**

In parallel to this privatization programme, the Thatcher administration deliberately copied the US by injecting competition into its airline, telecommunications and financial services sectors. The motivation was ideological, but with a clear sense of national self-interest. It was believed that Britain would gain a competitive advantage over the rest of continental Europe by deregulating early. In airlines, where bilateral deals were necessary, the UK sought out equally liberal countries such as Ireland and the Netherlands.

Lesson 4: the American deregulatory experience was channelled into Europe by the Thatcher government in the UK. In so far as it is useful to talk about an Anglo-American approach to industrial policy, it is this period which demonstrates the two countries working most harmoniously in friendly competition. No other country on the Continent has been as influenced by the American example as the British.

THE JAPANESE – ALSO LIBERALIZERS

Because it is unfashionable to recognize that Japan has been liberalizing in its own right, it is easy to forget that it, too, was moving ahead during this period. What is difficult for foreigners to assess is how much change came as a result of internal evolution, and how much as a result of American pressure. In financial services, for example, the USA has been able to gain only limited access for American firms, even though in international monetary affairs (from the Plaza Accord of 1986 onward) Japan has been cooperative in aiding currency stability and overcoming the overvaluation of the dollar in the mid-1980s.

In telecommunications, the picture is different. In 1985, NTT (Japan's equivalent to AT&T) was both partially privatized and deregulated. By the end of the decade a competitive fringe had been added to the dominant NTT and KDD (which hitherto had monopolized international tele-communications traffic); in particular, foreign companies could take a stake in consortia to handle international telecommunications.

In this particular case, there had been consistent US pressure over the years, but this was not always decisive, though it did ensure that US developments during the 1960s (when deregulatory pressures first grew)

Figure 3

Examples of Privatisation

Year	Sector	Country	Comments
1984	Telecommunications	UK	Privatisation of British Telecom
1985	Telecommunications	Japan	Privatisation of NT&T
1986	Energy	UK	Privatisation of British Gas
1987	Aviation	UK	Privatisation of British Airways
1990	Energy	UK	Privatisation of electricity companies
1990	Travel/Finance	Hungary	Privatisation of IBUSZ (travel and financial services group)
1990	Telecommunications	Mexico	Privatisation of Telmex
1991	Consumer Electronics	Hungary	Privatisation of Lehel (refrigerators)
1991	Aviation	Holland	Privatisation of the State Aviation College
1992	Energy	Canada	Privatisation of Petro Canada in progress

Source: Financial Times

and onward fed through into the Japanese debate. What is clear is that in opposition to both NTT and the relevant Ministry of Posts and Telecommunications, there were important forces pushing for liberalization which focused on the Ministry of International Trade and Industry and the general electronic supply industry.[2]

Hard diplomatic pressure from the USA has been important in opening up parts of the Japanese industrial scene. There are forces within Japan (MITI in particular) which will concede quite liberal regulation, in the interests of the equipment supply industry which seeks to expand its exports and could suffer from retaliatory protection. Clearly, though, there are sectors of the Japanese bureaucracy (the Finance Ministry, and the Ministry of Post and Telecommunications) which are far from liberal in their thinking. **Lesson 5: foreign pressure (Mrs Thatcher was to weigh in publicly later in the decade on telecommunication issues) is clearly needed to keep up the deregulatory process.**

CONCLUSIONS

By the mid-1980s, a considerable head of steam had built up behind the liberalization of key sectors – using both deregulation and privatization as tools.

The US generally acted as the catalyst, reflecting the fact that it probably possesses one of the most sophisticated regulatory regimes in the world which routinely endeavours to inject competition into the industries under regulation. Some of the key pressures in telecoms and financial services came from companies which reckoned they were getting a raw deal from the existing regulated environment.

In Japan, the US has generally found it necessary to apply considerable diplomatic pressure to get significant liberalization in sectors which matter to the outside world.

In Europe, there was a possible fleeting historical moment when the radical Mrs Thatcher both responded to American deregulatory developments, but also took them one stage further through the concept of privatization (which made little sense in the US which had such a limited experience in nationalized industries). What Mrs Thatcher's Britain did was to act as a beachhead for the US emphasis on liberalization. A question we will ask later is the extent to which the 1992 process and the collapse of the old Soviet system were affected by the liberalization developments of the first half of the 1980s.

For the global economy, these political developments matter. On the one hand, the dismemberment of AT&T and the privatization of giants like British Telecom and NTT has ushered a new set of giant players onto the world scene. At the same time, the deregulatory process has also had an international aspect. In most cases, deregulation has given greater market access to foreign companies than they had hitherto. This is starting to prove important as the newly liberated companies start to define a world role for themselves.

So political liberalization and deregulation has been an important development which will facilitate the globalization of companies – a development that the IT revolution has been making ever easier. Economic nationalism, however, can still act as a barrier.

4

THE GLOBALIZATION OF BRANDS

THE QUINTESSENTIAL GLOBAL shopping centre used to be Anchorage airport in Alaska. For time-zone reasons all the late-night European-bound planes from the Eastern Pacific would descend on Anchorage in the early hours of the Alaskan morning to be refuelled and resupplied. Japanese, Koreans, Filipinos, British, Germans, Italians – the whole motley crew – would disembark under the watchful eye of a stuffed polar bear.

For an hour or so, the weary, jet-lagged travellers would be left in what was effectively one large duty-free shopping mall in the icy depths of Alaska. Unlike typical shopping malls elsewhere in the world, this one makes few concessions to the local industries, apart from some limited supplies of pemmican and smoked salmon. It is, instead, a global mall selling nothing but global brands. Scotch whiskies such as Johnny Walker Red, J&B Rare, Ballantine's, Bell's, or Chivas Regal; perfumes by Yves Saint Laurent, Chanel, Givenchy and Christian Dior; cigarettes included not only the ubiquitous Marlboro, but also Camel, Winston, Benson & Hedges and Kent; luxury goods such as Gucci bags and scarves by Hermès; watches from classic Swiss names such as Rolex and Omega, as well as their Japanese challengers, Seiko, Citizen and Casio.

This is the Aladdin's cave world of the duty-free store. Nothing is stocked unless it has a brand name instantly recognizable without subtitles to the vanguard of the Global Citizen – the inter-continental air traveller, ranging from business executives to tourists – including the free-spending Japanese who have celebrated their emergence as international travellers by spending lavishly on luxury brand names.

Putting aside the more unearthly parts of the Anchorage experience (the below-freezing weather and the communal jet-lagged disorientation of the consumers) it actually reflects the way that world consumer markets are globalizing. It is the end product of the technological and political trends described in previous chapters.

This is a consumerist world in which brands and products fight for display space with an intensity never experienced before. Successful national brands are becoming continental ones, with a handful breaking out to become global brands of the potency of Marlboro, Coca-Cola, the Sony Walkman, Heineken, Holiday Inn, Lipton's Tea, Veuve Clicquot, Johnny Walker Black Label or Nike.

THE POTENCY OF BRANDS

As the Soviet hold over Eastern Europe crumbled in the late 1980s, the market researchers moved in. One key study was of 600 Soviets, Czechs, Yugoslavs, East Germans and Hungarians. Despite decades of supposed isolation from western influences, these potential consumers were surprisingly well-briefed on the leading western brand names. For instance, of the whole sample only three Poles and one Russian were unaware of Pepsi-Cola's name. Following Pepsi in the awareness stakes were Coca-Cola, Nescafé, Nivea, Chanel, Levi's, Johnny Walker, Maggi/Knorr, Guinness Book of Records, McDonald's, Philips and Gillette. Perhaps surprisingly, Japanese brands had not yet reached the visibility they have achieved elsewhere in the world. Despite that, Sony, Panasonic, Hitachi, Toshiba were placed 14–17th.[1]

Given the depth of anti-capitalist propaganda to which such consumers have been subjected, this level of awareness of western brands was impressive. But, above all, the study symbolizes the growing penetration of a limited number of brands into the global consciousness.

It is easy to be dismissive about the economic importance of brands. Somehow, the creation of a successful brand does not seem to have the glamour (one might almost say 'reality') of a research-based product breakthrough like the development of a new drug or the creation of an apparently new product such as a Sony Walkman.

Instead, many of the brands we deal with are in apparently trivial or non-essential sectors such as hamburger chains, cigarettes, alcohol, *haute couture* and the like. There is a perception that one cannot build long-term industrial competitiveness for nations on such industries. Surely the industries which really matter are more obviously science-based and manufacturing-intensive such as computers, automobiles and so on?

Perhaps. However, many of these high-recognition brands have been around for far longer than companies like IBM, Apple or Sony. Some such as Coca-Cola, Budweiser or Knorr have existed for over a century (and aspirin dates from 1893). Many others such as Lux, Birds Eye, Camel, Persil and Heineken have been around for over 50 years. There are commercial symbols that have a very long life – like that of Nipper, the dog that first listened to His Master's Voice on an early gramophone ninety years ago, and is still used today by the Japanese electronics company, JVC. These are mature, but resilient brands which should be around for many more decades. How many automotive or electronic companies can be sure they will be around that long?

Obviously successful brands do not rest on the kind of technological

Figure 4

Historic Brands

Brand	Country of Origin	Product	Date
Schweppes	Germany, UK	Soft Drinks	1798
Colgate	UK	Toothpaste	1806
Levis	USA	Jeans	1850
Nestlé	Switzerland	Beverages	1866
Coca-Cola	USA	Soft Drink	1886
Omega	Switzerland	Watches	1894
Martini	Italy	Liquor	1896
Fiat	Italy	Automobiles	1899
Gillette	UK	Razor Blades	1902
Max Factor	USA	Cosmetics	1909
Hitachi	Japan	Domestic Goods	1910
Marlboro	USA	Cigarettes	1924

Source: Adrian Room, <u>Dictionary of Trade Name Origins</u>, Routledge and Kegan Paul, London 1982

breakthroughs which produced the original transistor radio. However, one should not be overly dismissive of the technologies involved. Successful, well-managed brands will normally be sustained through continuous small-scale technological modifications over a period of decades. In a sector like detergents there are regular advances, such as the recent shift to superconcentrated brands which clean a lot of laundry with a very small portion of detergent. Nothing earth-shattering, but offering perceived improved performance to the customer.

What is happening in today's triad world is that the brand-driven giants – firms like Procter & Gamble, Unilever, Levi Strauss, Mars, Kellogg's, Philip Morris, Coca-Cola, Pepsi-Cola, Nestlé, Grand Metropolitan, LVMH (Louis Vuitton-Moet-Hennessey), Shiseido et al – are making a once-and-for-all grab to fill the branding vacuums exposed by the lowering of barriers of national markets and the increasing internationalization of business. Since branding has been Anglo-American led, the most mature market for brands is West Europe and the USA. The battle is now quite intense for brand dominance in Japan. For many of the branders, the battle is in its early stages in emerging parts of the world like the rest of Asia, East Europe, Africa and Latin America.

. . . and a battle it truly is. Firms like Unilever, P&G, Philip Morris and Nestlé are giant companies by any standard. They know the stability of branding patterns. They know that many of the leading brands in 1920s America are still the leading brands today. They all therefore know that whoever can establish their brands as leaders around the globe today will go a long way to establishing a lead position for years to come in products such as cigarettes, alcohol, personal care products (shampoos etc.), breakfast cereals, cosmetics, instant coffee and so on – not only for existing products, but for improved products or even new ones sold under the same brand ('brand extension', as it is called).

There is a healthy debate about the significance of such developments. At one extreme end, there are marketing gurus (such as Theodore Levitt of Harvard Business School) and advertising executives (such as the Saatchi brothers) who argue that world tastes are homogenizing – that consumers all round the world are quite rapidly becoming more similar in their tastes, thus permitting the development of genuinely global brands advertised and marketed world-wide. In this way economies of scale in marketing as well as production can be attained, the producer can withstand competition and consumers are given a product that embodies optimum quality and value.

THE FORCES AT WORK

At the level of international élites there is little doubt that a homogenization of tastes is occurring. Travel is certainly one factor at work. Coca-Cola, for instance, got its initial international impetus during and after World War 2, as the US authorities made sure that their armed forces would find their creature comforts anywhere in the world where they were posted. In a more diffuse way, the development of international tourism has increasingly exposed ordinary citizens to the variety of foreign products. Thus visitors to the USA became aware of fast food marketed from coast to coast. Visitors to the Mediterranean picked up a liking for ouzo, paella and lasagne. Visitors to Japan (a much rarer breed) acquired an understanding of sake, sumo, sushi and wood block prints. These travellers may not rush back home to continue their acquaintance with, say, Japanese food, but they are aware of images and products and this awareness sensitizes them to the next advertisement which uses a Japanese theme. Thus Unilever introduced in the UK a range of ice-cream products branded 'Gino Ginelli', in order to capitalize on the reputation of Italian ice-cream – even though none of the products came from Italy.

Films, television and pop music have probably been even more potent channels for spreading arresting images around the world. Where would the Marlboro cowboy now be without 80-odd years of Hollywood westerns to create the stereotypes from which this extraordinarily potent brand image could grow? Even today, images of James Dean, Marilyn Monroe, and the younger Marlon Brando are used round the world for marketing purposes, once again testifying to the strength of Hollywood's iconic influence. One part of the battle between Coke and Pepsi turns around their use of pop music stars in their commercials.

Quite simply, an increasing number of today's consumers grow up listening to a common core of pop singers and watching a common core of Hollywood blockbusters and hit television programmes. The more sophisticated consumer will start to share some reading tastes, perhaps some experiences in highbrow music, almost certainly some artistic knowledge. None of this means that the day-to-day life of a young executive in Tokyo, New York or Paris comes anywhere near to being identical – but it does mean that, year by year, the core of common experiences is growing.

SPREAD OF A MARKETING ETHOS

In no way, however, do consumer tastes develop passively. The development of brands is highly influenced by competition between the consumer giants. Companies like Unilever, Procter & Gamble or Kao cannot dictate world tastes, but they should be viewed as skirmishing armies, probing the defences of consumers around the world to see what products are strong enough to be shifted to more than one country.

This makes sense. A product which sells well in one country will generally have qualities which will make it sellable somewhere else in the world, particularly in countries with related cultures. In these circumstances, why reinvent a product which, perhaps with some modifications, can be introduced from elsewhere? What holds true for products may also then hold true for brand names and advertising strategies. For all those reasons, companies have a vested interest to push potential international brands.

The Anglo-Dutch food firm, Unilever, is the kind of company which is at the heart of this process. On the one hand it is responsive to local tastes, so that in the early 1990s for instance, it was using 85 varieties of flavouring in the chicken soups it sells across Europe (it has taken measures to see how far it can rationalize such diversity). On the other, it is constantly on the search for products which can be 'rolled out' globally with minimal modifications. So when it acquired Chesebrough Ponds in 1987, it was able to take that company's best-selling spaghetti sauce, Ragu, and roll it out across Europe with only one slight modification to the brand name in Germany to meet trade description rules.[2]

On a global basis, Unilever has been successful with Timotei, the best-selling shampoo outside the USA. The brand started as a failed deodorant in Finland where its name means 'grass'. A local Unilever executive spotted the marketing potential of a mild natural brand and transferred the formula to shampoo. In 1975, the product was successfully launched in Sweden, where it was given a distinctive pack. The product was then launched back in Finland and rolled out round the rest of Europe, on an image of Scandinavian herbs and a somewhat virginal blonde model who washes her hair outside in a bucket or blows dandelion seeds into a boyfriend's face. When taken to Japan, the third modification of the basic ad produced a runaway success with Timotei taking 10 per cent of the market.

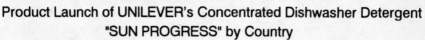

Figure 5

Product Launch of UNILEVER's Concentrated Dishwasher Detergent "SUN PROGRESS" by Country

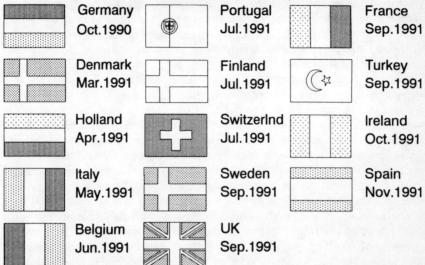

Germany Oct.1990	Portugal Jul.1991	France Sep.1991
Denmark Mar.1991	Finland Jul.1991	Turkey Sep.1991
Holland Apr.1991	Switzerlnd Jul.1991	Ireland Oct.1991
Italy May.1991	Sweden Sep.1991	Spain Nov.1991
Belgium Jun.1991	UK Sep.1991	

Source: UNILEVER

Coca-Cola is an even clearer example of how the brand-driven companies now view the world. Coke has 46 per cent of the world's carbonated soft drink market. Its ambitions are boundless. In the words of Roberto Goizueta, the Coca-Cola chairman: 'By the year 2000, we will have Coca-Cola available within an arm's reach of desire of the 6 billion people who will be housed on this planet.'[3] This is not just a question of running advertisments, it is a question of building up the bottling, manufacturing and distribution infrastructures of markets all round the world. So, in early 1992, Coke announced the creation of a privately owned business in Moscow to manufacture the famous syrup and to establish 2,000 retail outlets in the city. In India, it was planning a joint venture to get itself back into one of the few countries it withdrew from in the 1970s after a dispute with the government. In Japan, it spent $500 million on 130,000 vending machines, which are so crucial to sales in that country. In China, it has 13 joint venture plants and is clearly getting prepared for the long haul in a country of giant potential, but limited current per capita income. All this activity is, of course, in addition to the traditional 'Cola wars' with Pepsi in the USA where Coke's market lead is rather narrower.

The Coke story is one of the clearest examples of what is involved in the development of a global marketing strategy. Coca-Cola has a global brand name which is now recognized in every part of the globe. However, advertising is only one part of the process. Establishing such a brand needs a supporting supply and distribution system (including stringent quality control, since a quality mishap in one market can have global repercussions), which may often have to be created from scratch. It also involves putting competitive markers down in countries such as China where western consumer patterns are still extremely weak. It involves getting ever closer to an understanding of the cultural forces at work in all a company's key markets (Coke puts an increasing effort into forecasting entertainment trends worldwide). It also involves opportunism.

On the day in November 1989 when the Berlin Wall was finally breached, Coca-Cola's Atlanta head office ordered its Berlin colleagues to hand out free cans of Coke to the East Germans who came through the wall to look at the consumer goods that had been denied them so long by their communist masters. Given the way that Coke's image has been quite consciously developed around the American way of life, and, for much of the Cold War, had actually became an unofficial symbol of the capitalist system in general (leftist writers often referred to alleged US imperialism as 'Coca-colonization'), this move was highly significant. Each can which was consumed that day could be interpreted as a small demonstration of the victory of the free enterprise system over communism. In its way, the power of Coke's image (along with that of Marlboro, Pepsi, Levi Strauss and others) had actually played a part in destroying the original allure of the Marxist ideal. Coke had paid its dues. It had a right to be part of the celebrations on that heady day in Berlin.*

LIMITS TO GLOBALIZATION

Despite the potency of global brands such as Coke, they are still only a relatively small part of the world economy. The vast majority of products that consumers currently buy are still national or regional ones. There is considerable debate about how many products are really suitable for the global branding process.

Language, for instance, is still a barrier. Brand names with some potency in one language have unfortunate connotations in another. Classic cases are two soft drinks, France's Pschitt and Japan's Pocari Sweat – both of which have unfortunate connotations in English. The attempt to sell a deodorant called 'Silver Mist' in Germany was hindered by the fact that 'mist' is the German for manure, while Coca-Cola's carbonated beverage 'Mellow Yellow' had to be renamed in Thailand because in Thai 'yellow' means 'pus'; the product name was shortened to 'Mello' for the Thai market.

---

* Ironically, one of the more tasteless (but funny) comedies about the Cold War, Billy Wilder's *One, Two, Three*, was about the attempts of a Berlin-based Coca-Cola executive to bring the American way of life to the Coke-deprived denizens of the East. While it was being shot in Berlin in 1961, the construction of the Wall started. The film was deeply nihilistic and savage toward (amongst other targets) Coke. The latter's executives can argue that real life has exonerated them.

Life styles do differ from country to country and it would be arrogant to assume that these differences will be totally eradicated – though some of them may be narrowed. To take just one example – breakfast habits. The British and Americans have long accepted pre-prepared cereals such as cornflakes as the heart of this meal. The British consume an annual 13.3 pounds per person, with the Americans slightly behind at 10.1 pounds. Continental Europeans, on the other hand, still favour breakfasts of bread, cheese, eggs and meat, so the French, for instance average only 1.8 pounds of cereals per year.[4]

In Japan, breakfast traditions are totally different, emphasizing rice, raw eggs and pickles. In these circumstances, it does not matter how powerful the marketing clout may be of General Mills, Nestlé, Kellogg and Quaker; they have a long hard slog ahead of them to convince all cultures to adopt a cereal-based breakfast. What they can hope to do is increase the relative importance of cereals in each market, and to ensure that it is their brands which dominate. The brands may well be global, but their relative penetration of different cultures will be much more varied than is the case for Coke.

Cultural patterns affect global marketing in more complex ways. To pick one example, the impact of land prices will have a significant effect on product design and marketing. At one extreme is the USA where land is cheap, thus allowing everything from houses to automobiles to be large. At the other is Japan which is desperately short of space, with families crammed into apartments which are tiny even by European standards, and where one cannot, for instance, in Tokyo buy a car unless one has a parking space available for it.

Such extremes immediately make it difficult to develop standard products. It is far from accidental that the Detroit automakers have found it much more difficult to break into the Japanese market than the luxury European car-makers who work in an automotive market which has more of the space constraints which are found in Japan.

Within product categories such as consumer durables for the home, space constraints become one very obvious barrier to the development of global products. Refrigerators made for the American lifestyle have very little place in Europe, and still less in Japan.

But space is only one factor affecting the would-be global marketer. With washing machines, housewives round the world are used to different water temperatures, with the Japanese, for instance, using cold water for washing, which not only demands a specific type of washing action, but needs detergents with different chemical formulations from those used with warmer water elsewhere in the West. On top of complications like this, there are different stylistic preferences; the Germans like designs which give the impression of engineering quality, while the French value a stylish appearance over a functional one.

But such indicators only scratch at the surface. Deeper, more subtle national characteristics can still play havoc with the marketer's instinctive desire to standardize marketing strategies. There are problems with humour – the British enjoy humorous ads, the Germans don't; likewise race – Benetton got themselves into serious problems in the US with a campaign which seemed innocuous in Europe which involved a naked black lady holding a white baby; and, not surprisingly, sex – US ads are notoriously strait-laced while the French tolerate the widespread use of naked females to promote products that often have nothing at all to do with the body.

An extra level of complexity is provided by different regulatory approaches to advertising in general, and how different products can be handled. A few countries still ban television advertising or insist that all adverts are carried between certain hours. Some disapprove of comparative advertising ('knocking copy'), while an increasing number restrict the advertising of tobacco (Japanese consumers cannot comprehend the shock felt by visiting British or American visitors who see television ads for cigarettes in which an actor may be seen coming from a work-out in a gym and then reaching for a pack of cigarettes).

None of these differences is particularly serious, though they may tell us something about the deeper cultures of the countries concerned. The row about the allegedly racist Benetton ad, for instance, graphically illustrates how sensitive by world standards the US political culture is to racial and gender issues. Non-American politicians ignore this fact at their peril as Japan's ex-Premier Nakasone found when he blamed America's economic and social problems on the lack of racial homogeneity in the USA.

REGIONAL IDENTITIES

After a period in which an enthusiasm for global marketing moved to the fore, the tendency now is to emphasize the importance of broad regional differences. A major exposition of this approach was an article in the *Harvard Business Review* of May–June 1991 which summarized a survey of 12,000 executives in 25 different countries. Using cluster analysis, the authors identified a set of distinctive managerial attitudes.

They identified three main groups of cultural allies. The first group included the classic 'Anglo-Saxons' (Australia, Canada, Britain, New Zealand, the US) and Singapore: these countries came out as the least cosmopolitan of the sample (though one can argue about whether a lack of languages in an increasingly English-speaking world actually tells one a great deal about whether a management has global vision or not).

The second group is (with the exception of France) based on the use of the romance languages (Spanish, Portuguese and Italian). Taking in Argentina, Brazil, Italy, Mexico, Spain and Venezuela, there was amongst other characteristics a relatively high reliance on trade policy for industry protection.

Group 3 includes representative from the German-speaking world,

France, the Netherlands and Scandinavia. It was this group which was most cosmopolitan (on the criteria used in this survey).

Beyond these groups there are the cultural islands of Japan (strong emphasis on the work ethic), South Korea (protectionist, putting country ahead of company), India (protectionist) and Hungary (very focused on economic regeneration).

Such a study is not of massive use to a marketer, but it does serve to remind one that the world is still beset with cultural differences. On the other hand, it does show that it is possible to group countries in terms of cultural similarities, with linguistic links being particularly important. The search for international marketing patterns falls within an intermediate position on a spectrum which will range from purely local marketing at one end, to global marketing strategies at the other.

First of all, just using purely economic analysis, one can identify some simple patterns. As societies grow richer, the pattern of their consumer needs will change. African peasants will need basic foodstuffs, clothes and products like seeds and hoes – what they will not need is hamburger chains, Gucci shoes or Mercedes Benz cars (the occasional pickup truck is another matter). At a higher level of income, consumers will start to become interested in convenience foods, shampoos, video-recorders and the like. At the richest levels, consumers get the taste for fancy brands of Scotch whisky, fashionable holidays, powerful autos and so on.

What the marketer can do is take information about per capita wealth and decide at what point a particular country is likely to move into the kind of consumer patterns which the USA or other industrialized countries may have adopted some years ago. Products and marketing strategies which worked well in the US can then be used as a benchmark when considering how best to tackle the emerging needs of the newly-rich consumers. Even if products have to be modified to meet local cultural needs, and if advertising campaigns must be designed afresh, the global marketers will know that an underlying susceptibility to a particular type of product will tend to emerge at a particular level of development. They will know advertising campaigns which have worked in the past, elsewhere in the world. These can be used as a basis for experimentation. What we therefore see is the development of marketing strategies which may target 10–15 countries simultaneously, as Unilever did with Ragu. Global marketing today is, then, not best typified by the relatively standardized campaigns of Coca-Cola or McDonalds, but by intermediate cases where the corporate giants are starting to try rolling out marketing campaigns which have worked well on one continent to other parts of the triad world.

A nice example is breakfast cereals where Kellogg's, Nestlé and General Mills are shaping up for a Coke-vs-Pepsi-style global tussle which will leave the world eating a great deal more of branded, pre-prepared cereals – a need which is not always self-evident in cultures which have treated breakfast in a different way.

In this sector, Nestlé – strong in Europe, but weak in cereals – and General Mills – strong in cereals in the USA, but weak elsewhere – have formed a joint venture, Cereal Partners Worldwide (CPW), to internationalize General Mills' cereal brands such as Cheerios and Golden Grahams (plus Shredded Wheat and Shreddies which the joint venture picked up from a smaller competitor along the way). In Europe, the venture initially avoided traditional Kellogg's territory in the UK, and has started with France, Spain and Portugal. In future, the idea is to build on Nestlé's strength in Asia, Africa and Latin America to roll these products into relatively untapped markets which can only grow in the future.

There are two angles to this story which are worth noting. Firstly, this is a classic example of a global roll-out of brands which had been nurtured in the USA. The joint venture was put together hurriedly over 1989–90 because both partners knew they had little time to lose. The second lesson is that it is far quicker to license or buy brands than it is to build new ones from scratch. In food, the big players have been Nestlé (with its acquisitions of Rowntree and Buitoni), Philip Morris (Jacobs Suchard) and France's BSN (the manufacturer of Danone yoghurt which acquired Belin biscuits and Panzini pasta). As products compete for shelf-space in retail outlets, only the best-selling (most-recognized) brands will be given room.

Nestlé is a big, self-confident company with at least one mega-brand, Nescafé, under its control (in the late 1980s, Nestlé was producing 200 blends of coffee to satisfy its markets worldwide). Despite that, it could not conceive of developing its own cereal brands; even if it found the right magic formula, it would take from ten to thirty years to establish a totally new brand in an already oligopolistic market. Far better to do what it did with General Mills and buy into existing, under-exploited brands, so that it can concentrate on the global marketing which it knows well.

It is this potential of internationalizing existing brands which is behind a series of major acquisitions in brand-driven industries such as alcohol and perfumes. Unilever has been moving into perfumes (buying Calvin Klein and Elizabeth Arden), along with the French luxury goods company, LVMH (Christian Dior, Givenchy plus a stake in Guerlain), L'Oréal (Helena Rubinstein and a stake in Lanvin) and Procter & Gamble (Max Factor). As one looks into whiskies, beers and wines one finds the same picture – of the giants circling their smaller competitors, picking them off one by one. Guinness, in a fiercely-fought takeover battle for Distillers in the late 1980s, successfully acquired global brands such as Johnny Walker whisky to add to its own armoury of brands.

The brand-led giants are now beginning to raise the stakes. Just as their high-tech counterparts in other sectors are spending more on research and are increasing the number of product launches, so the branders are moving in a similar direction. In perfumes, for instance, the giants are using their financial muscle to launch an increasing number of new products, and to relaunch old ones ever more aggressively. The sums of money are, for a perfume, nowhere near the sums needed for a new automobile ($40 million is the range of money that a Unilever or an Estée Lauder could currently spend launching a new perfume in the USA alone), but are still beyond the reach of small companies marketing in only one country. The stakes for staying in the game are being constantly raised. As M. Antoine Riboud, chairman of BSN (a major French player in the brand-led food sector) has been quoted as saying: 'In this business, the number one makes a lot of money, the number two can make a decent living, the number three just suffers.'[5]

. . . and that sums up what the global branding battles are all about. It does not particularly matter to the global giants if the brands they are selling are true global brands or not; what does matter is that they control the top two or three brands in as many countries in the world as possible. For some, the battle is still to get fully established throughout the triad world. The real giants, however, are well ahead of that particular game. The Cokes, the Pepsis, the Unilevers, Nestlé's and the Philip Morrises are starting to lock up the next generation of consumers – the Indians, Chinese, the East Europeans and the former Soviet Union.

One final note: in all this discussion of brands, the Japanese have been conspicuously under-represented. Yes, they do have firms which are slugging it out in the brand-driven sectors. Suntory is no mean competitor in whiskies; firms like Shiseido and Kao are up against the Unilevers of the world. Yes, their manufacturing companies have shown brilliant marketing skills as they have driven their automobiles and consumer electronic goods worldwide. However, Japan has not had a history of branding in consumer goods, generally relying on the overall name of the producing company. Thus the coming of Asahi's 'Super Dry' beer, which doubled Asahi's market share almost overnight, was one of the first times that the vigorous promotion of a brand really worked.[6] On top of this in-experience is the problem of handling cultural diversity overseas, for there is no way that any company is going to maintain a global brand for decades unless it is fully sensitive to the cultural variations with which the world is filled.

Perhaps a sign of the times is the way that Nestlé and Coca-Cola are seeking to globalize canned ready-to-drink coffee, despite the fact that this beverage is a Japanese development – originally sold in vending machines outside railway stations. Nestlé and Coke have entered a joint venture in Japan to compete in this market. The lessons they learn from this experience will immediately be fed back into their own global networks. There is little sign that there are any Japanese companies in a position to compete against them outside Japan.

So very different from the strong Japanese competitive position in automobiles and consumer electronics. But then the culture behind branding is (primarily) American . . . and culture can still provide competitive advantages to nations.

5

CORPORATE STRATEGY: FAST, FLEXIBLE, FAR-SEEING?

THERE IS NO hiding place for the corporate giants. The revolutions in communications and transportation technology, the shortening product cycle, the internationalization of business are rewriting the rules, creating global competition at every conceivable level. Executives do not just have to focus on producing the right products at the right time. They are having to restructure their product development and manufacturing systems. In some cases, they are even having to redefine the industry which they are in. Simultaneously, they are having to develop strategies for each of the major continents, which is pushing them into problems of managing in a multi-cultural world. On top of all this, many of them are moving into the political unknown. Industrialists who could once count on a cosy relationship with their parent governments are being cast loose as the concept of protected national champions increasingly becomes obsolete.

All these challenges are hitting executives with increasing speed and intensity. To hesitate is to lose competitive momentum. In many cases, delays in coming up with strategic responses to this more brutal world can be fatal.

This is an environment which renders many past strategies irrelevant. The world of Henry Ford is dead – as is the world of Alfred Sloan, whose multi-divisional structure turned General Motors into a colossus which bestrode the world scene for so long.

Executives are having to feel their way into a future in which classic industrial organizations are ripe for tearing apart. Just as the model of the command economy has failed the competitive test at the national level, so is the classic Detroit-style, hierarchically-organized approach faltering at the level of the corporation.

New models are emerging, but their relevance to tomorrow's information-abundant world still has to be demonstrated. Executives still have an immense amount to learn from Japan's 'lean production' methods; however, serious questions still remain about how far one can generalize from the experience of Toyota and the other Japanese corporate giants. Again, the model of Japan and Germany suggests that 'families' of companies may give their members a competitive advantage over those companies which come from a more individualistic competitive environment. At the same time, the structural change occurring both within and around American giants such as IBM raises the possibility that the classic vertically-integrated, hierarchical multinational company is dying, and that new more flexible structures of competition and cooperation may be emerging.

The truth is that executives and management gurus round the world are all just guessing which strategies and structures will guarantee survival in the coming century. The slogan 'Think globally – Act locally' is appealing, but it is not self-evident how to combine global coordination and control with local adaptation and autonomy. The only certainties are that executives must assume that the emerging battle ground will be a multi-cultural one; that information barriers will continue to fall; and that lessons from the past will be of limited use to those seeking to plot a strategy which will stand the test of the coming decades.

THE DECLINE OF DETROIT

One symbol of what is happening is the fate of Motown – Detroit. For three-quarters of a century, Detroit was a symbol of all that was powerful in the American industrial sector. First, there was Henry Ford who perfected the classic mass-assembly factory. His approach was then perfected by Alfred Sloan who, in putting together General Motors, perfected the system of decentralized divisions, sharing a reasonable proportion of mechanical parts and joined in a coherent marketing strategy.[1] For decades, this formula worked well. In 1952, the then president of General Motors, 'Engine Charlie' Wilson, went on record as saying that what was good for the country was good for General Motors. Detroit was then at the zenith of its dominance of the world automotive industry.

During the 1960s, this classically simple organizational structure became more complex as computers allowed corporate headquarters to start coordinating activities which – pre-1939 – they would never have attempted to do. Thus Ford created Ford Europe to start the integration of its previously independent subsidiaries in Germany, the UK, Belgium, France and other locations. The dream was to create a world car which could be developed for production and sale around the world.

For a while, Ford and GM were able to make their global strategy work. Within the US they saw off the competition from European upstarts like Volkswagen and Renault, and even from Chrysler which, weak within the US, was unable to build itself a sustainable operation in Europe and was forced to retreat back to the Americas in the 1970s. In so doing, Chrysler became one of the first of the corporate giants to fail in the attempt to establish a genuinely inter-continental presence.

However, it is the fate of Detroit's Big Three in the 1980s which is of particular significance for this book. Both Chrysler and Ford faced major crises in the early 1980s from which Ford, in particular, drew important lessons. By studying Mazda, the Japanese company in which it took a 25 per cent stake in 1979, it realized just how far the Japanese industry had moved ahead of Detroit in the field of lean production. The American company launched a crash 'PJ' ('Post-Japan') programme which focused on slimming Ford down, speeding development times, drastically improving quality peformance and improving relationships with suppliers. Although this has not saved Ford from losses in the early 1990s, the company has learned significant lessons, such as with the building of its plant in Hermosilla in Mexico in the mid-1980s. Ford drew heavily on Mazda's Japanese experience and produced a plant with the best quality record of all the world's mass-assembly auto plants surveyed by the MIT team.[2]

GM took longer to learn. Like Ford, it had links with one of the smaller Japanese auto manufacturers (Isuzu) but, unlike Ford, it never put a serious effort into building links with its partner. Instead, it did some learning from the Japanese, through the GM-Toyota NUMMI joint venture in California, in which an old GM factory was converted to joint production of Chevrolet/Toyota cars. In general, though, it drew the wrong conclusions in the early 1980s, assuming that salvation would come primarily from the application of advanced electronics and automated production – despite the fact that the Japanese were showing that this was only partly the answer; good production engineering and the development of teamwork were also part of the solution. So GM invested heavily in high-tech companies; and, in creating its Saturn division, it sought to demonstrate that the application of advanced automation in a freshly created division could lead to an operation fully competitive with the Japanese.

Effectively GM failed. After losing $2 billion in 1990 and $4.5 billion in 1991, it finally had to bite the bullet. It announced that it would be closing six assembly plants and 15 other facilities by 1995, losing along the way some 74,000 blue and white collar jobs. Overall, this would mean that the workforce will end up just half of its 1985 size.[3] This can only be described as a massive down-sizing in response to a general strategic failure in the face of growing competition from Japan and faster-reacting competitors such as Ford.

THE GLOBAL SHAKEOUT

GM is only one of a long line of companies throughout the USA and Europe which have been forced to announce similar slash-and-burn rationalizations. Within the USA, there are cases such as Firestone which, during the mid-1980s, while trying to remain independent, lopped 50,000 from its workforce (which was roughly halved), but still ended up being acquired by the Japanese competitor, Bridgestone. IBM cut 53,000 jobs in the late 1980s, and announced in late 1991 that another 20,000 would have to go, some of them forcibly. In 1990, McDonnell-Douglas, the American aerospace company, announced it would be shedding 11 per cent of its workforce and in late 1991 began negotiating to sell 40 per cent of the company to Taiwanese interests. In early 1992, another aerospace company, United Technologies, announced the elimination of 13,900 jobs and the closure or consolidation of more than 100 facilities around the world.

Within Europe, British Steel cut its labour force by 112,000 between 1980 and 1990, ending with just over 50,000 employees. In October 1990, the Dutch electronics company, Philips, announced cuts of between 45,000 and 55,000 from a global workforce of 285,000, and let 24,200 of them go in the first nine months of 1991. Other significant announcements have included 35,000 lay-offs by Fiat (1990), 15,000 by Electrolux (1990), 6,000 by Anglo-Dutch Unilever (1991) and 3,400 by the Dutch automotive company DAF (1990).

Such deep rationalizations have been the typical response of companies finally becoming aware of how desperately their competitive position has slipped. Although tragic in terms of individual employees and, often, whole communities, such butchery is often the first grim step toward staunching financial losses, and thus buying time as survival plans are put into place.

Philips is a good example of how such rationalizations can be managed. Once the company had faced up to how badly it had fallen behind the Japanese competition, it rethought its overall strategy and shifted focus more purely toward consumer electronics. It thus got out of a number of sectors such as information technology, white goods (where it had a joint venture with the American company Whirlpool), and telecommunications (where it had a joint venture with AT&T). It also pulled out of some of its pan-European collaborative research efforts. For European industrial policy, all this was an apparent disaster, since Philips was one of the few local companies which could conceivably be a significant player in such strategic sectors. On the other hand, this intensive restructuring at least pulled the company back into the black over 1991, thus buying it time to see if one of its new consumer-oriented products would come good over the subsequent couple of years.

As with all such rationalizations, the easy steps come first. Cutting back on 'non-core' activities and pruning the dead wood are relatively simple (if unpleasant). Once that is done, management has to put product strategies in place which will produce the next generation of profits needed to sustain growth. In the case of Philips (a company with a strong research tradition), the odds are that it will pull itself around. It is hard to be as optimistic about a number of the other companies which have been slashing employment since the turn of the decade.

One can, in fact, see the current wave of rationalizations in terms of Joseph Schumpeter's cycles of 'creative destruction'. In this case, companies are responding to two challenges – the globalization of competition (in particular the rise of Japan) and the accelerating impact of the information revolution. The application of computers, fax machines, and direct-dial telephones has meant that it has become possible to shrink managerial bureaucracies by hacking out whole layers of management which, in earlier, pre-electronic days were essential to coordinate the activities of complex operations. The need for coordination is still there, but the electronic neural paths of the modern corporation are now robust enough for decision-makers to be able to communicate with each other with a speed and precision which previous generations of executives could only dream of. At the simplest level, the word-processor has meant that the automatic assumption that each executive had his/her own secretary is now invalid. Similarly, the fax machine and direct overseas dialling means that complex international divisions are become less necessary as an intermediary between company headquarters and decision-makers scattered throughout the globe.

So, when GM and the others reach for the axe, they are not necessarily damaging themselves. Instead, they are often belatedly coming to terms with the organizational realities of today's world. Just as the clerks of the nineteenth century who transcribed document after document with quill pens were eradicated by the advent of the typewriter, so the middle manager of the post-1945 era is being eradicated by the electronic wave

Figure 6

THE FALLING COSTS OF LONG-DISTANCE TELECOMMUNICATIONS

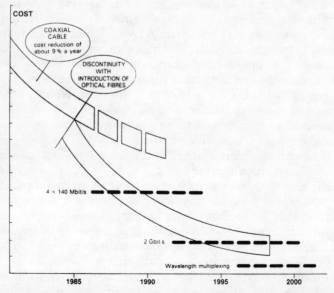

Source: Reproduced from H Ungerer & N P Costello: Telecommunications in Europe, Brussels: Commission of the EC, 1988, p.43

which is transforming the way that any organization – let alone global ones – is being run.

Cutting out layers of bureaucracy, however, does not necessarily guarantee that the creativity of the executives who are left will improve. Managements who have their eyes turned to the wrong competitive targets will go under, however much they may have hacked away at their bureaucracies.

THE LESSONS FROM IBM

IBM is, like General Motors, one of those bellwether companies by which the health of the US economy has recently been judged. To those of us writing about corporate issues in the 1960s and 1970s, IBM's onward march seemed unstoppable – but it, too, is in crisis. The big difference from GM is that IBM's response has been very much more sophisticated – and it tells us a great deal about how the world is changing.

IBM is a classic example of how the IT revolution has redefined the nature of competition in key industrial sectors. Quite simply, over the course of the post-war era, IBM came to dominate the world of mainframe computer – and 'dominate' is the correct word to use. Throughout the 1970s and early 1980s its share of the world's data processing market came close to 40 per cent. For much of that time, IBM was under heavy pressure from the antitrust authorities both in the USA and Europe to demonstrate that it was not abusing its position of dominance. Both in Japan and West Europe, industrial policy was aimed at producing companies which could at least survive in the face of IBM's competitive challenge. Few thought that anything would stop IBM pulling ahead of older industrial giants such as GM and Exxon.

Ironically, IBM has proven to be a victim of the technologies which gave it so much wealth for so long. As microelectronic developments put ever greater computing power into microchips, the role of mainframe computers came under steady attack. IBM was forced to legitimize this development when it launched its Personal Computer in 1981. This was a major commercial success, but IBM was unable to control the wave of competitors which it unleashed, and it was thus unable to engineer a controlled shift away from mainframe computing toward the decentralized computing power which came from each office desk increasingly having its own PC.

Effectively, IBM misjudged the speed at which developments in computing technology would hit at its strategic core. First, it was very slow to realize that the switch to desk top computing was unleashing an avalanche of competition from (often small) companies which had low overheads, could move extremely fast and, in the case of companies like Compaq, produce higher quality products than IBM envisioned. This failure of vision meant that IBM spent a decade in which it slowed its decision-making and produced unattractive commercial compromises in an effort to maintain the kind of industry control that it once had in mainframes. The result was that IBM's share of the world computer industry fell from 36 per cent to 23 per cent in the 1980s – and to compound this disastrous performance, it even failed to maintain its hold on the Personal Computer market, dropping from 27 per cent market share to 16.5 per cent by the early 1990s.[4]

Its response has been two-fold.

First, realizing that it no longer has the in-house skills or cultures to keep the lead in all parts of the industry, it has become one of the foremost exponents of the strategic alliance concept, whereby companies enter alliances with other independent companies (normally to cooperate in one or two very distinctive areas). In IBM's case, this has involved entering alliances with companies such as Apple (primarily for the creation of new imaginative software), France's Groupe Bull (in which IBM is taking a small equity stake), and Germany's Siemens (collaboration on the productions of 16- and 64-megabit DRAM chips). In addition, in Europe alone, over 1990–91, IBM spent $100 million to buy into some 200 software and computer-service companies. Elsewhere in its empire, it was starting to make computers for Wang and Mitsubishi. In chips, it forged an agreement with Intel to push the downsizing of computers toward the goal of getting a computer on a chip.

Secondly, in late 1991, it announced a programme of radical de-centralization of power within its system to give considerable autonomy to business units such as Personal Computers and Workstations ($14 billion revenue in 1991), Storage Products (tape and disk drives: $10.8 billion), Software ($10.6 billion) and a number of other activities, possibly including its semiconductor business. Some of its traditional operations (typewriters and printers, for example) were hived off into autonomous or quasi-autonomous enterprises.

The idea is that IBM headquarters at Armonk will retreat from making operating decisions and will become much more of a holding company. The autonomous business units will be given profit-and-loss responsi-bility, will be expected to hit financial targets, but will increasingly be free to choose how closely they will work with other parts of the IBM family, and could even be allowed to float some of their shares on the market, thus winning an even greater sense of independence.

The full implications of this reorganization will be dealt with later. For the moment, what matters is that IBM is facing up to global competition in an even more ambitious way than firms such as Ford started to do in the mid-1980s. Both Ford and now IBM have realized that rebuilding competitiveness is not just about slashing costs. It is about redefining the very way in which even (perhaps, particularly) the corporate giants do business. There is an urgency within today's executive elite. Massive competitive change is inevitable and irresistible. All one can do is take some initial defensive steps, and then redirect executive attention to the

Figure 7

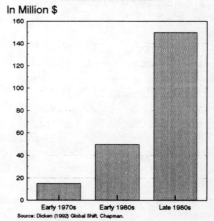

SEMICONDUCTOR	YEAR
Discrete Devices	1948
Integrated Circuits	1960s
1K DRAM	1970
4K DRAM	1973
16K DRAM	1976
64K DRAM	1978
256K DRAM	1983
1M DRAM	1986
4M DRAM	1989
16M DRAM	1992*

MILESTONES IN THE DEVELOPMENT OF SEMICONDUCTORS OVER TIME

* Initial Production

Sources: Economist; Financial Times; Langlois
(1988) Microelectronics. Unwin Hyman; Malerba
(1985) Semiconductor Business. Pinter.

NEW CHIP PRODUCTION PLANT
Minimum Investment
In Million $

Source: Dicken (1992) Global Shift. Chapman.

real sources of global competition, while redesigning the structures within which they work.

THE IMPERATIVES

Accepting that companies are having to develop strategies for an extremely fast-moving world, are there any general patterns which can be identified?

1. GETTING THE TECHNOLOGY RIGHT

Firstly, it is clear that all companies must continuously monitor the impact that new technologies are having on their industries.

In some cases, technology is actually redefining the business sector in which a company is doing business. IBM's experience with the computing world is a graphic example of the way IT has revolutionized one key sector. Another concerns the British company Reuters which has developed a world lead in the field of computerized financial trading systems. Originally, Reuters was a conventional newswire service feeding worldwide news to the British newspaper industry. As newspapers gradually lost ground to television, it seemed that Reuters would gently fade away. In fact, it discovered that it had developed a lead in the electronic transmission of financial information, and worked hard to build up a global network of terminals through which currency movements could be tracked and then traded. At present, 40 per cent of foreign currency trades are made through a Reuters system. This company is moving on from mere currencies, and is aiming to develop a system which will allow clients to trade stocks, options and futures on a single screen. In so evolving, Reuters has been at the very heart of the development of 24-hour financial markets. It has come a long way from its mundane beginnings.

There are other examples within the financial services sector of the way that IT developments are blurring industry boundaries. In particular, the development of electronic money-transfer systems, credit cards and automatic teller machines (i.e. 'hole-in-the-wall' cashpoint machines) have transformed the banking industry. Technologies such as these have allowed non-banks such as Sears Roebuck, General Motors Acceptance Corp and a number of savings and loans operations (building societies in the UK) to become major financial institutions carrying out many of the transactions which used to be a banking monopoly.

Even if technology does not produce completely new sectors, it is proving a potent force in blurring boundaries between apparently distinct industries. When this happens, established companies on either side of the divide are forced to act, even if there is no guaranteed route to survival. As we write, the erosion of the barriers between telephone systems (carrying voice messages), telex-style systems (carrying information) and television (carrying sound and pictures) is well under way. Effectively, the digital revolution is moving toward a world in which a single transmission media can simultaneously carry television signals, complex computer interactions and telephone conversations. Additonally the distribution between the telecommunications network operators and the providers of value-added telecommunications services (such as on-line data-bases or dial-a-weather-forecasts) is blurring.

There is lively debate about how comprehensively companies should respond to this convergence of computing and telecommunications. The Japanese electronic giant NEC has a specific strategy in which it seeks to foster the convergence of its computer and communications equipment activities. Fujitsu is another Japanese company which seeks to combine these two sectors. Various western companies have sought to achieve such results via strategic alliances with apparently complementary companies. Thus AT&T tried first to enter Europe via two doomed alliances – one with Philips (with a consumer electronics bias) and another with Olivetti (a company with a computing tradition). Canada's Northern Telecom formed similar alliances with computer companies such as Apple, DEC and Hewlett-Packard.

In another kind of intelligent response to technological developments, a company can use technology to rejuvenate old products or effectively create new ones. Sony has been at the centre of a number of such breakthroughs made possible by developments in solid-state electronics.

Figure 8

Convergence of Communications and Computing Technologies

	1847-	1870-	1920-	1940-	1960s	1970s	1980s
Communications Technology	* Telegraphy	* Telephony	* Sound Photo * Facsimile * Telex	* Radio * Television * Tape Recording * Direct Distance Calling	* Colour Television * Communications Satellites * Digital Communications * Electronic Switching	* Facsimile Transmission * Packet Switching * Optical Fibre * Video-Disks	* Cellular Radio * Private Satellites * Integrated Service Digital Networks * Electronic Mail * Tele-Conferencing * On-line Enquiry * Computer Aided Design * Computer Aided Manufacturing * Videotext * Materials Planning and Stock Control * Remote Sensing Devices
Hybrids					* Stereo Hi-fi Sound	* Teletext * Paging	
Computing Technology	* Analytical Engine	* Punched Card Business Machine	* Electro-Mechanical Calculator * Differential Analyzer	* Transistor * Electronic Numerical Integrator and Computer * Electronic Calcultor	* Structured Programming * Mini-Computers * Integrated Circuits	* VLSI * Spreadsheets * Micro-Processors * Applications Generators * LSI * Database Mngt Systems	* Wafer Scale Integration * Dataflow Processor * Expert Systems * Transputer * Optical Disk Storage * Portable Computers

Sources: Dicken (1992) Global Shift. Chapman;
Flamm (1988) Creating the Computer. Brookings;
Commission of the European Communities (1987).

53

The original transistor radio, for instance, was a classic example of how an apparently mature product could be rejuvenated by the application of microelectronics. The video recorder in its initial guise was a bulky, expensive product aimed at professional television studios: what Sony (and Philips and the Matsushita Group) did was to miniaturize the product by applying microelectronics until, in the 1970s, they had a product which was both cheap and compact enough to become a staple product within the home. Finally, Sony had the genius to produce the Sony Walkman, a product which was in its way as brilliant a conception as the original transistor radio. Once again, the miniaturization made possible by electronic developments allowed the development of a totally new consumer product. Sony had once again hit the jackpot.

In today's world, though, the intelligent application of new technologies has to be far more pervasive than merely to help the production of conceptually brilliant new consumer products. All the lessons from Japan's developments of the Lean Production system are that technology is now being used to speed development times, to increase the flexibility of productions systems, without in any way compromising their overall dedication to quality.

It is important to stress that the Japanese lead in Lean Production has not been developed just by the application of new, flexible technologies.

There is some important social organization underpinning this post-Ford era. Having conceded this, the challenge to western companies has been extreme. It has been most obvious in the automotive sector, but throughout other key sectors such as consumer electronics and semi-conductors, Japanese companies have been showing their mastery of contemporary industrial production techniques.

There are other, non-Japanese cases of companies which have gained considerable competitive advantage by discovering creative ways of applying new technologies to their businesses. Italy's Benetton is a good example. Founded in 1965 in a disused henhouse in north-east Italy it had, by 1990, become the world's largest consumer of raw wool, selling imaginatively designed woollen garments through 5,900 shops in 82 countries. Originally a knitwear manufacturer, it eventually moved into retailing, where it realized that by electronically linking the stores to the design, manufacturing and warehousing operations, it could gain an advantage over its competitors by producing garments in undyed wool, then dyeing them at the last moment to hit the changing fashion requirements of end-markets. The intensive use of electronics allows management to monitor what is happening in each market (by the late 1980s, the world was divided into 70 areas,), and to shorten the time needed for orders to be scheduled through factories. The current generation of electronic equipment allows Benetton to capture the model, colour and size of all garments sold in key shops round the world. This gives the company advance warning of changing demand patterns, and thus permits optimum scheduling of production. The use of computer-aided design means that the company can produce a much greater variety of garments than would otherwise be the case. By the end of the 1980s, its annual production of 50 million garments came in the form of 3,000 designs using around 200 different colours.[5]

Within the airline industry, airlines realized that there was competitive advantage to be won from moving early into computerized reservation systems. American (the Sabre system) and United (Apollo) moved early into this business, and positively sought to include other companies in them. For a while (until the competition authorities caught up with them), they were able to play competitive games in which, rivals alleged, the controlling airline's flights were shown most prominently. Ultimately though, these reservations systems have proved a good investment. In 1990, for instance, American was earning more from the Sabre system than it was from its conventional airline business.

STANDARDS BATTLES

A further way in which corporate strategy interacts with technology is in the area of standards, because, just as companies can win by getting their brands accepted globally, so they can also gain a competitive advantage by getting their technological standards generally accepted.

There is nothing particularly new about this. If one thinks back over the history of, say, recorded music, there were no guarantees that consumers would ultimately settle on, first, 78 revolutions-per-minute records, then 33 rpm long-playing records and, finally, 45 rpm singles. In each case, the format which won out did so over alternative ones of which few of us are even conscious. Whatever happened to the 16⅔ rpm record?

The increasing pace of technological change means that companies are faced with standards-determined marketing at decreasing intervals. Thus the long-playing record has been superseded not just with one product but with a variety. Not only have both the audio tape and the compact disk been competing to replace the LP, but they have been evolving in their turn, as both Philips and Sony have tried to establish their variants of digital compact cassettes as an alternative to CDs.

One only has to look back to the development of video recorders to see the importance of such battles. Three different standards struggled for recognition on world markets. Philips was into the field early with its V2000 system, but took slightly too long to settle on one fixed standard. Sony was recognized as having the most sophisticated product (Betamax), but was too restrictive in licensing the technology. It was therefore left to JVC (and its Matsushita parent company) to walk off with the prize through the VHS system, which it licensed widely, thus developing a critical mass of software dependent on the VHS system. As consumers increasingly bought or rented VHS tapes, they became increasingly dependent on VHS hardware which further strengthened the demand for VHS tapes, and so on. This saga explains why Japanese consumer electronics firms like Sony are so determined to secure access to the Hollywood film and record catalogues. They see this as allowing them to give their next generation electronic products a competitive initial kick by simultaneously launching attractive films and records on the relevant software.

Sony, Philips and, to a lesser extent, Matsushita have been key players in these standards wars. The first two, in particular, have cooperated quite closely in setting mutually beneficial standards, starting with the initial audiotape cassette, and taking in a lot of developments in compact disc technology. They both know that a product which can be given solid initial support simultaneously in Japan, West Europe and the USA (which now has no real consumer electronics champion in its own right) will tend to win over products which have to establish themselves sequentially in the three centres of the triad world. Although they will still find themselves pushing some mutually-incompatible products (digital compact cassettes are a case in point), in general, they know the importance of working together to develop mutually-acceptable standards where and whenever possible.

Developing the industry standard is not always a key to success, however. In consumer electronics Philips developed the standard for the original audiotape cassette systems, but lost out to the Japanese. A similar process occurred in personal computers, as described earlier. Since the original PC case, IBM and its competitors have been in an interesting battle, where IBM has been trying to make subsequent proprietary standards stick with greater force, while the competition has been aiming to develop 'Open' standards which would effectively allow equipment and software from different sources to link together without any one company trying to dictate on what terms this connection should be made. The jury is still out on this contest.

General Motors has pioneered an equivalent approach to factory automation with MAP (Manufacturing Automation Protocol) which is designed to let equipment from a variety of manufacturers be used together.

Elsewhere, governments can come into the standards-setting arena. Sometimes, they simply have to be the key setters of standards: for instance, no one is going to start manufacturing television sets until it is clear how the broadcast signals will operate. Increasingly, such standards setting is seen to have a place to play in industrial policy. In the first wave of television standards creation, the fact that Europe and the USA ended with three distinct standards was of commercial importance – particularly in Europe where the French could use the SECAM standards to protect French industrial interests, and where the PAL licence used elsewhere in Europe was used positively to force Japanese television manufacturers to show competitive restraint. As we write, there is a complicated battle taking place around High-Definition Television (HDTV) standards, with the USA, Japan and Europe all aware that the precise standards chosen will affect the competitive position of Japanese consumer electronics companies against the rest – though there is a convincing argument that today's consumer electronics companies are so globally alert that they will adapt quite easily to whatever standards are set on each continent.

Most industrial sectors will have some standards which are of commercial significance. From the foregoing, one can see it is sometimes up to the companies concerned to find ways to get their standards accepted as *de facto* global ones. In other cases, it is still up to governments to set standards, but they will normally do so with an eye to improving the competitive position of indigenous companies. In either case, either company or government is motivated by a knowledge that standards are an important weapon in the search for global competitive supremacy.

2. BRANDS: THE GLOBAL ROLLOUT

Mastering high technology is not the only route to a global presence. The testimony of firms such as Coca-Cola, Philip Morris, McDonald's, Nestlé, Unilever, Grand Metropolitan, Kellogg, General Mills, Levi Strauss, Walt Disney, Guinness, Heineken, Seagram, Suntory, Nintendo and Kao is that a dedication to the black arts of marketing can be just as effective in breaking into global markets as producing a series of research and development breakthroughs – and often a successful brand may be far more durable than products which rest on a relatively short-lived patent.

In an earlier chapter we have touched on the issue of global brands. Although we sided with the sceptics who challenge the idea that the majority of products are ever going to be suitable for global branding, there can be no doubt that all companies should examine their marketing strategies to see how far they should at least start to go down this route. This is because the lesson from brands is that, once one is established as one of the leading two or three in its field, it becomes a potent force which can often be maintained as a leading brand for decades on end – providing the company behind the brands is astute enough.

What we are seeing today is a rush by consumer products companies to stimulate consumer markets in the economies which are currently edging into some form of prosperity, while establishing brands wherever this is possible.

An example of this process is the joint venture called Cereal Partners Worldwide (CPW) formed between General Mills and Nestlé in the late 1980s as described in the last chapter. General Mills was seeking to take its American expertise in breakfasts cereals into a world where Kellogg had often arrived first. Nestlé had a very strong global presence with products like Nescafé, but was weak in cereals. Hence the purpose of the joint venture was to roll out General Mills' branded products through Nestlé's global marketing networks. Within Europe, they have been spreading Cheerios, Golden Grahams and (a recent acquisition) Shredded Wheat through southern European countries like France, Spain and

Portugal, which have been relatively unaffected by the Kellogg cereal breakfast offensive which has been so effective in North European countries like the UK. In the future, such products can be rolled out through Nestlé's marketing channels in Asia, Africa and Latin America.[6]

This is a classic case of two companies setting out to cover the world with established brands and their variants in one particular market sector. What is happening in breakfast cereals is being replicated in cigarettes, razors, detergents, alcohol, fast foods, clothes, instant coffees, perfumes, lavatory cleansers, margarines, hotels, soaps, confectionery, shampoos, toothpastes and so on. Where products can be branded, they are eased into the awareness of the global citizen. Once in the global consciousness, they will be hard to eradicate.

Extending the geographical boundaries of the consumer society is the territory of the truly giant consumer goods multinationals – the Unilevers, Procter & Gambles and Coca-Colas of the world. Where consumer markets are already well developed, more subtle strategies are developing. All sane marketers are aware of the dangers of over-standardization, but still the competitive pressures are on the multinationals to rationalize their marketing campaigns. This kind of product launch was employed by Gillette with its Sensor razor (introduced in 1989) with a common name and marketing strategy in 19 countries on both sides of the Atlantic. On the other hand, one can find companies in the same industrial sector which take different positions on whether to go for global or regional brands. In domestic appliances for instance, the American company Whirlpool is tending to go the global route, while its European competitor, Electrolux, is keeping local brands in existence alongside its pan-European ones.[7]

However, even if brands are not standardized, it is still possible to take a marketing strategy from one country and apply it to an equivalent product in a second country. One such example is the campaign for Nestlé freeze-dried coffees in the UK (Nescafé) and the USA (Taster's Choice), in which a sophisticated man about town and his attractive neighbour borrow the coffee from each other and, over a sequence of advertisements, develop a romantic relationship – keeping the coffee link active. Although not to everyone's taste, these serial advertisements worked well in the UK and so were adapted for a similarly positioned product in the USA. Similarly, Coca-Cola used the same basic McCann-Erickson storyboard for a TV commercial (big tough athlete shares drink with young fan) developed in the USA to feature football star 'Mean Joe' Greene of the Pittsburgh Steelers in its campaign in Thailand where it used a local soccer star, Niwat, and in Argentina the soccer player Diego Maradona.

Marketing is not just about devising the correct branding strategy however. It is also about devising marketing strategies which keep the pressure on the competition. Once again, the Japanese seem to be leading the way in the key area where technology and marketing intersect – that is in the number of products put on the market, and the speed with which they can be developed.

Japanese companies put much less emphasis than their western competitors on formal market research. Instead they follow a 'scatter-shot' approach, in which companies follow hunches, cover their competitors' products through reverse engineering and throw a wide variety of products at the market, with the minimum 'time-to-market' possible, and then wait to see which products succeed or fall by the wayside. Special 'antennae' shops for product launches area developed, and then monitored closely for consumer reaction. Successful products can then be reinforced by clusters of related products, and unsuccessful ones can be quickly dropped.

Production technology comes into the equation, because if one is dealing with products of the complexity of the automobile, one needs the kind of production flexibility pioneered by the Lean System to produce models in the shorter, more idiosyncratic, runs which today's individualistic consumer demands.

Speeding product development is not, however, just a question of good technology, as the case of the British pharmaceutical company, Glaxo, shows. Glaxo's success with one anti-ulcer drug called Zantac turned it into Britain's largest company by capitalization (1991). Zantac was not the first anti-ulcer drug to hit world markets, but the Glaxo management gambled that, by shortening the time-to-market for Zantac from the normal ten years to five, then they would ultimately win the global marketing battle. So the scientists carried out all the development stages in the laboratory simultaneously (although such speed carries increased cost and risk). Secondly, the drug was launched in every large market in the world at the same time, instead of being rolled out one by one. Third, it was priced at a premium to strengthen the impression that this was a distinctive product. Everything in this strategy worked smoothly, and Glaxo became the second largest drugs company in the world.[8]

This is a very clear example of the rewards that are potentially there for companies which can speed development times, while simultaneously marketing globally. The financial risks may grow. But the rewards grow higher too.

GETTING THE GEOGRAPHY RIGHT

Technology and products are only part of the picture. Equally important is knowing how to position the company round the globe.

The emerging conventional wisdom is that companies must establish themselves throughout the triad world. This is the basic tenet of an author such as Kenichi Ohmae. If companies are not established throughout the globe, then they fail to gain the scale economies needed to sustain the company in an era of intensified competition.

There is much truth in this argument, and one can identify at least three different kinds of companies which have to consider globalization as a major strand in their strategy.

The technologically-driven ones need to spread research and product development costs across as wide a set of markets as they can develop. The aircraft and aero-engine manufacturers are a classic example of the forces at work here, with Boeing, McDonnell-Douglas and Airbus in the former sector, and General Electric, Pratt & Whitney and Rolls-Royce (with Snecma as a bit player) in the latter, fighting a global battle for survival. There are immense barriers to entry into both industries, and the Japanese have no immediate prospects of breaking into them as an independent player. Despite that, all the western aerospace companies are being forced to develop strategies which include some form of partnerships or alliances with Japanese and other Asian companies, in order to improve their chances of picking up a decent share of the fast-growing Pacific Rim market.

In the commercial jet sector, the mighty Boeing has found it sensible to bring in Japanese risk-sharing partners in the development of the 777 wide-bodied jet. McDonnell-Douglas entered the 1990s faced with the prospect of being driven into a poor third behind Boeing and Airbus by the mid-1990s. Its reaction has been to look for equity investors and risk-sharing sub-contractors in Taiwan, Japan, Korea, Singapore and Indonesia. There is a possibility that at least part of McDonnell-Douglas' operations could become an Asian equivalent of Airbus Industrie – a regional champion for a range of governments. All these aerospace companies know that success in North America and West Europe is not enough. If they fail also to establish themselves in Pacific Rim markets, they will lose the scale economies which are critical to long-term survival.

It is a moot point how many other industries are driven purely by scale economies in production and development. Semi-conductors, pharmaceuticals, much of computing and telecommunications equipment manufacturing, automobiles and consumer electronics would all seem to be sufficiently scale-led to require some form of triad strategy. In a number of these sectors, the Japanese have an advantage in that they are moving outward from a market which has, until recently, been extremely difficult to penetrate – originally for protectionist reasons, now primarily for cultural ones. Inevitably, this has given industries such as Japanese automotives and consumer electronics an extra competitive edge, particularly when western companies have been extremely slow to react competitively within Europe and North America.

A second reason for adopting a triad strategy is where companies are market driven in sectors where tastes are homogenizing. Even with brands, there are scale economies. It matters, for instance, to Pepsico that Coca-Cola has traditionally been much stronger globally, controlling 46 per cent of the international soft-drinks market, and deriving 80 per cent of its profit from selling Coke, Sprite and Fanta sodas in non-US markets.[9] By failing to slug it out with Coke on an equal basis all round the world, Pepsi has been ceding its competitor the lion's share of the faster-growing, most profitable markets, thus endangering its competitive position within the USA.

In cases like the Pepsi/Coke or Kellogg-Nestlé/General Mills battles we are dealing with competitive global roll-outs: large parts of the globe are still under-exploited in branding terms. Competition between the branded giants turns around the comparative speed and effectiveness in which they can establish their presence in successive countries and regions. If, within the USA, the leading brand in 1925 was still (in 19 out of 22 standard products) in the same position today,[10] the rewards for winning global brand leadership today can only be described as immense.

A third reason for developing a global strategy is to follow's one's clients. If they go global, or if the centre of gravity of one's chosen industrial sector shifts as new competitors move to the fore, then component suppliers have to adapt their strategies. In the past, this was why American auto-component companies like Borg-Warner moved abroad. Today, it explains why the Japanese component suppliers like Bridgestone (tyres), Nippondenso (automotive electronics) and Calsonic (catalytic converters etc.) have moved so actively into the USA. They have been following the key customers, the Japanese automotive giants, as the latter have set up transplant factories in North America. One can find similar developments in any industrial sector. It is even starting to happen in telecommunications where the more ambitious telecoms players feel that the giant multinationals would increasingly like to buy all their global telecoms business through one company. Sprint, the third largest long-distance carrier in the USA, is now offering such services. On the data front, in 1991, it won the contract to run Unilever's entire European data network, beating off competition from AT&T, British Telecom and information technology firms like Digital Equipment and EDS.[11].

In industries such as automobiles and consumer electronics, where the centre of gravity has moved to Japan, non-Japanese component suppliers have an interesting dilemma. Japanese transplant operations – particularly in Europe – are not completely closed to indigenous component suppliers. However, overall product design and, thus, a great deal of purchasing policy is carried out in Japan. An initial way to break into this system is to form joint ventures with Japanese component suppliers close to the transplant assembly lines, but this may merely legitimize the presence of the Japanese suppliers. The more ambitious approach is to seek to supply the Japanese assemblers anywhere in the world, including within Japan itself. Thus a British component company, GKN, sells products to the Japanese transplant community in North America. Another such British company, Lucas, has entered a joint venture with Sumitomo to make brakes in the USA, and is signing licensing deals with the Japanese in a bid to win business in Japan. A few companies have gone further to cement relations with the Japanese corporate headquarters. The British chemical company, ICI, has established a technical centre in Japan at least in part because it missed the chance of getting close to the Japanese consumer electronic companies as they started to dominate the electronic media: through its technical centre in Tsukuba Science City, it hopes to demonstrate that it is a serious, quality-driven player in the plastic films needed in this fast-moving market which is now driven from Japan. By working more closely with product designers in Japan, the outsider companies hope to increase their chances of winning contracts throughout the global operations of the Japanese giants.

This brings us to one other reason for selective investments round the globe: the world's most innovative markets now vary between different product sectors. In many cases, US markets are still the most innovative. So, if one wants to monitor environmental, life-style or movie developments, then a presence in California is essential. Although there were other reasons why Sony invested in Columbia Pictures, it was part of a traditional response by the Japanese company to life-style developments in this opinion-forming state.

Michael Porter developed this argument in his book, *The Competitive Advantage of Nations*, in which he argued that different countries develop the early movers in a particular industry. Thus, in agricultural chemicals, Du Pont moved its European headquarters from Geneva to Paris to get closer to the major agricultural centre in Europe. In small copiers, Xerox's involvement in Fuji-Xerox has allowed it to take part in an industry which is now led technically by Japan. In domestic appliances, Philips moved its relevant headquarters to Italy.[12]

From the Fuji-Xerox and earlier ICI examples, one can see the growing strategic importance of Japan. In consumer electronics, for instance, Japan has become the prime source of innovation, and Philips, the main European presence in this sector, has responded by strengthening its presence there. In a related move, it has been using Taiwan as its main focus on the residual black and white television sector. This reflects the way that the whole East Asian Pacific Rim has become the world's lead centre for low-cost electronic assembly.

Within Europe, the UK has become a world centre for the hotel industry, and the Inter-Continental chain switched its headquarters from the USA to reflect this fact. The UK has also quite consciously used deregulation policies to stimulate competition within the telecommunications and financial services sectors. This paid off when IBM switched the headquarters of its telecommunications division out of the USA to the UK (the first time IBM had ever let this happen). Within the world telecommunications sector, it is generally acknowledged that the UK is now providing the most competitive market in regards to mobile telephony and other telecommunications developments. The result is that companies like the American Baby Bells (the offshoots of AT&T's divestiture) are investing in the UK to explore branches of business which regulators in the USA still deny them.

GEOGRAPHICAL RETRENCHMENT

Not all companies will be able to sustain a truly global presence, and some very interesting questions are going to be thrown up by those who decide they are going to have to build their future strategy on a presence in only one or two continents. This may be permissible because of the particular logic of the relevant industrial sector in which the company finds itself. Retailing, for instance, may be one of those industries where it is genuinely difficult to transfer experience across national borders, let alone across oceans. Marks & Spencer, the British retailer par excellence, has found it hard to make inroads into the Canadian market with its own stores, or the US market, where it acquired the Ivy-League clothier Brooks Brothers.

In most cases, though, we are going to see companies retreating from an inter-continental strategy because they are, quite simply, unable to establish themselves competitively outside their home economy. Chrysler is a classic case of a company which has beaten a geographical retreat, having failed to establish itself in Europe during the 1960s and 1970s. More recently, there have been other significant retreats within the automotive industry. Both Rover and Peugeot have withdrawn from the American market. Volkswagen still sells there but has stopped manufacturing in the US, having failed to consolidate its early marketing success with the VW Beetle model. As a company, VW can supply the US market from production facilities in Mexico, Canada, Brazil or Argentina, but the fact that it is clearly putting considerable trust in the importance of cheap labour assembly is not particularly reassuring when the Japanese are showing it is possible to invest in the USA and be competitive.

In early 1992 Federal Express withdrew from the intra-European express delivery market after heavy losses – clearly a case where local market characteristics proved resistant to the formidable reputation the company has developed in the US.

Having said that, it is not possible to adjudge corporate strategies as being successes or failures until some years after the key decisions have been made. Some of these retreats (those of Peugeot, Chrysler and Rover) have clearly been moves by companies which have decided they no longer have the strength to be world players. Volkswagen can still argue that it has potential export platforms in countries like Mexico, Canada, Brazil and Argentina, and that it has not totally given up marketing in the USA. Only time will tell whether its export platforms are indeed sturdy enough to compete with the Japanese transplants which seem to be performing more effectively than VW was able to do on US soil.

The main question is, though, whether there is any room in an industry like automobiles for independent players of the size of Fiat, Peugeot or Chrysler which increasingly seem to have continental ambitions only.

Our guess has to be no. In industries of this technological complexity, a purely continental player will just not sell enough cars to allow the development of a product range broad enough to fight off the world players. These questions even have to be raised of a company such as BMW which has been notably successful in developing a global niche of high-performance, relatively luxurious cars. As we write, sales are dropping in Japan in the face of intensified competition from the indigenous Japanese auto companies which have been moving up-market on the back of their success in standard models.

What is true for automobiles seems equally true for most of the electronics sector and other research intensive industries such as chemicals, pharmaceuticals, aerospace etc. Yes, of course, there will be industries where regional and other niche strategies are possible. At the level of the industrial commanding heights, though, such sectors look as if they will be the exception, and not the rule.

THE METHODS OF GEOGRAPHICAL EXPANSION

The one thing which is common to all companies contemplating their international strategies is a sense of urgency. Barriers to international expansion are falling fast. Competition can come from any part of the world. Those who are left on their starting blocks will find it very difficult to make up the lost ground.

The slowest way to expand is through greenfield plants – building new facilities in key markets. This has tended to be the Japanese way of expansion. It has the virtue of being relatively uncontroversial, politically, but each plant does take time to plan, build and then expand. Particularly when the investment is in a new territory whose political or market potential is unclear, the temptation is to build the plant in stages. Inevitably the first investment will tend to be quite small, probably less than is economically viable in the long term. It may well take an expansion of the initial investment to reach a truly economic size. All this may take a decade or more. Given the number of countries in the world, such a greenfield expansion route is for the very cautious.

At the other extreme is the route favoured by the Anglo-Americans – expansion by acquisition of existing companies. This is a politically high-risk strategy which has the benefit of buying management, production facilities and market share in one fell swoop. It avoids the risk that a greenfield investment may run into resistance at the planning and construction stage. Because a company is normally buying a going concern, some of the market uncertainties are reduced.

Politically, though, this strategy runs the risk of considerable local outcry, as American companies used to find in Europe and as Japanese companies have found, as when Fujitsu tried to buy Fairchild. In addition, there is much evidence to suggest that the purchasing company often pays far too much for its acquisition. The reason why a company may be vulnerable to a bid is that its management has somehow or other fallen down on its job. Sure, in buying a company, one is buying its market share – but one is also buying a management which may be incompetent or hostile or both. If one is not careful, there may be unexpected liabilities, such as the property and Third World debts

Figure 9

METHODS OF EXPANSION: Examples of Companies Engaged in Licensing, Franchising, Joint Ventures, Take-overs and Greenfield Investments, 1989-1992.

Origin	Licensing	Franchising	Joint Venture	Take-over	Greenfield
USA	•Coca Cola (US)/ Britvic (US/UK) •Philip Morris (US)/ Tabak (Czechoslovakia) and Krakow Tobacco Factory (Poland) •Apple (US)/Sharp (Jap) •Texas Instruments (US)/ Ricoh (Japan)	•McDonald's (US) •Opel (US)/Yanase (Japan) •Pepsico (US) •Ford (US)	•Hughes Aircraft US/ JVC (Japan) •Chevron (US)/ Kazachstan (oil) •Morton International (US)/Robert Bosch (Germany)	•Ford (US)/Jaguar (UK) •Philip Morris (US)/ Jacobs Suchard (Switzerland) •Pepsico (US)/Wedel (Poland) •IBM (US)/ Muszertechnika (Hungary)	•Motorola (US)/Tianjin (China) •Texas Instruments (US)/Avezzano (Italy) •General Motors (US)/ Szentgotthard (Hungary) •Coca Cola (US)/Gdynia (Poland)
Japan	•Hitachi (Japan)/Olivetti (Italy) •Sony (J)/Samsung (Korea)	•Mazda (Japan) •Toyota (Japan) •Nissan (Japan)	•NKK (Japan)/Bethlehem Steel (US) •Honda Motor (Japan)/ Guangzhou Motor Cycle (China)	•Fujitsu (Japan)/ICL (UK) •Sony (Japan)/Columbia Pictures (US)	•Mitsubishi (Japan)/ Aachen (Germany) •Hitachi (Japan)/ Landshut (Germany) •Canon (Japan)/Brittany (France) •Toyota (Japan)/ Burnaston (UK)
UK	•ICI (UK)/Hungary, Czechoslovakia •Pilkington/PPG (US)	•Rover (UK) •Burger King (UK) •Body Shop (UK)	•Atlantic Television (UK)/ Channel 2 TV Romania (Romania) •Laura Ashley (UK)/ Japanese United Stores (Japan)	•SmithKline Beecham (UK)/Saechsiches Serumwerke (Germany) •Unilever (UK/NL)/NMV (Hungary) •Unilever (UK/NL)/ Pollena Bydgoszcz (Pol)	•ICI (UK)/Puerto Rico •GKN (UK) and Tochigini Fuji (Japan)/Tochigi (Japan)
France	•Rhone-Poulenc (France)/ Regeneration Pharmaceuticals (US)	•Citroen (France) •Renault (France) •Peugeot (France)	•Total (France)/Komineft (Russia) •France Telecom (France)/Deutsche Telekom (Germany) •Club Med (France)/ Carnival Cruise Lines (US)	•Bull (France)/Zenith (US) •SNECMA (France)/ Speco (US) •Rhone-Poulenc(France)/ Chemlon (Czechoslovakia)	•Société Ciments Francais (France)/ Turkey •Orsam (Lafarge Coppee) (France) and Ajino-moto (Japan)/ Venice (Italy)

which European banks incurred when they bought into the American financial system in the late 1970s and early 1980s. Britain's Midland Bank became a potential takeover victim in its own right when its purchase of California's Crocker Bank went disastrously wrong.

Given the financial liberalization which took place in the 1980s, the global acquisition route suddenly became extremely attractive to a set of 'financial engineers' who proved just how fast it could allow a firm to move. In fact, the 1980s were marked by a set of Australian and British companies who appeared, seemingly from nowhere, to become global forces.

Although many of these 'meteors' fell to earth around the turn of the decade, there were some spectacular performances. The most extreme case was, probably, that of the British advertising agency, Saatchi and Saatchi, which was created in the 1970s, won some notoriety (and acclaim) for its political advertising on behalf of Mrs Thatcher's conservative party in 1979, then went on a global acquisition spree. By the mid-1980s it was the largest advertising network in the world, having acquired American giants such as Ted Bates and Compton. After that, the structure started to fall apart as the firm proved incapable of managing the conglomeration of companies it had acquired. That, however, is not the point. The main lesson of this episode is the fact that Saatchi and Saatchi built itself into the world's largest presence in its particular industrial sector within fifteen years of its creation.

What the Saatchis were up to was part of a wider movement. From Australia, there was a set of entrepreneurs such as Rupert Murdoch (News International), Alan Bond, Robert Holmes à Court, Warren Anderson and Kerry Packer who played many of the same games, though only Rupert Murdoch (who, in the process, turned himself into an American citizen) finally survived on the global scene. In Britain, the equivalent figures were Robert Maxwell, Sir James Goldsmith and Lord Hanson (of Hanson Trust). Maxwell eventually made the classic mistake of paying too much for his acquisitions and mysteriously fell over the side of his yacht after embezzling over $1 billion from his companies round the world (including the pension fund of one of the authors' wives!). On the other hand, Hanson Trust is a company which has grown almost entirely by acquisition, but which has survived and has won its way into lists of the top 100 non-American industrial companies purely by playing the international acquisition game in an extremely disciplined way. Others such as Murdoch's News International got themselves badly over-stretched financially but, providing they can keep their bankers happy, will end up as substantial global empires which have primarily been built by skilled financial engineers.

Put like this, the acquisition route will seem of dubious validity. Many of these meteors were children of the era which produced junk bonds, Michael Milken and the savings and loans disaster. A number of the edifices they raised proved insubstantial, and were swept away as the financial tide turned in the late 1980s.

However, substantial, mainstream companies can also play this game. There will be disasters such as Ford's quixotic purchase of Britain's specialist car manufacturer Jaguar for a vastly inflated sum, but acquisitions can be used to buy a company into the global number one or two slot which indicates they may have the scale to survive global competition. The battle between consumer products companies like Procter & Gamble and the Anglo-Dutch Unilever has at least in part been fought through tactical acquisitions on either side. Procter & Gamble, for instance, outbid Unilever for Richardson Vicks, while the European company subsequently went on to purchase Chesebrough-Ponds. Unilever has also used acquisition to build itself into one of the world leaders in cosmetics – specifically, its 1989 purchase of Fabergé and Elizabeth Arden allowed it to run neck and neck with L'Oréal. In a different sector, the British chemical company, ICI, hauled itself into the world's number one slot in coatings (i.e. paints) via its 1986 purchase of the American giant, Glidden.

Both the ICI and Unilever moves show that acquisitions can be used to give a company world leadership in specific industrial sectors – and that such acquisitions can be made to work. The alternative strategy of internal, organic growth might eventually have achieved the same result but, first, a competitor might have moved to the fore by acquiring the target companies instead. Secondly, organic growth might well have taken decades to achieve a position which an overnight acquisition in fact achieved.

A further point is that mastery of financial engineering techniques is just as much a strategic skill as learning the secrets of Japan's Lean Production system. This is where companies from the Anglo-American financial tradition currently have a lead over Japanese and, probably, continental European competitors. Coming from open financial markets in which any company can initiate and/or be the target of a hostile bid, all sizeable companies learn how to play the acquisition game. Even when the financial activity seems to have no clear industrial logic, alert companies can still benefit.

The moral of this is that being fully integrated into a lively financial centre such as the City of London can give inherent strategic advantages. This may be one of the reasons why British companies seem to perform on the global scene rather more strongly than the troubled history of the British economy would seem to predict. In many cases, their technological strengths may be suspect, but they come from a dealmaking culture. As nationalistic barriers are falling fast, this speed of reaction may allow them to (in boxing parlance) more than punch their weight.

There are also various ways to expand which fall somewhere between the greenfield and acquisition routes. One such is franchising, whereby a company allows foreign investors to operate facilities (be they a hotel or hamburger joint) under the parent company's guidance. The advantage of this strategy is speed of expansion, but it can lead to problems with quality control. McDonald's, for instance, franchises widely within the USA, but has been much more cautious as it has moved overseas, since it has felt the necessity to ensure that US-style standards are maintained, even when moving into strange industrial cultures which may not value US-style service so highly, and may have to experiment to find (or supplement) local produce to provide, for instance, the potatoes which produce the required quality of french fries. On the other hand, Coca-Cola has used franchising techniques quite extensively in expanding globally so fast. This has saved it from having to establish new bottling plants and marketing teams all round the world.

Licensing of technology is another strategy, though this can sometimes act as a two-edged sword. Historically, this was how companies tried to exploit the Japanese market. In the face of Japanese cultural and legal resistance to inward direct investment, many foreign companies licensed their products or technologies to Japanese companies which may now be major global competitors to them. Thus, for instance, the post-1945 Japanese automotive industry was revived around the models built under licence from France's Renault and two long-defunct British companies, Rootes and Austin. A number of western companies now regret the casualness with which they licensed their technology in the 1960s and 1970s when Japanese competitive capabilities were becoming apparent.

Despite this caveat, licensing will continue to have a legitimate role in corporate strategy. For instance, there will be an increasing number of sectors where a new competitive balance will emerge in each part of the triad world. Inevitably there will be companies which are profitably established in one continent, but which do not feel they could successfully establish themselves as a major force in another. In these circumstances, licensing one's more successful products makes perfectly good sense.

GEOGRAPHICAL ORGANIZATION

Undoubtedly, the hardest decision any company will have to make is how to organize for a world of global competition.

In theory, the picture is clear. There is obviously some sort of continuum from a purely nationally-focused strategy to some kind of 'transnational' approach in which executives are drawn from all round the world, and decision-making becomes 'polycentric' – that is when business activities are run from wherever in the world decision-making seems most logical. To some extent, this debate about the ideal organizational structure is a battle between management school gurus such as Christopher Bartlett and Sumantra Ghoshal (Harvard and Insead) or Michael Porter who differ about the relative importance which should be given by a company to locating in strongly competitive home bases.

But this is also a debate in which the Japanese are involved, which is hardly surprising since Japanese companies are late-comers to the international scene and are having to shoe-horn a process of organizational change, which older-established 'western' multinationals took decades to perfect, into a much shorter timeframe. In this debate, Kenichi Ohmae, the managing director of McKinsey in Japan, and Sony's Akio Morita have been particularly influential. Their emphasis is on companies becoming 'insiders' in key global markets by replicating the systems (including research and development, and engineering) which they have developed at home (effectively, this is a 'cloning' strategy). Beyond that, though, they see a further stage in which the company is effectively denationalized. Morita talks of 'global localization': the ability of a company to think globally while taking the needs of local markets and cultures into account.

In practice, this trick of melding the scale economies of going global with the needs of local markets is extremely difficult, and tends to be both time-consuming (when global competition requires speed of decision-making) and likely to require compromises which satisfy no one. An example is the way Honda ran into trouble with its 1990 Accord model. The 1986 model had been successful in both Japan and USA, but in subsequent years demand patterns in these two key markets diverged. US consumers increasingly wanted a reliable, high quality means of everyday transport, while Japanese consumers wanted a status symbol. Effectively, Honda's engineers were required to produce two different cars, but did not have the resources to do so (you can be the ninth biggest auto producer in the world and still be too small). The result was a compromise design which sold well in the US, but did disappointingly in Japan. Any executive with global responsibilities will know Honda's dilemma, and there is no single blueprint which will work for all companies. One can, however, point to some trends.

First, there seems to be a swing away from over-powerful geographical divisions. Increasingly, product divisions are being given global responsibilities, sometimes even to the extent of shifting the headquarters of the relevant divisions out of the home country (Nestlé, Unilever, Procter & Gamble and IBM have all gone some way down this road). This may on occasion lead to insensitive product development, but the thinking is that it is easier for strong product development and marketing teams to build cultural sensitivity into their operations, than it is for a geographical division to master all the nuances of the formation of product strategies.

At the same time there is a passing need to de-nationalize management structures. At a superficial level, this is is sometimes started by the adoption of English as the common working language throughout a company – which is, of course, a form of cultural imperialism by the Anglo-Americans, but also reflects the fact that 'Standard English' has become the language of international business and diplomacy. Automatic interpretation devices will undoubtedly reduce the need for common linguistic skills in decades to come. For the moment, though, language is a barrier – particularly for Japanese companies seeking to integrate non-Japanese executives into their systems.

The de-nationalization of executive structures has to be worked from both ends of the executive spectrum. At the level of boards of directors (or, at the very least, international advisory boards), there is a strong case for involving a variety of nationals. In older established multinationals such as Unilever, ICI, IBM and a number of the major international banks this process has gone quite some way. Japanese companies are lagging behind. Sony has appointed a German and American to its board. By 1990, Kyocera had three non-Japanese on its board.

It is more difficult to give non-home national executives a decent career structure, which will give them a chance to influence the overall direction of the company. All too often there is a 'glass ceiling' to their careers, whereby they will be considered for top posts in the relevant national subsidiary, but will find it very difficult to fight their way upward to positions of real responsibility in the corporate headquarters. This is not just a stricture on newer multinational players such as the Japanese. Very few non-Americans have made it to board level in American multinationals, and the picture is no better when looking at most European companies. It may be that Japanese companies will be best advised to internationalize the boards of key subsidiaries. Thus, for instance, ICL, the British computer company, which is 80 per cent owned by Fujitsu, has representatives from Fujitsu (Japan), ICL (UK), Northern Telecom (Canadian) and Nokia (Finland) as well as Viscount Davignon (Belgian), a former European Community Commissioner. No one can complain that that board is too dominated by the Japanese hierarchy.

On the financial front, there is a trend toward getting listings on a number of overseas stock exchanges. This is still very much a minority strategy, but has to be seen as an indicator of how seriously a company genuinely holds global ambitions. The advantages are that it is one step forward in the internationalization of a company's equity ownership and will give a company access to a larger potential pool of capital than a purely national base will. A leading British company, ICI, now has about 11 per cent of its equity in US hands as a result of its decision to get a listing in New York. In theory, such listings should lead to a higher price for the company's shares, which can have both offensive and defensive importance.

The disadvantage is an immense amount of paper-work, particularly if the company is seeking a listing in the USA, where the SEC is a particularly demanding regulator. This immediately discourages companies from countries like Germany, France and Switzerland where disclosure requirements fall some way behind American standards. However, in a world where financial skills are one weapon in a company's competitive armoury, an unwillingness to accept such scrutiny will hamper companies in their search for the cheapest, most flexible sources of capital. As long as companies believe that technological competitiveness is all that matters, this lack of financial flexibility may not be a problem. If, however, one believes that 'financial engineering' is another area bestowing global competitive strengths, then slowness in internationalizing financial strategies will be a competitive disadvantage.

STRATEGIC ALLIANCES

For a large number of companies, the options are more limited. For a variety of reasons, their global coverage is limited. Their problems are less to do with internationalizing their management structure, and more about how they turn themselves into global players when they currently may be no more than significant players within one continent.

Many such companies feel they do not have the time to expand through a succession of greenfield investments. On the other hand, they may well feel inhibited from playing the mergers and acquisitions game. In these circumstances, a large number of managements start thinking of strategic alliances – that is, links between independent companies which fall short of a full equity relationship.

Some companies may have such a strategy forced upon them because they are in sectors where foreign ownership is either forbidden or highly controversial. This is certainly true of industries with a security dimension – defence industries, much of aerospace, airlines etc. It is also true of many of the industries which are in the process of being deregulated such as financial services and telecommunications. In such sectors, there are whole clusters of companies which are either state-owned or clearly marked as being out of bounds to foreigners. In these circumstances, a company wanting to develop a global strategy is forced to work with overseas competitors in a variety of ways which fall short of an acquisition of one company by another. These can include the creation of joint ventures, one company taking a minority stake in the other, collaborative research or just straight marketing collaborations.

To the uninitiated, the results often appear as a set of rather arbitrary corporate links. Just to scratch the surface, in airlines, one has links between SAS, Swissair and Austrian Airlines; Lufthansa and JAL; and between KLM and Northwest. In computing, one can point to IBM and Groupe Bull; the unsuccessful 1986 reciprocal marketing agreement between AT&T and Olivetti; AT&T and Sun Microsystems (to develop software); Intel, AT&T and Olivetti (development of a multi-processor version of Unix); and Sony and Apple (the development of multi-media computers). In automobiles VW and Ford have a deal to develop a van; Renault and Volvo have an active joint venture. In aerospace, British Aerospace and General Dynamics set up a wide-ranging collaboration in 1990; while Pratt & Whitney, Rolls-Royce, Mitsubishi Heavy Industries and others are working together to produce aero engines. At a more general level, Daimler-Benz and Mitsubishi sought to develop a deepening relationship across their entire corporate environments. It would be possible to fill whole pages with lists of such alliances. The important question is how significant they actually are.

On the one hand, one can quote an Olivetti executive: 'In the 1990s, competition will no longer be between individual companies, but between new, complex corporate groupings. A company's competitive position no longer depends only on its internal capabilities; it also depends on the type of relationships it has been able to establish with other firms and the scope of these relationships.'[13] Given the significance of many of the players in such alliances (IBM, NTT, VW et al) one cannot dismiss the phenomenon too easily.

On the other hand, there is a long literature on joint ventures and other such initiatives which fall short of full mergers, and the conclusions are generally cautious. Any such alliance is bound to be fragile as the balance of power between partners varies over time. The alliances which work best are ones where the partners have strictly complementary strengths.

However, many of the alliances in industries such as telecommunications, airlines or computing do not promise well. They are between companies which are, ultimately, competitors, even if they can hide from this fact because they are currently strong in different continents. The trouble with such alliances is that they are often seen as alternatives to full mergers which would leave one set of managers in a dominant position. Ultimately, even in industries such as telecommunications, a narrow range of companies will win out on a global basis. Most of today's wave of alliances should be seen as purely temporary moves in industrial sectors where the true rigours of global competition have still to be completely accepted. In sectors such as telecoms, it will take decades for governments to accept the full logic of such competition. In others like automobiles we are probably much closer to an intense restructuring of the industry. The Volvo-Renault deal is one of the last-gasp plays of companies which are ultimately unable to stay competitive even within their home continents. The VW-Ford deal is a reminder that even the true giants cannot be guaranteed continued independence over the next couple of decades. As companies move through the period of alliances, we will see a corporate shakeout not just within continents, but between them.

THE SUN-PLANET RELATIONSHIP

Patterns are starting to emerge, such as when a few giant companies come to dominate particular clusters of lesser players – as a sun is surrounded by dependent planets. In computing, IBM is quite clearly emerging as a central node for a wide range of alliances, as is Fujitsu through its links with Amdahl, ICL and Siemens. In airlines, alliances seem to be coalescing round a handful of companies – Delta, United and American in the USA, JAL in Japan, some combination of British Airways, Lufthansa and (perhaps) Air France in Europe, and companies such as Singapore Airlines in the rest of the world. In Aerospace, Boeing, McDonnell-Douglas, Pratt & Whitney, General Electric and (just possibly) Rolls-Royce are developing a similar role. In automobiles, it is the big three in

Japan, Ford (rather than the less agile General Motors), perhaps Volkswagen in Europe which are emerging as the dominant players.

This is in fact a select group of giant companies which are becoming global systems integrators. Sometimes, they will actually acquire companies dependent upon them. However, just as often, they will leave those companies apparently independent but, in reality, increasingly bound by the fate of the ultimate integrator. Sometimes, the subordinate companies will be left 'independent' because economic nationalism is still strong enough to block transnational mergers which might otherwise make strategic sense. In other cases, they will be left alone because the information technology revolution is permitting the development of 'virtual' corporations – that is, groups of companies, working towards a common goal, linked not by common ownership but by shared electronic systems which allow them to plan and work in unison.

This is particularly common in the defence industry, in which a major project such as the development of a new bomber may involve the activities of upwards of 2,000 companies.[14] One can see the emergence of similar clusters of companies around a whole series of major global projects, such as a new Boeing passenger jet (which increasingly will involve Japanese sub-contractors) or a transnational collaboration such as Europe's Tornado aircraft and its planned successor, the European Fighter Aircraft. In the automobiles sector, one finds firms like Nissan putting in place global communications networks linking suppliers from all round the world into the central design process.

As the electronic networks at the heart of such developments become increasingly sophisticated the traditional logic of vertical integration (buying up one one's suppliers) is undercut. Control is exercised less and less through formal ownership relationships, but by a voluntary shared commitment, aided by modern electronics, to achieve a certain goal set by a systems integrator. Companies which have worked together on one major project will inevitably find it easier working together on subsequent ones. Sometimes this will lead to mergers between key players. However, in today's world, this is not essential. Companies can work together on a long-term basis without necessarily losing their formal independence. Ultimately they will all be dependent on the economic health of the 'virtual corporation' to which they belong.

MULTIDIMENSIONAL CHALLENGES

We live in a world in which all the past certainties of executives are under challenge. The pace of competition is increasing, as is the range of countries from which that competition may come. In a wide number of industries, there are clearly far too many companies seeking to be global players – and a corporate bloodbath is thus inevitable. At the same time, the information technology revolution which is responsible for these changes in the external competitive environment is also changing the nature of internal corporate organization. In a negative sense, this explains some of the massive shakeouts taking place within long-established multinational companies. In a different sense, it is permitting companies to manage their relationships with both customers and suppliers in a new, apparently more flexible, way.

The intensity and variety of the challenges to management and workforces are actually very frightening. Managers can no longer be single-dimension figures, good merely at technology or financial control or whatever. Companies which survive will be run by executives who can fine-tune corporate systems to the multi-dimensional challenges of today's competitive environment. Understanding the full range of ways in which technology is affecting the global business environment is probably the single most important task of today's managers. However, their responses to these challenges must be culturally and financially sophisticated and produced at a speed which would astound executives used to the much less complex and more sedate business environment of a few decades ago.

6

RISE OF JAPAN: HAVING IT BOTH WAYS?

THE LEXUS STORY

VISITING STATE-OF-THE-ART Japanese factories is to visit the temples of modern capitalism. To appreciate them, however, one must put oneself in a contemporary state of mind. In a religious shrine the emphasis is on unchanging ritual with roots going back many centuries. The spectator must approach them with an acute sense of continuity over time. In a factory, the secret is very different. It is to spot the significant technological changes which have taken place since one's last visit – to see how the pace and variety of operations has changed. For non-engineers, this appreciation can be difficult. Occasionally, though, the layout of a factory tells a story even to the layman. Since late 1989 the place to visit has been the Tahara plant in Toyota City.[1]

On the surface, this looks a conventionally impressive modern automotive plant. Plenty of industrial robots in action. Some workers on the shop floor – but not many. The key, though, lies with the automobiles being assembled. One is the Crown, an upmarket but otherwise routine Toyota model. Suddenly one's eyes are drawn to a second model which is being assembled alongside it. The assembly lines are basically the same – they cross over and under each other as the two models make their way across the plant to the end of their individual assembly processes – but the second model is very different. It is the Lexus, Toyota's competitor in the luxury car market. This is the Japanese answer to Mercedes, Porsche, BMW and Rolls-Royce.

Yes, there are occasional signs that this car is something special. It is, for instance, given protective covering at certain stages on the line where its paint could get scratched. However, the true significance of this plant is that a car which is as prestigious as the Lexus is being routinely churned out on assembly lines which work every bit as fast and smoothly as those for the relatively routine model, the Crown.

To the unitiated, this may not seem much. However, it is actually the visual symbol of the 'Post-Ford' revolution. Run well, today's assembly plants can produce whatever the consumer wants, in whatever quantity – however small. Japanese companies like Toyota can now deliver crafts-man quality on mass assembly lines. The fact that the Japanese have mastered this art is a symbol of how the Japanese economy has now moved to the forefront of the world of global competition.

THE RISE OF JAPAN

In 1945, Japan was a wrecked society. Cities had been fire-bombed or, in two cases, devastated by nuclear weapons. Its industry was in ruins. Its subsequent industrial rise – along with the collapse of the Soviet system – has been one of the two most important developments of the late twentieth century.

For the global business system, though, it is the rise of Japan which has been of crucial importance. On the one hand, Japanese companies have been redefining the very nature of global competition. On the other, a growing understanding of the system which produced Japan's success has posed questions to all competing governments. Japan has apparently benefited from a superb industrial policy. Can competing societies copy the Japanese recipe for company-government relations?

At the same time the Japanese success story rests on peculiar foundations. Certainly, Japanese companies are emerging from a very introverted and nationalistic business culture. Has this really given them an unfair advantage in world markets? How much effort should western competitors be putting into trying to get Japanese competitors to play by the same rules?

THE SEARCH FOR UNDERSTANDING

In the late 1960s, it was possible for books on multinationals to be written with minimal references to Japan. Servan-Schreiber's *Le Défi Américain*[2] was an early bestseller in this field, warning the laggard Europeans of the multinational phenomenon. He found American companies the only ones worth writing about. However, as the 1970s progressed and trade frictions increased, awareness of Japanese competition grew. The search for an understanding of the Japanese phenomenon started.

In 1979, the first bestseller in this genre hit the bookshops. This was Ezra Vogel's *Japan as Number One*,[3] which noted that the world was dealing with a new phenomenon. He emphasized the close relationship between Japanese companies and relevant government bodies such as MITI (the Ministry of International Trade and Industry) or the Economic Planning Agency in the more immediate post-1945 period. While calling for a reinvigoration of US industrial policy, he also identified some of the cultural differences between Japan and the USA – particularly emphasizing the importance of group loyalties, which would be difficult to replicate elsewhere.

Since Vogel's bestseller, airport bookshops have rarely been without a couple of brisk-selling (occasionally, meretricious) studies of the Japanese phenomenon. For a while, such studies focused on the cultural distinctiveness of Japan. Thus William Ouchi's *Theory Z* argued that Japan's emphasis on group-oriented, participative decision-making was an ideal managerial style, inherently better than the more autocratic approaches of western executives.[4]

The books tended to stress the importance of principles such as lifetime employment, the elaborate consultation procedures within companies, and the 'descent from heaven' whereby senior officials retire into high-ranking positions in the companies they have been overseeing.

An almost idyllic picture emerged of an economic superpower in which officials, managers and workers pulled together in one great happy family. It took a while for some dissenting voices to be heard.

From within Japan itself there were occasional cries of anger, such as those expressed in Satoshi Kamata's 1973 book, *Japan in the Passing Lane*.[5] This recorded what it was actually like to work for Toyota as a temporary assembly line worker; it described a work-force which, though relatively docile, was driven hard by a somewhat oppressive management structure.

This alternative picture of a workaholic, driven society is one that is held widely outside Japan. Its classic expression was given by the European Community's Roy Denman who caused a considerable stir in 1979 when he livened up an EC Commission report (which was then leaked to the press) on EC–Japanese trade relations with a reference to 'a country of workaholics who live in what Westerners would regard as little more than rabbit hutches'.[6] The sensation these comments created in Japan was probably only matched by the row which brewed twelve years later when it was disclosed that the new French prime minister, Edith Cresson, not only believed 'There is a world economic war on', but had earlier referred to the Japanese as 'ants' whose aim was 'to conquer market share and then kill the competition'.[7]

Within slightly less emotive political and industrial circles, attention turned increasingly to the role of the Japanese government. The role of bodies like MITI and, at an earlier stage, the Economic Planning Agency were subjected to detailed scrutiny in studies such as Chalmers Johnson's *MITI and the Japanese Miracle*.[8] Johnson argued that the Japanese system is a distinctive form of a 'capitalist developmental' state, which can be put alongside more traditional forms of capitalism and communism. This analysis stressed the importance of targeted intervention – the process whereby the government-industry network identified the next industrial sectors Japan needed to conquer. The way that allegedly competing companies were brought together into pre-competitive research consortia was also noted.

Gradually, through the 1980s, an accumulation of studies such as this developed into a full-fledged school which argued that the Japanese success story rested on unfair foundations. Clyde Prestowitz's *Trading Places*[9] was one of the more influential. Paying particular attention to the semi-conductor industry, he analysed the methods whereby the Japanese had decimated an apparently thriving US industry. Everything from MITI's start-up aid, to unfair trading practices such as dumping, through to weak US trade negotiatiors were implicated.

The work of Karel van Wolferen[10] put Japanese industrial policy into a much wider social and historical perspective. The picture he painted was of a fragmented power structure in which the bureaucrats had, since 1945, played a dominant role in steering the corporate sector toward its onslaught on world markets. However, he also stressed that this fragmentation meant that Japan was difficult to live with, in that few Japanese in a position to negotiate agreements with foreigners were ever going to be able to implement them. Thus, should foreigners seek redress for a particular trade practice, not even a prime minister could implement a commitment in Japan which ran against the interests of other competing groups. The implicit argument was that the Japanese would remain uncomfortable commercial and diplomatic rivals.

THE MANAGEMENT LITERATURE

The literature focusing on company-government relationships has tended to be read in an adversarial light. However, in parallel with such studies, other authors have been building a picture of how the Japanese managerial system actually works at the corporate level. Here, the picture is more complimentary – though no less scaring for Western competitors.

As mentioned above, these works initially focused on the superficial differences between Japanese and western management styles. The emphasis on consultation, the lack of status differentials, the principle of life-time employment, all attracted favourable comment when put against the autocratic, status-ridden, individualistic management styles of the west.

Fairly rapidly, though, it became apparent that Japan's success rested on much more than a participatory management style.

For one thing, it was argued, the ferocious competitiveness of Japanese companies on world markets is built on a generally very competitive domestic market. Studies such as *Kaisha* by James Abegglen and George Stalk[11] showed how vicious this competition could be. Cases such as the way Honda blasted Tohatsu (the market leader in motorcycles in the 1950s) into bankruptcy, and then ruthlessly fought off the subsequent challenge of Yamaha, passed into the business school folklore. The lessons drawn from such cases were the importance of obsessive dedication to going for market growth, and the use of product proliferation as a competitive weapon (in a critical 18-month period, Honda released 81 new motorcycle models against Yamaha's 34). None of this owed anything to government support (in fact MITI had actively discouraged Honda from entering the automotive market). It owed everything to a competitive dynamic within Japan which produced fleet-footed corporations, who when they moved overseas were able to pulverize unprepared, slower-witted American and European competitors.

One paradox quickly emerged. Certainly, Japanese companies were devastating global competitors, but the methods they used relied heavily on lessons initially learned from the West. There was, for instance, the extraordinary case of the American W. Edwards Deming who, while barely known in his home country, became a guru in Japan through his advice on the importance of quality control. It was this emphasis on quality which was to allow Japan to make such rapid inroads into western markets from the 1970s on. Many have commented on the irony whereby one of the most prestigious awards available to Japanese companies is the Deming award named after this subtly influential American consultant.

However, it was not just the emphasis on quality which was important. What leading Japanese executives came to master was the overall secret of production management. They achieved this by visiting Detroit, then the capital dedicated to the mass production techniques initially perfected by Henry Ford. Western competitors did not at first realize that after these Japanese executives returned to Japan, by constant experimentation and incremental improvements, they pushed the bounds of factory automation forward far beyond the vision of American organizational innovators such as Henry Ford or Alfred Sloan.

In so doing, Japanese management has effectively pushed the world into 'Post-Fordism' – an era in which factories are starting to reclaim some of the flexibility which pre-mass production facilities once (not very efficiently) enjoyed.

The study which tells this story so clearly is of the world auto industry – *The Machine which Changed the World*.[12] By studying about half the world's automotive plants, an MIT-led team was able to demonstrate how much more effective the Japanese ones are in comparison with those in the USA or West Europe. In particular, they showed how the Japanese have both shortened development times and reduced the minimum volumes needed to produce a car economically. When combined with an emphasis on quality and the 'Just-in-Time' system for reducing inventories, these improvements have turned the Japanese into formidable competitors on the world scene.

The key point about a key study such as this is that it does not really support the classic conspiratorial view of Japan's success. Sure, MITI played a role in encouraging the industry in the 1950s. Yes, the industry was kept closed to foreigners through to the early 1970s. There's also no denying that MITI was active in the early 1980s in encouraging the industry to invest overseas to reduce trade frictions.

However, it was not a MITI programme which taught Eiji Toyoda and Taiichi Ohno (the geniuses behind Toyota's post-1945 drive to world eminence) how to build flexibility into Henry Ford's classic Detroit mass-assembly model. Similarly, the commitments to quality, the reduction of inventories and the speeding of development times have come primarily through the actions of executives – not through government programmes.

Recently, other studies have turned to the wider organizational structures of the Japanese corporate system, paying particular attention to the *Keiretsu* – the grouping of companies round some combination of bank, trading house or large industrial firm. Harvard Business School's W. Carl Kester (1991) distinguished the groupings which date from the pre-World War 2 *Zaibatsu* groupings ('horizontal *Keiretsu*' such as Mitsubishi and Mitsui); newer bank-centred groups such as those centred round the Industrial Bank of Japan and the Sanwa Bank; and the (also relatively recent) 'vertical *Keiretsu*' which have built up round key manufacturers such as Toyota, Nissan, Hitachi or Nippon Steel.

One can debate precisely how distinctive this form of organization actually is. In Germany, for instance, there are clusters of companies which focus on particular universal banks. The links binding the major clients of, say, the Deutsche Bank may not be as close as those binding the Mitsubishi or Mitsui family of companies – but links there are of a nature which one would not find in the US context. Secondly, as one looks round the industrial landscape of countries such as Italy or India, one finds clusters of family-based enterprises which have many similar characteristics (bar the dynamism) of the *Keiretsu*. Certainly, no one can look at the Fiat-dominated Italian environment and argue that that sprawling industrial groupings are unique to Japan.

Keiretsu have now started to feature in the Structural Impediments Dialogue between the US and Japanese authorities; the Americans argue that these groupings are an unfair institutional barrier to foreign competitors. Even those who are not overly hostile to the *Keiretsu* identify the ways they may work in favour of Japanese companies. On one front, they have been at the heart of the financial system which has allowed Japanese companies to plan for long-term growth. At the same time, the vertical *Keiretsu* have helped foster a deep relationship between core company and suppliers which clearly allows Japanese companies to work more closely together through the development cycle than would be true elsewhere in the world. Significantly, many major western companies are working with suppliers in order to deepen relationships in line with what they sense is happening in Japan.

In fact, one can argue that some aspects of the *Keiretsu* system are hangovers from Japan's proto-capitalist, pre-world war days. Just as some of their employment practices have to to be tested in a period of genuine global competition, one can argue that the full range of *Keiretsu* practices have still to be tested for their ultimate economic rationale.

A SYNTHESIS

If one adds the literature of the policy analysts, the cultural observers and the management schools, then a complex picture emerges, in which culture, government policies and sheer management abilities all feature.

Very importantly, the Japanese success story has not come out of a vacuum. This was a nation which took modernization seriously from the moment in the 1860s when it opened its frontiers to the wider world. Its 1905 victory over the Russian navy in Tsushima Straits gave a clear initial indication of its potential. Nor was its ability to wage – however misguidedly – the 1941–45 Pacific war against the USA and its allies the action of a technologically primitive state.

ENTER THE BUREAUCRATS

The 1945 defeat clearly devastated the Japanese economy. However, thanks to the fact that the bureaucracy was not purged by the occupation forces to the extent to which the politicians and business executives were, there was a major institutional shift in favour of an activist bureaucracy . . . and for the two or three decades after 1945, this bureaucracy was of paramount importance. It was these bureaucrats who masterminded the targeting and support of emerging technologies, while administering the protection of wide swathes of the Japanese economy.

This peculiar history of Japan's post-1945 institutions is important. A very weak political system meant that, much more than in other parts of the world, ministers were tools of their ministries. In addition, the breaking of the pre-war industrial groupings meant that the bureaucrats were in no danger of being thwarted by politically influential, self-concerned industrial lobbies. They could thus create development goals without having to worry too much about those sectors which were due to lose out (agriculture being the main exception).

The bureaucrats in MITI and the Economic Planning Agency worked well and created a much-vaunted system of 'administrative guidance'. They involved the Japanese corporate establishment in their planning. They set intelligent goals for the economy. They had an array of protectionist and financial tools to steer industrialists in desired directions.

It was in the mid-1960s that Japanese goals turned to what we would now call high technology. In 1966 (a year before the publication of *Le Défi Américain*) the need to develop a countervailing force to IBM was first spelled out. Within ten years, a system for allowing Japanese companies to come together in pre-competitive research collaborations was in place. It was one of these, the VLSI Technology Research Association, which from 1976 to 1979 gave the country's electronic industry a chance to start catching the American microelectronics industry – a change they eagerly grasped. At the time, the significance of such initiatives was not fully appreciated elsewhere in the world. It took the announcement of the Fifth Generation Computer project in 1981 to ram it home to the world that it was no longer the USA which was the dominant industrial challenger, but Japan.

THE ROLE OF MANAGERS

It is totally misleading to lay all Japan's success at the door of the under-staffed ministries in Kasumigaseki (the district in which the ministries cluster). The bureaucrats may have pointed in the right direction. They needed good quality managers who could ultimately strike out on their own.

Once again, the 1945 military defeat provides a key. Having lost the war, and having had a 'Peace' constitution imposed on them, there was nothing comparable to the military-industrial complexes which emerged in the USA, the United Kingdom and, usually to a lesser extent, in other western countries. In the absence of such a military-oriented sector, the best Japanese executive talent went into mainstream, commercially-oriented industrial sectors. Instead of designing products like tanks or missiles, they could concentrate on things such as automobiles and consumer electronics which filled a direct consumer need.

When in 1962 President de Gaulle (significantly a general) called Prime Minister Ikeda a 'transistor salesman', the French leader was illuminating an important point. To him (as would have been true of equivalent American or British leaders) products such as transistor radios were just not serious. Within Japan, however, the picture was different. Radios were one more step in the worthy process of catching up with the West.

The quality of Japanese management clearly goes a long way toward explaining how Japan moved ahead of the west in key areas of product development and manufacturing technology. After all, it needed intelligent managers to see the importance of Deming's teaching about the importance of statistical quality control. Again, the creation of the *Kanban* ('Just-in-time') system of inventory control was the result of creative thinking within Toyota. Above all, the success of Japanese companies in cutting development times so drastically is evidence of managerial expertise at a very high level. The ability to develop the necessary vision and to rethink classic production engineering certainties in the light of the electronic revolution, while keeping workforces well-motivated and compliant, points to a mastery of the overall management process which goes far beyond that shown by the competition elsewhere. Sure, there are still some residual questions about the ability of Japanese managers to handle research creativity and to manage cultural diversity. However, even if Japanese management does have some weaknesses in such areas, the strengths it has demonstrated in recent decades are such that to raise questions like these is merely quibbling.

A ROLE FOR CULTURE

Clearly, there are cultural forces at work as well. For instance, one can argue that the relatively strong commitment of work-forces to their companies should be explained at the level of deep culture. Specifically, the Confucian tradition in Japan is often cited to explain why this country seems naturally adapted to the rhythms of today's industrial life. This tradition, it is argued, provides a culture in which education is valued, and where respect is given to those in authority, in return for a paternalistic acceptance that those in authority have obligations to look after those below them.

Such a culture is particularly well suited to today's industrial age. The obedience-obligation bond between worker and boss helps provide an atmosphere of peaceful industrial relations. At the same time, the emphasis given to education means that the big Japanese companies are working with a well-educated workforce. As they move into the 'Post-Ford' industrial world, they can rely on the flexibility of shopfloor workers who boast a much higher proportion of university qualifications than is true of anywhere in the west outside the USA. This well-educated workforce is relatively attuned to demands for quality and flexibility.

If one then takes into account the relative ethnic homogeneity of Japan, then one sees one more factor working toward a degree of social cohesion not often found elsewhere.

One should not scoff at such arguments. The lack of commitment to training and a relative unconcern with higher education is clearly a drag on the economic potential of most countries in Western Europe – Germany probably excepted. Again, sociologists such as Weber have long argued that certain ideologies are better suited to the development of capitalism than others. What this emphasis on Confucianism is doing is adding a gloss to earlier arguments. Protestantism, with its emphasis on the obligation on individuals to better themselves, is certainly well-suited to the cut-and-thrust of capitalist competition, but it may not produce executives and workforces with a natural eye for detail. What the Confucian tradition may have done is to provide a culture which is particularly suited to the large-scale, bureaucratic, technologically-sophisticated organizations which are at the heart of today's world of global competition.

Having said all that, one can allow oneself a little scepticism. After all it should never be forgotten that the era of industrial peace now found in Japan was won quite brutally in the late 1940s and early 1950s. In fact, Japanese labour relations were actually quite violent both between the wars and in the immediate post-1945 era. It took a period of conscious union-busting in the early 1950s to produce the era of compliant company unions now the norm in Japan.

XENOPHOBIA

This cultural homogeneity has had its darker side. Certainly, there can be no disguising that the country has been motivated by a deep patriotism which has sometimes tipped over into xenophobia. Although uncomfortable for the rest of the world, these passions have undoubtedly been beneficial for the Japanese industrial effort. Certainly, during the catch-up period, the determination to overhaul the industrial West was an important motivating force. This drive to overcome foreign competition was exemplified by the cases of companies like Komatsu with its well-publicized 'Encircle Caterpillar' strategy.

The strength of these feelings has made Japan a difficult economic partner, because they have produced a culture with a particularly strong anti-import, anti-foreign bias. It was this which produced such nonsenses as the attempt to block imports of foreign skis on the grounds that Japanese snow had special characteristics.

Whatever its enthusiasm for exports and, even, investment overseas, Japanese management has not championed the opening of its own markets to imports. To some extent managers have been able to hide behind the fact that the Japanese distribution system is particularly Byzantine in its nature, and very hard for foreigners to crack. On top of that, the *Keiretsu* system has developed intra-group loyalties which make them hard to penetrate, even by other Japanese. In this case, the country's very industrial structure might almost seem to have been designed to work against foreign suppliers. This is certainly an argument used by the American semi-conductor industry which has argued that, as the centre of gravity for this industry has moved from Silicon Valley to Japan, the American industry does not get prompt access to leading edge semi-conductor fabrication machinery, which is in Japanese hands and is offered first to Japanese fabricators within established *Keiretsu* networks.

At the level of the bureaucrats, the growth of genuine internationalism has been patchy. MITI has probably moved fastest among the ministries, but foreign players were having problems as late as the late 1980s with ministries such as the Ministry of Posts and Telecommunications. This body fought a tough rearguard action to prevent the British company Cable and Wireless from winning an effective stake in the IDC telecommunications consortium. At a non-ministerial level, bodies like the Tokyo Stock Exchange fought fairly tenaciously in the 1980s to avoid accepting foreign securities traders as members – giving lack of space as their ostensible reason for refusal.

To non-Japanese, all this resistance to foreigners is reprehensible. On the other hand, a defence can be made. All countries have xenophobic tendencies. In the United Kingdom, one of the authors had a relative who even in the mid-1980s would not buy German cars, and would surreptitiously kick any Japanese one that came his way; his memories of the Second World War still seared him.

Certainly, within Western Europe, anti-Americanism was once as strong as some of the anti-Japanese sentiments found today. Both the authors of this book, for instance, started writing on multinational companies in the 1960s, during the general period of anti-Americanism which *Le Défi Américain* represented. Certainly, no European with an honest memory can complain that Japan was developing industrial policies to counter IBM at around the same time. We were certainly trying to do so in Europe. The main difference is that the Japanese came up with effective policies. We, in Europe did not. However, we were all aiming at the same goal.

Even so, there is still a sense that the Japanese industrial culture remains more nationalist than most. For instance, when in 1989 the irrepressible US corporate raider T. Boone Pickens tried moving into Japan by buying a minority stake in Koito Manufacturing (part of the Toyota Group), he met with a resistance which can only be described as visceral. Japanese culture is not yet comfortable with the concept of a hostile takeover bid, and the reaction to an American practitioner of this black art was particularly savage.

HOW DISTINCTIVE A SYSTEM

The Japanese system is a strong system which has borrowed widely from the west, and has proved particularly skilled at adapting and improving important western techniques.

However, there are many aspects of Japan's industrial culture which seems alien to western observers. The questions therefore are: to what extent are we dealing with a distinctively non-western industrial system? To the extent that we are, is the system converging toward an increasingly standardized western model? Or will the Japanese system remain culturally distinctive?

At the micro level of the company, one is dealing with institutions which are fundamentally recognizable in western terms. The fact that they have emerged from a distinctive environment has led to emphases which make them seem quite remote.

EMPLOYMENT PRACTICES

The emphasis that leading Japanese companies have put on life-time employment, job rotation to produce generalists rather than specialists, and elaborate consultation instead of authoritarian decision-making is distinctive. However, such practices are not unique: young executives entering leading western companies like IBM, Royal Dutch-Shell or Volkswagen have normally had expectations of job security not much different from those of their Japanese equivalents starting careers with Toyota, NEC et al. Again, though few western companies have gone to Japanese lengths in fostering consultative devices such as quality circles, the evidence from books such as *In Search of Excellence*[13] is that the best American companies stress the importance of participative management to a very high degree.

Some Japanese practices do however remain distinctive. One thinks, for instance, of *Ringii*, in which proposals circulate round companies to pick up seal stamps from a wide variety of colleagues and superiors before a final decision to go ahead with a proposal can be given. One also thinks of the principles of extreme job rotation and a related respect for seniority over rewarding individual talent.

It is possible to argue that such practices contribute to the overall success of Japanese management. For instance, consultation between widely experienced generalists will mean that most of the implications of any particular decision are thought through before it has to be implemented. Similarly, life-time employment will help produce a total dedication to the interests of the corporation.

On the other hand, one can argue that these are managerial styles which have evolved by happenstance and which have not yet been fully exposed to critical analysis. After all, the extraordinary success of the Japanese catch-up decades meant that most mainstream Japanese companies have enjoyed relatively uninterrupted financial success, and have rarely had to analyse the actual effectiveness of some of their recent traditions.

Today, though, such pressures are growing. Competition for new graduates is increasing and the quality of their industrial spirit is declining as they start to question '5K' careers – that is involving work which is *kiken* (dangerous), *kitani* (dirty), *kitsui* (demanding), *kurai* (dark) and *kakkowarui* (unbecoming). There is also a small seepage of independently-minded Japanese executives into foreign companies establishing themselves in Japan. It is rare that these defectors are key players, but Japanese executives who feel themselves blocked in advancement now have alternative career structures.

For the first time for decades, companies are having to look at the downside of some of their practices. For instance, life-time employment means that companies are stuck with the inefficient and the unmotivated; slowly, companies are coming to accept that they will have to start sacking people.

Again, there is a growing awareness that there are disadvantages to an over-emphasis on generalists who are promoted purely on seniority principles. Japanese financial institutions, for instance, are finding that the specialists in their western competitors are better able to develop innovative financial instruments. They are therefore starting to think about the need to develop specialists who may be able to innovate as well.

There are signs that companies are having to become much more selective in choosing who they send overseas. Minoru Makihara, the president of Mitsubishi Corporation, claimed in one interview that the success of overseas ventures was closely tied to the capabilities of the individual sent out to head them. His company was thus having to focus on sending not the person who would be routinely scheduled to go, but the 'right' person – 'whether he or she is Japanese, American, British or whatever.'[14] Such thinking would have been seen as revolutionary ten years ago, but now reflects how Japanese management is having to come to terms with the next realities of the super-competitive world.

It will be interesting to watch the extent to which Japanese companies will maintain *Keiretsu* relationships as they move abroad. In general, one would expect such a strategy to raise the cost for Japanese companies of doing business globally. They would like to continue their supplier relationships as they move abroad, but that will inevitably mean that some of these suppliers will be operating on inefficient scale economies compared with leading local suppliers. If they fail to deal with a reasonable proportion of the more efficient local non-Japanese component producers then they will ultimately be cutting themselves off from good healthy sources of competitive pressure.

Ultimately, though, a simple export of *Keiretsu* relationships is bound to trigger American and, perhaps, European response. When the Japanese system was opaque, western victims could have little legal recourse. However, just as anti-dumping actions have developed a set of case law, so will accusations that collusive action in Japan is affecting competition elsewhere in the world. The use of anti-trust litigation in the American market will eventually speed the end of such collusion.

Figure 10

THE MITSUBISHI GROUP

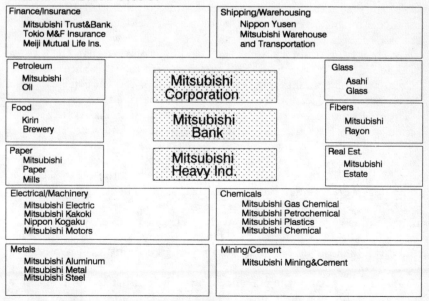

Source: Industrial Groupings in Japan, 1986-1987. Tokyo: Dodwell

THE FINANCIAL SYSTEM

During the 'catch-up' decades, Japanese companies undoubtedly benefited from a particularly generous financial regime, under which the
savings of ordinary citizens were funnelled into chosen industrial sectors
at cheap rates. As late as the 1970s, real interest rates for industrialists were
kept artificially low, allowing Japanese companies to build up their debt
on terms which were generous by world standards. Then during the
economic boom of the 1980s, as the Japanese authorities tried to counter a
sharp rise in the Yen, liquidity flooded into the system, leading to a boom
in both stock and property prices. Japanese companies began to see
themselves as financial manipulators, and for a while in the late 1980s they
were able to raise over half a trillion dollars for next to no cost. While
everyone seemed to benefit from a never-ending boom, observers started
talking about 'Zaitech', an age of financial engineering when mainstream
industrial companies unleashed their corporate treasurers to take
advantage of deregulated financial markets. This was the era when a
company such as Toyota prided itself on its financial surpluses, jokingly
referring to the company as 'Toyota Bank'.

For a while it looked as though the Japanese had discovered a perpetual
virtuous financial cycle. Industrial success would lead to profits which
would be fed back into the financial sector, guaranteeing ever increasing
profits to everyone. No matter that the Tokyo Stock Exchange traded on
multiples found nowhere else in the industrialized world. Japan was
different.

To western competitors, this all seems unfair – and to some extent it has
been. In practice, the Japanese authorities in the post-1945 period
installed a financial system suitable for a less-developed economy (which
was fair enough, though the Germans showed there were other ways for
recovering from military defeat). The key point is that the central
weakness of the Japanese political system meant that this anti-consumer
system was not dismantled at the point when Japanese industrialists were
clearly clawing the economy out of the less-developed status.

The really important question is whether the financial system is still
biased heavily toward industrial investment – and here there are
conflicting views. On the one hand, there is no denying that as late as the
mid-1980s, the real capital costs in Japan were 5.9 per cent versus 9.7 per
cent in the USA.[15] Again, the 1991 scandal when the giant securities
companies were found to be reimbursing their key clients against losses on
securities trading was clear evidence that the Japanese system remains
highly collusive (and biased against foreigners – none of whom received
such guarantees). Obviously, a Japanese industrial giant, with such
guarantees behind it, can plan ahead with a certainty not available to
western competitors.

On the other hand, the evidence is that such disparities in real capital
costs are declining quite rapidly. Financial deregulation in Japan and the

globalization of financial markets have been making it easier for foreigners to borrow in Tokyo and for Japanese to lend overseas if higher real returns can be found there. In addition, work by Timothy Luehrman and Carl Kester of Harvard Business School[16] is suggesting that, once adjustment is made for the different structures of the US and Japanese systems, the real after-tax cost of capital was roughly equivalent where companies faced the same risks. There will be distortions as long as Japanese equity investors remain relatively inexperienced in assessing the prospects of foreign companies. However, the cost of capital gap should increasingly be an irrelevancy.

COMPANY-GOVERNMENT RELATIONS

Perhaps the biggest single advantage the Japanese industrial sector possesses is that the overall political system remains hopelessly biased towards the interests of well-financed special interest groups. Inevitably this means that the corporate sector is rarely challenged by countervailing domestic political pressures. Japan has a political system unrivalled within the industrialized world in which, as the old joke says, money does not just talk; it screams.

At one level, the relationship of companies and ministries is merely an example of what other countries have often tried to create – and have failed. All that has happened in the Japanese case is that in finding a positive role for ministries such as MITI, they went about the job of indicative planning effectively, while others like the French and (pre-Thatcherite) British failed. The question of whether innovations such as pre-competitive research collaborations were particularly unfair is an interesting one. However, if these are put into the context of the big transnational nuclear research or aerospace collaborative programmes which the Europeans have been fostering since the 1950s, the only distinctiveness of the Japanese efforts is that they proved to be more effective at identifying commercially-important work to support.

Against the complaint that the Japanese put financial support into research programmes which effectively subsidized companies in the early stages of developing new technologies, one can argue the importance that US defence spending has had for getting Boeing into the forefront of civil aviation, or the central role of the Apollo moon programme in giving a kick start to the US micro-electronic industry. In the Japanese case, the sums of money have not been extreme. Once again, the accusations may turn mostly on the effectiveness of their financial support, not on the principle of their trying to provide any at all.

However, the Japanese corporate sector has particularly benefited from the way that the interests of consumers and employees have been consistently under-represented. This explains, for instance, why there was so little consumer resistance to a financial structure which favoured industrial borrowers at the expense of corporate lenders. It explains also why there is so little public concern about levels of corporate collusion which would have raised howls of public protest in more polarized political systems such as that of the United States.

On top of this, industrial interests have clearly captured particular ministries. The Ministry of Posts and Telecommunications is very close to NTT, the Japanese telecoms giant. Similarly, the Ministry of Finance is extremely close to the financial interests it is supposed to regulate and promote. This is the ministry, par excellence, which has benefited from the *amakudari* system whereby, on retirement, high officials descend from heaven into well-paid top managerial positions within the companies they have spent their careers promoting and regulating. It is thus hardly surprising that this ministry has proved ineffective at injecting real competitive urgency into the financial services industry. Effectively, this is a ministry which has put the promotion of the financial services industry before its tight regulation.

There are, however, dangers for Japanese industrialists in working under a weak political system skewed in the favour of narrow industrial interests. For one thing, narrow-minded industrialists often need protecting from themselves. To take financial services, for instance, it is clear that Tokyo is being damaged as a credible international financial centre precisely because the bias toward the big Japanese corporations is still so marked.

Secondly, the weakness of the overall system means that Japanese companies are increasingly badly represented by the Japanese diplomatic system in international disputes. Quite simply, western negotiators rarely believe that their Japanese opposite numbers can deliver change when they go back to Tokyo. So the temptation is to promote change in Japan by relatively crude bilateral threats elsewhere in the world. For instance, if aspects of the *Keiretsu* system really are collusive against foreigners, then the increasing temptation is to take action at the level of the US anti-trust authorities. If one cannot trust the Japanese political system to put backbone into its Fair Trade Commission, then one might as well fight the damage done by such collusion in a country like the USA where one can get rulings stemming from the effects of collusion across the Pacific.

In a closed Japanese system, then, the peculiarities of the Japanese political system would not be of much interest to others. However, as Japanese trade and investment penetrate the rest of the world, the effects of the system start to be felt elsewhere. Their political system is undoubtedly distinctive but, as it is biased toward industrial special interests and against foreigners, it itself is becoming a political issue at the global level. If Japan is to be accepted at a global level, political change will have to be forced upon it – a process which is already under way.

THE NEED FOR ADAPTATION AND REFORM

If one views Japan as a superb industrial machine constructed on idiosyncratic institutional and cultural foundations, this raises some very interesting questions indeed.

For one thing, Japan has effectively achieved its industrial catch-up campaign. In most of the main industrial sectors, its companies now rank with the world's best. To what extent are the institutions which propelled them to the fore adequate for a world in which they must stake a claim to the future? To what extent will the Japanese system evolve to support their industries in their new world role?

INTERNAL AND EXTERNAL PRESSURES FOR CHANGE

We have earlier given some examples of how growing competition within Japan is forcing modifications of traditional employment practices, such as the principle of life-time employment. But change is coming more widely.

Starting from a very low level, there are signs of movement at the level of corporate ownership. Until quite recently, mergers and acquisitions have been an insignificant part of the corporate Japanese scene – but the number of companies who are clearly in significant financial pain is starting to grow. These include the smaller Japanese auto manufacturers such as Subaru which survived the boom years of the 1980s at least in part because US protectionism gave all Japanese exporters to the US a subsidy at the expense of the American consumer. Such companies have been forced to turn to bigger protectors (Subaru turned to Nissan). A generation of smaller Japanese players can be identified who are more likely than not to be swept out of business as the realities of global super-competitivity hit Japan.

Another area of some spontaneous movement is the relationship of MITI (and other dominant ministries) and their client companies. Although the structures for targeted intervention are still in place, the effectiveness of this system seems much diminished. The largest Japanese companies have been amassing cash mountains, so they no longer need the cheap credits which went with the classic targeted intervention process. Secondly, the nature of targeting has changed irrevocably as the Japanese have caught up with the rest of the world. No longer can they simply track the structure of the US economy, moving toward those sectors where the US were still ahead of Japan. Today, the Japanese are having to guess what the technological and commercial shape of the twenty-first century will look like, just like IBM and the rest of us.

THE EXTERNAL PRESSURES

Increasingly, though, movement is coming not just for domestic reasons, but because powerful foreign governments require change. It is American pressure which has been particularly important, and to some extent the USA has become the champion of the Japanese citizen which the Japanese political system has not provided. In financial services, telecommunications and airline regulation, policies have changed significantly because of such pressure. As far as the Americans have been concerned, they have seen it is their responsibility to impose western, 'Anglo-Saxon' standards on the Japanese environment. By creating 'level playing fields', the US would force Japanese companies to compete on equal terms.

A great deal of Japanese movement has come about because of such pressures. Even if one takes MITI, the ministry which has probably moved fastest, its conversion in the mid-1980s to the need to encourage imports owed much to the protectionist pressures building up in the USA and elsewhere. If Japanese companies could be persuaded to invest overseas, and if imports into Japan could be stepped up, the worst of anti-Japanese trade measures might be avoided.

Most other reforms have come under even more explicit pressure.

One very obvious area of pressure has been on Japanese financial practices. In 1983, a Yen-Dollar Committee was created between Japan and a United States, which was increasingly irritated (and frightened) by the heavy capital flows from Japan to the US, which threatened to undermine the value of the Yen, thus further increasing the competitive capabilities of Japanese exporters. As a result of these pressures, controls on interest rates slowly began to be dismantled, signalling the end of a system which had been biased against savers in favour of industrial borrowers.

In parallel, the pressures grew to allow western financial institutions into Japan. In particular, the resistance of the Tokyo Stock Exchange was challenged, and US and European securities houses were allowed into Tokyo to compete with the Japanese financial giants such as Nomura and Nikko.

Admittedly, it has been fashionable to argue that such financial liberalization has been a sham. In particular, it is affirmed that the only cause of change in the mid-1980s was that the bigger Japanese financial institutions wanted to expand overseas in their own right. If Tokyo financial markets were kept closed, they would face resistance as they tried to move into global financial centres such as New York or London. Therefore, it is argued, the reforms which were tolerated by the Ministry of Finance were just enough to keep the foreigners happy, without really changing the nature of Tokyo's financial markets.

There may well be some truth in these accusations, though it should be noted that the Japanese authorities allowed western financial institutions to carry out activities in Tokyo which would not have been possible for a purely Japanese competitor. Thus western banks were helped to find a way of trading securities, in apparent contravention of Article 65 which is meant to stop such 'Universal' banking.

In fact, this liberalization was to have its effect in early 1990 when the Tokyo authorities failed to avert a major collapse of Japanese stock markets which led to a near 50 per cent fall in the Nikkei index over the following ten months (which then put pressure on the grossly over-inflated property market). By spring 1992, markets had still not rebounded, and an even deeper collapse was under way.

One alleged reason for the authorities' failure to manage this fall was that foreign securities houses, though insecurely established in Tokyo, had been pioneering techniques such as programme trading which meant that the workings of market forces were both speeded and intensified. The Ministry of Finance and the Japanese securities houses finally found themselves unable to fine-tune the Tokyo Stock Exchange with the effectiveness they had had in the past.

At the same time, the liberalization of interest rates (though still not complete) was putting pressure on banks, which were having to come to terms with the Bank for International Settlement's insistence that they work with capital reserves equivalent to those maintained by major non-Japanese competitors. As stock prices fell, the Japanese banks no longer had access to the cheap credit they had relied on in past decades, but still had to raise their capital bases to meet BIS requirements.

Doubtless the bubble economy would have burst some time. However, the financial liberalization which has taken place – at least partly because of heavy foreign pressure – means that it will only rise again in a form much closer to the Wall Street model.

Telecommunications is another sector where liberalization has taken place at least partly as a result of foreign pressure. As with financial services, there were some internal forces pushing for deregulation, but this was another case where the Americans used their diplomatic clout to side with bodies like MITI who were pushing for openness.

This also gives an idea of the fault lines within Japanese society regarding the liberalization process. Whatever the legislation said about allowing foreign companies into telecommunications consortia in Japan, the Ministry of Posts and Telecommunications tried all it knew to avoid implementing the letter of the law. This particularly affected the British company, Cable and Wireless, which wanted to be an active player in the IDC (International Digital Communications) consortia. The MPT was determined that the British should be allowed only a passive role. Unusually, Cable and Wireless refused to take such treatment quietly. Top executives made speeches attacking the MPT position, while Mrs Thatcher also entered the fray. Eventually the MPT gave ground, but this was only after considerable external pressure had been added to the discreet opposition of MITI. Once again, it was foreign pressure which had been the key.

Like it or not, the Japanese are doomed to live with such rather galling outside pressures for some time to come. Undoubtedly nationalistic politicians will resent pressures and will refine the arguments about how Japan can say 'No'. However, there are now voices such as Sony's Mr Morita who do support a number of foreign criticisms of the Japanese system. He has publicly accepted that this gives Japanese companies an unfair competitive advantages over foreigners. In particular, he cites the long hours worked by Japanese workers, and the way that *Keiretsu* meant that Japanese companies can get away with paying low dividends, and squeezing component suppliers on prices.

However, even if Japanese policy-makers don't fully accept such arguments, they are stymied by the fact that their companies now need access to overseas market and investment opportunities. These will increasingly be blocked should Japan fail to move more toward the Anglo-American industrial culture.

So the Japanese have been forced to tighten their control on the exports of strategically significant goods and materials in the aftermath of the Toshiba-Kongsberg incident when sophisticated metal milling equipment, suitable for producing silent submarine propellors, was sold to the Soviet navy. Japanese executives may not have been universally happy about such restrictions, but if firms like Toshiba were not to be penalized in the more important US market, they had to come to terms with such Cold War controls.

Pressures are clearly building up in other areas. In financial services, the Japanese are under pressure to accept US standards on insider trading on securities – a concept that is alien to the free and easy world of Japanese financial management. Similarly, the relatively casual acceptance of gangsters is another part of the corporate culture which will come under criticism. In the past, the Japanese political establishment has found it hard to get angry about such practices, but when foreigners start to react, life gets more serious. A case in point was the 1991 set of scandals involving the giant securities houses such as Nomura. Once international pillars of financial probity such as the World Bank started to drop the Japanese securities houses because of their links with the Yakuza (gangsters), the scandal began to incur financial costs on a global scale. Similarly, the litigious US community understandably took to the law courts to argue that the special deals between the securities giants and privileged Japanese clients had effectively damaged the interests of non-Japanese outsiders. Should they be awarded compensation in American courts, what started as a purely Japanese affair will once again end up costing Japanese companies financial penalties over and above those imposed within Japan itself.

Again, in the area of anti-trust policy, it is pretty obvious that the Japanese will have to tighten their policies to avert yet more diplomatic rows with the American judicial system. The *Keiretsu* system is now under scrutiny, as is the Japanese distribution system which is so very clearly anti-consumer and (presumably) anti-competitive.

It is understandable that there should be some Japanese resentment of such extraterritorial pressures. However, they are becoming global players, and that means living by the standards which dominate the world economy. As explained in the next chapter, these standards are predominantly determined by the USA. The Japanese system will just have to come to terms with this unpleasant fact of life. As President Truman allegedly put it: 'If you can't stand the heat, get out of the kitchen'. As far as the super-competitive era is concerned, the Japanese are undoubtedly 'in the kitchen'. They had better get used to the heat.

QUESTIONS FOR THE TWENTY-FIRST CENTURY

It should be clear from this chapter that we are impressed with the quality of Japanese management, but one can point to some weaknesses.

The first question is whether they will continue to be so technologically dynamic now that they have more or less caught up with best western practices. Certainly, the task of mapping out the technological paths for the next twenty or thirty years is going to be a great deal more complicated than it was in the 1960s and 1970s when the cooperation between MITI and the Japanese industrial community was at its closest. An imaginative tracking of the American economy was what was needed then. Today, there are no clear road maps. Japanese companies are having to guess about technological futures along with the rest of the international business community. How good will their judgement be?

One cannot automatically assume that their overall success will continue. For one thing, non-Japanese companies with access to key technologies are getting much tougher on their licensing policies – and some of Japan's past success lay in getting cheap licences from western competitors who were not fully alert to the cost of strengthening Japanese competition. Again, within Japan there is a considerable debate about the quality of Japanese creativity, reflecting worries about an educational system which stresses rote learning more than individual creativity. It could be that the Japanese employment system which values continuity of employment and generalists may work against them in this area. Certainly, one hears Japanese research managers talking of the attractions of locating research in countries such as Britain where they can go out and recruit specialists in a particular field without having to worry about their loyalties to other companies.

On the other hand, the virtues of scientific creativity can perhaps be over-stressed. After all, the creation of most consumer-oriented products rests not on scientific breakthroughs, but on the intelligent and systematic application of known technologies to a particular business problem. Japanese companies are steadily deepening their research base. The number of patents they are filing is running at high levels. There is certainly no a priori reason why they should not be as creative as is necessary. Just as the American burst of Nobel prizes in science started after the country's economic strength was established, so it is quite possible that Japan's economic strength will produce the outstanding science in good time.

There are similar worries about the country's ability to master the software which is increasingly important in developing successful products. Once again, the jury must remain out. It is true that they have had difficulties in establishing global standards in sectors such as computing where they have considerable hardware skills. On the other hand, a lot of effort is going into mastering the automation of software development and there is no particular reason why they should not close the gap on the more individualist west, as they have done before in other sectors.

Certainly Japanese companies will have to come to terms with a domestic society which is less dominated by corporate needs. New graduates will still be appropriately educated by western standards, but there are both labour shortages and entrants into the labour force who are increasingly reluctant to accept the long hours and dehumanizing conditions of their fathers. The odds are that companies will have to become more sensitive to short-term financial pressures than has been true in the past. As growth rates continue to fall toward OECD averages, the cost of failure in the Japanese system will increase. Companies will have to take a shorter-term financial view, and not all will manage to make the transition.

Perhaps the greatest question mark lies over the ability of Japanese companies to come to terms with internationalization.

Up till now, they have not really been tested. For obvious reasons they have been latecomers as multinational investors. Even today, a giant firm like Toyota has less than ten year's experience as an investor in the USA, and still has to complete its first factory in western Europe.

Most people have assumed that the first wave of Japanese investment has been unequivocally successful. Certainly, one can point to the impressive initial penetration into American and European markets of the Japanese automotive industry. In consumer electronics, a firm like Sony has clearly established itself very thoroughly at the heart of the American and European markets.

. . . and yet, doubts are starting to emerge. For one thing, there is some evidence from McKinsey that Japanese investment in the USA is significantly less profitable than that of the indigenous competition. Slow decision-making and a tendency to produce over-standardized products were among the explanations given for this. Certainly in Europe there are many small Japanese operations which must currently be of a size well below the optimum needed to be fully profitable.

The Japanese ability to manage cultural and political complexity is only just beginning to be tested. Some Japanese companies are already having to reorganize their overseas projects. Honda is reorganizing its whole global set of activities. Sony and its Japanese imitators have been pouring money into their Hollywood holdings on a scale which means they will have to be extraordinarily successful if they are to get a decent return on their money. (Apart from making a major investment in Italy, Sony and Matsushita could not have invested in a business culture more remote from the Japanese one than that of Hollywood.) Bridgestone has still failed to turn its Firestone operations around.

Our bet is that the 1990s will see some quite spectacular disasters amongst the less cautious Japanese overseas investors. We believe that the cultural coherence within Japan, a factor which has worked in favour of the Japanese industrial machine, will work against Japanese companies as they move into the wider world. A few Japanese companies are now starting to build credible career paths for non-Japanese employees – Sony leading the way with an American and German on its main board. In general, though, however nice sounding the statements of Japanese management principles are ('global localization' etc.) it is rare to come across a Japanese company with a convincing policy in this respect. Although American companies have come under attack in the past for insensitive management practices (being anti-union), they at least were sound on practices such as treating racial minorities sympathetically, and knowing how to avoid accusations of sexual discrimination. It is precisely in such areas that Japanese culture has values extremely different from those found in the USA. Readers must make their own minds up about the significance of the hostility of feminist and black groups to Japanese investment in America.

Despite all this, there can be little doubt that the bulk of Japanese companies which rely on solid technology and product development will continue to grow quite happily. We would, however, predict some investment disasters where Japanese managers have to come to terms with more culturally complex situations. The Japanese investments in Hollywood will probably produce some of the first such major disasters; we can see nothing in the history of Japanese management to suggest that it will be able to manage the cultural anarchy of Hollywood. The philosophy behind the investments made great sense (helping to establish hardware standards by guaranteeing the necessary flow of movies and so on). The managerial complexity of producing the necessary software flow will almost certainly prove too great, even for a manager as talented as Akio Morita.

Having said that, we will be delighted to be proved wrong . . . and if these Japanese managers do successfully manage their Hollywood investments, then we will accept that they can manage absolutely anything!

THE ASSIMILATION OF JAPAN

It is irresponsible to be too pessimistic about what will happen to Japan in coming decades. The ideas of the total eclipse of Japan, or of a war with it, is totally implausible.

Yes, there will be tensions between the USA and Japan, and it is still just possible for Japan to say 'No' and retreat into itself. However, this is extremely unlikely. What makes much more sense is a scenario in which the coming decades see the final assimilation of Japan into the world political-economy. Obviously, there are tensions at this moment, but what we are seeing is a once-and-for-all cross penetration of trade and investment which is unique in its speed and volume.

This is not just about Japanese companies going overseas. It is also about western companies establishing themselves in Japan, which will almost certainly remain a culturally complex market, though a steadily less forbidding one. This penetration will be led by sectors such as computers, consumer electronics and suppliers to the auto industry since Japan has become a lead market for such products. The western companies may not erect large plants (for Japan will remain an expensive, labour-short location for investment): but they will have operations large enough for them to monitor market developments within Japan, and to be credible when they seek to establish relations with the headquarters of Japanese companies.

In the reverse direction, there will be a shakeout among Japanese overseas investors. These companies will have to learn how to come to terms with a post-Catch-up world, in which they will have to be not just masters of product development and manufacturing technology, but able also to manage global operating networks. Many will flourish, but some will find they cannot master a world of cultural diversity and will have to follow the path of many a European and American company before them, and retreat to what they hope is a defensible home base (in this case, back in Japan).

Japan will develop as a vibrant, innovative consumer market for products such as automobiles, consumer electronics and fashion. This will ensure the steady interest of the world's companies in these sectors. If Japan is where the 'Early Movers' reside, then they must all be represented there. Tokyo will continue to develop as one of the key trend-establishing cities in the world. As Manhattan's decline goes on, Tokyo will inherit its role as the semi-futuristic megalopolis symbolically representing the strand in the modern world.

This two-way assimilation process will continue to speed up. The Japanese will start the relatively slow process of coming to terms with a world of foreign investors, where foreign executives must be given proper career paths if Japanese companies are to survive. The xenophobia within Japanese society is already decreasing, but attitudes will still need a lot of changing before foreigners are treated on broadly the same terms as nationals.

In the reverse direction, much of the emotion surrounding Japanese overseas investment will disappear. It is only natural that the initial wave of Japanese investment has stirred resentment. It has built up extremely fast compared with the equivalent expansion of American, British or Dutch multinationals. It has had to deal with pre-existing racial tensions. Above all, the Japanese transplants have been an unwelcome reminder of the USA's loss of its industrial leadership.

These resentments will pass as Japanese investors are absorbed into local cultures. This is what has happened to nearly all previous cultural invasions, from that of the Barbarian hordes who swept through Europe, 1,500 years ago, to the American multinationals who moved globally in the post-1945 era. Japanese companies will grow more adept at internationalizing their management structures. The steady stream of innovative products from their factories will be seen as just another set of products which discerning consumers will appreciate. At the less visible level of component supplies, the Japanese penetration will concern few except direct industrial competitors. At the cultural level, Sumo wrestling, Kabuki theatre, Japanese architecture and so on will be absorbed as another set of ingredients into the cultural smorgasbord which is today's world.

Assimilation, though, requires behavioural changes both by the newcomers and the established communities. Who will make the most adjustments – the Japanese or the outside world?

As we see it (and however unpalatable this will prove for a proud culture), it will be Japan which will have to adapt most to the new world. At the managerial level, companies will have to struggle to improve the career prospects of non-Japanese executives. At the cultural level, the Japanese will continue to learn English, while relatively few foreigners bother to master Japanese. Although western managements will continue to learn from their Japanese counterparts, it will be the Japanese who will be faced with the more wrenching changes as western standards of competition, the openness of distribution systems, equal opportunity employment and other policies are forced on them – sometimes by political pressure.

As the French have already discovered, it can be galling to possess a proud, rich, distinctive culture in a world which is partially homogenizing around the English language and American culture. The Japanese, coming from a particularly remote and nationalistic culture, will find this very difficult to stomach.

Twenty or thirty years ago, when President de Gaulle sneered about the Japanese prime minister being a 'transistor salesman', the Japanese could hope to have things both ways. They could become an industrial superpower, but on their own terms. In practice, life is going to prove more complex than that. Japanese companies will remain at the forefront of the world economy – but it will be under Anglo-American rules.

7

WHAT'S GOOD FOR AMERICA?

DURING THE SUMMER of 1991 Brother Industries, the Japanese typewriter and printer manufacturer, complained to the US Federal Trade Commission that SCM Corporation (supplier of the famed Smith Corona typewriter, one of America's best-known brands) was dumping imported electronic typewriters in the US and thereby endangering jobs in Brother's typewriter factory in Kentucky. The claim was unsuccessful, but it illustrates the degree to which the US has become entwined in the global marketplace (indeed, SCM is now owned by Hanson of the UK).

Mitsubishi big-screen televisions are made in California by a factory employing 700 Americans, but Zenith – the only surviving US TV manufacturer – will make all its sets in Mexico by 1993. Some General Motors cars have a higher import content than the Toyota, Nissan and Honda cars made in the USA. Robert Reich, the Harvard academic, was right to ask 'Who is Us?' in an article in the *Harvard Business Review*;[1] increasingly the nationality of corporate ownership is no guarantee that the home country will derive the lion's share of the benefits, and foreign-owned firms often make a greater contribution to economic welfare and competitiveness than their domestic counterparts.

It was not always so. In January 1953 the President of General Motors, 'Engine Charlie' Wilson, was nominated by President Eisenhower to be Secretary of Defense. He told the US Senate Armed Services Committee: 'For years I thought what was good for our country was good for General Motors and vice versa . . . It goes with the welfare of the country.' There were few then who disagreed with his underlying premise. Yet almost forty years later, GM – its market share eroded by Japanese car exports and transplant production – announced the closure of several of its plants and the elimination of over 74,000 jobs by 1996. By the beginning of 1992 Honda had overtaken Chrysler as the third largest auto producer in the US, and President George Bush took the chief executives of the three US carmakers to Tokyo in order to pressure Japan into buying more American cars (over half the very small number of American car exports to Japan are made in Ohio by Honda).

By the 1990s, the idea of the 'American Century' was a bad joke for US industrialists and their workforces alike. For them to accept that the US was no longer at the cutting edge of world industrial power was a bitter pill to swallow. Although the collapse of the Soviet Union meant an end to the era of superpower rivalry, Americans found that the fruits of victory were meagre – indeed, that the struggle for supremacy was now couched in economic terms and the chief rivals were Europe (notably reunited Germany), the newly industrialized 'Pacific Tigers' of Hong Kong, Taiwan, South Korea and Singapore, and above all Japan. Although the American ideals of democracy and free market capitalism seemed to be taking the world by storm, America was not the prime beneficiary: its domestic economy was burdened by the twin deficits of public expenditure and balance of payments, a decaying infrastructure and increasing industrial competition from abroad.

Books about America's decline became one of the few growth industries in the US, notably Paul Kennedy's best-seller *The Rise and Fall of the Great Powers*,[2] which pointed to excessive foreign strategic commitments, or 'imperial overstretch', as a cause of underinvestment and loss of competitiveness in the US. Although others pointed out that America's decline was only relative, a result of the economic miracles in Germany, Japan and elsewhere that had been promoted and encouraged by America, and that the US remained the most powerful country in the world – as its leadership in the war against Iraq in 1991 showed – this was small consolation to the ordinary American citizen, increasingly fearful that the American Dream of liberty and increasing affluence could no longer be attained.

This psychic malaise matters to the rest of the world precisely because America's past economic and political strength made American values enormously influential and attractive. After World War Two, the US was a colossus bestriding the world, offering military security to its allies in return for a commitment to contain the spread of communism and to rebuild their economies on the basis of freer trade and investment. This strength allowed America to set the agenda for how the world economy should be run. Sometimes this was done formally, as with the creation of the Bretton Woods system of fixed exchange rates (with all currencies tied to the US Dollar) and the US dominance in the International Monetary Fund and the World Bank. More subtly, the USA demonstrated a free enterprise system which was held up as a beacon to a less entrepreneurial world.

The 'American Way' was one of relatively unfettered competition in which the consumer was king. The US constitution had combined a weak legislature with a strong legal tradition. Companies could act without too much fear of arbitrary governmental intervention, except in times of war. If anything, a tradition of bringing top industrialists – such as GM's Charles Wilson or Ford's Robert McNamara, who both served as Secretary of Defense – or their close advisers into government meant that the corporate sector had a political prestige not found elsewhere in the world, where aristocratic or military reputations far outweighed mere commercial success. The American élite was well used to multiple careers; President Eisenhower had been a distinguished general, Secretary of State Kissinger was a former Harvard professor, and Time Inc's Clare Booth Luce became Ambassador in Rome. Senior politicians and civil servants routinely left public service to take executive positions in industry: Robert Hormats, former Treasury Assistant Secretary of State for Economic Affairs, became Vice-President of Goldman Sachs and Secretary of State George Shultz returned to the Bechtel Corporation.

The global political situation reinforced the prestige of businessmen. The fact that the US and the USSR drifted into the tense Cold War era shortly after the Second World War meant that the virtues of the American way of life (with special emphasis on Free Enterprise) became the raw material for a propaganda blitz which covered the world. Free Enterprise and the American Dream were presented as two sides of the same coin.

Underlying reality did not always square with the public image. There has always been a strand of populist, anti-Big Business sentiment in the American political culture. John D. Rockefeller's Standard Oil Trust was broken up in 1911 after Ida Tarbell and other journalists had exposed its predatory business tactics; fifty years later the crusading lawyer Ralph Nader compelled GM to halt production of the Corvair because it was 'Unsafe at Any Speed'.

At the popular level of a Hollywood cult film such as *It's a Wonderful Life* (directed by Frank Capra and released in 1946), this distrust of big business and of government by distant bureaucrats carried great resonance. In that film, the enemies of James Stewart's small town family-run Savings and Loan are Mr Potter, the local bank owner and industrialist who dominates the economic life of Bedford Falls, and the Federal Government bank examiner, whose surprise visits and insistence on regulations being followed interfere with the S&L's public-spirited lending practices. Hollywood Westerns often represented the coming of large-scale ranching (with its barbed wire fencing off the prairie) or the expansion of the railway companies as corporate villains threatening the individual settler.

The importance of this is that public distrust of private monopoly power led to political reaction. Since the late 1880s, when the world's first anti-monopoly legislation was passed by the US Congress, there has been a strong, distinctively American approach to the regulation of key industries – be they railroads, airlines, telephone or power companies. Each industry's circumstances are different, but in general the power of the companies was defined by law, and the interest of the consumers was taken into account. State ownership of industry was avoided. We argue in this chapter that this framework of regulation to guarantee competition is not only alive and well, but is a pattern which the US is exporting to the rest of the world.

Beneath the free-enterprise rhetoric, however, there was a large sector of the US economy – the 'Military-Industrial Complex' that President Eisenhower warned about in his 1960 farewell address – which has always been heavily dependent on government spending. Whenever an American complains about the evils of governmental intervention in industrial policy elsewhere in the world, one merely has to point out that companies such Boeing and IBM benefited from the long period of the Cold War, when federal money and preferential purchasing policies enabled them to develop costly technologies which the commercial market could not have supported.

THE EMERGING SHOCKS

The 1950s and the 1960s were the glory years for US corporations. They dominated the key technologies, though the Soviet space effort, the early success of Volkswagen and the successful commercialization by Japan of the transistor radio were indicators that new challengers were waiting in the wings. American multinational corporations expanded their investments through the world. Those were the years when everyone was frightened of American industrial and technological hegemony. This spread overseas of American-owned firms was indeed a real 'American Challenge'[3] to claim industrial and technological supremacy. It was felt by the Europeans, the Japanese – and had long been felt in the Third World. It was not just General Motors, Esso (now Exxon) and IBM that the world respected. It was also firms like Chrysler, Citicorp, Pan Am, Socal, Firestone, Honeywell, McDonnell-Douglas – ironically, corporations that have either been merged with other companies or are now fighting for their independent survival.

The first serious psychological shocks came in the 1970s. The Vietnam War went badly and the US effectively had to concede defeat. The Bretton Woods system collapsed as it became evident that the US was no longer able to sustain confidence in the dollar as the keystone of the system of fixed exchange rates. There followed the OPEC revolution of the early 1970s in which the Anglo-American oil companies lost control of the oil industry.

The resultant explosion in oil prices produced a boom in oil revenues to assorted desert sheikhdoms and kingdoms. As the Arab and other oil producers started recycling these petrodollars, US citizens were suddenly aware that various foreigners were buying up American real estate – and US public opinion was not certain that it liked the experience. The concern about Arab investment peaked in 1981 when the Kuwait Petroleum Company bid $2.5 billion for Santa Fe Petroleum. Although this deal was cleared by the relevant authorities, the political row rumbled on for several years as Congressmen argued that Kuwait was not offering reciprocal openness to US companies.[4]

THE 1980S: TIME FOR GLOOM AND INNOVATION

By the early 1980s, worries were running far deeper. The Arabs could be dismissed as lucky possessors of natural resources. What was much harder to explain away was a deepening crisis over the competitive position of the big three automakers of Detroit (GM, Ford and Chrysler), the very symbols of America's prowess in manufacturing mass production. American industry was being challenged on its home territory by a wave of imports (notably from Japan) and by a rapid expansion of inward direct investment from all around the world.

The automotive crisis started in the late 1970s with a crisis at Chrysler which was primarily caused by bad management. To pull Chrysler round, however, its new president and CEO, Lee Iacocca, would have to lay off 50,000 out of the company's 110,000 total employees, as well as having to plead with Congress for a loan guarantee to keep the company in business.

This was merely a prelude to the storm. The whole of Detroit was badly placed for the post-Shah oil shock of 1979–80. As consumers looked around for small, fuel-efficient cars it was the Japanese car-producers that could and did provide them, taking 25 per cent of the American auto market in 1979.[5] The US consumer started to appreciate the quality of Japanese imports and also the price: the Japanese had a cost advantage of between $1,500–$2,000 per automobile over American-made cars. Given Detroit's slowness (unfortunate, but understandable in the context of the 1970s) to realize that such a challenge was about to hit them, the US automobile industry sought a politically feasible answer to the problem. It worked for some form of trade protection, and got it through a 'Voluntary' Export Restraint agreement with their Japanese opposite numbers in May 1981.

After this the impact of Japanese business on the US increased steadily. As competition spread from one sector to another – from cars and consumer electronics to machine tools and semiconductors – and as Japanese transplant factories were set up on US soil, it was evident that the age of unchallenged American industrial dominance was over. The questions which remained were: whether the new challenges were temporary or permanent ones; whether this was purely a Japanese phenomenon; and – depending on the answer to the first two questions – could US competitiveness be revived?

Put this way, the question of the relative decline of the US economy looms large. However, it would be misleading to focus on just this issue, because during the 1970s and 1980s the USA initiated a wave of global liberalization which in many respects confirms the country's position as the most influential actor in the world economy. Some of the impetus for this deregulation and liberalization came from the conservative ideology of President Reagan and his advisers, advocates of supply-side economics. Reagan firmly believed in the beneficial effects of competition and, in general, his administrations acted consistently to support measures to reduce government regulation and promote competition.

President Reagan cannot claim sole credit for this signicant liberalization of key sectors. For instance, he inherited the process of airline deregulation as part of the populist legacy of his predecessor, Jimmy Carter. Similarly, challenges to AT&T ('Ma Bell', the telecommunications giant with a near-monopoly) had been working their way through the legal system for some years. It was thus an accident of history that Judge Greene's crucial 1982 ruling which dismembered this company should have fallen within Reagan's first term of office.

Thirdly, he inherited the loosening of the financial system triggered by the Wall Street 'Big Bang' of 1975, which abolished fixed commissions for securities trading. This initial liberalization was very much the result of internal competition, with the big institutional investors succeeding in breaking the cartel of established securities houses, at least in part by playing the New York Stock Exchange ('Wall Street') off against the competing American Stock Exchange and the Over-the-Counter exchange.

Big Bang effectively signalled the beginning of a new era, which was to flower in the following decade. It did not so much rewrite rules and regulations as cut the profit margins of Wall Street firms, forcing them into aggressive innovation. In 1978, Salomon Brothers moved into the mortgage market, and became the key players in 1981 when Congress passed legislation to remove the ceiling on interest paid to bank depositors (Regulation 'Q') and allow Savings and Loans Companies (the thrifts) to sell their mortgage loans to invest for higher returns. This incentive to invest in unfamiliar areas was supported by the continuation of Federal or State insurance of savings deposits (up to $100,000 per depositer per institution) which meant that depositors cared only for the rate of return rather than the soundness of the loan portfolio. In *Liar's Poker*,[6] Michael Lewis describes the mayhem as the inexperienced thrifts managers fell into the grasp of the Wall Street hucksters.

Meanwhile, Drexel Burnham's Michael Milken was demonstrating the value and power of junk bonds (securities backing loans to companies that compensated for the degree of risk by offering a higher rate of return) when skilfully packaged and marketed. Here Milken was not responding to any particular relaxation of official regulations, but was thinking creatively about the potentialities of the existing financial system. Junk bonds enabled takeover specialists to mount raids on under-performing companies by raising capital on the market rather than providing it from corporate reserves. Such threats encouraged companies to maintain or increase returns to investors, even if this meant maximizing short-term profitability at the expense of investment in research and development or increased productivity that would ensure the long-term viability of the firm.

The result of this financial creativity was to change the face of corporate

America in the 1980s, sometimes increasing its efficiency, but more frequently diverting the attention of top executives from thinking about how best to position their companies in the face of increased foreign competition. The 1980s were a traumatic time for America's corporate leaders. On the one hand, the decade was one of exceptional ownership turmoil as the attention of both foreign investors and domestic raiders fuelled by junk-bonds focused on the acquisition of any American corporation that had under-performing and undervalued assets. In addition, the regulatory changes in the airline and telecommunications industries were transforming those sectors and strongly influencing other governments (notably the Thatcher government in Britain) to attempt similar deregulatory initiatives.

In addition, a separate battle with foreign competition intensified during the decade. An increasing share of America's GNP was accounted for by foreign trade – up from a fifth in the 1970s to over a quarter in the 1980s. By 1980 there were few areas of manufacturing that were not exposed to import competition, and increasing pressure from beleaguered American firms for Washington to protect them. During the early 1980s the US Government became increasingly reliant on foreign financing of its budget deficit, while the strength of the dollar hindered American exports and sucked in imports. The impact of these 'twin deficits' was to turn America from a net creditor in 1981 to a net debtor in 1986. After coordinated international action to bring down the value of the dollar (the Plaza and Louvre Accords of 1985–87), which made dollar-denominated assets very attractive to non-American purchasers, foreign investment in the US increased significantly. In part this foreign direct investment – especially Japanese investment – was prompted by 'trade friction', as a means of circumventing actual or anticipated import barriers by producing goods inside the US market. Although the USA no longer enjoyed the economic predominance it enjoyed in the late 1940s and 1950s, it remained an important source of influence. Despite all the problems, its economy remained large and rich. When Japanese and European companies sought to expand, they both turned first to the USA. In a world of mass communications that encourages a degree of cultural homogenization, it is American culture that still provides the dominant icons which are recognized throughout the world. Whether these icons are Madonna, McDonald's Big Mac hamburger, Levi's jeans, American football, the Marlboro cowboy, or the whole pantheon of Hollywood's film and television stars, their cumulative global impact far outweighs that of any other country.

Even so, the overwhelming impression of the 1980s was one of lost American competitive strength. US citizens could see the deserted factories, could read about massive lay-offs, knew about the wave of new Japanese transplant factories in the US, and could see the effect that raiders fuelled by junk bonds could have on corporate America. Suddenly, American companies seemed to be challenged from every direction. The age of American economic certainty was finally gone.

THE SELLING OF AMERICA

During the 1980s the nature of competition within the USA took a major new turn as foreign direct investment in America accelerated. Although the economy had been built with a significant amount of foreign investment in the nineteenth century, during the twentieth century foreign ownership of American industry declined until after the second world war, and even then remained below the level of foreign penetration of any industrialized country except Japan. Thus the sharp upturn in inward investment was highly visible and politically sensitive. Where American multinationals once stalked the world, foreign multinationals now made the running in the United States.

As DeAnne Julius has explained, the US stock of inward multinational investment in 1977 was smaller than that in Canada and only slightly bigger than the stock in the UK. By 1985, the multinational investment was over twice as large as in Canada, and three to four times greater than stocks in Germany and the UK.[7] In 1988, for the first time since the first world war, inward direct investment into the USA ran ahead of the outward investments of American multinationals. Again, in 1977, foreigners controlled a mere 5 per cent of American manufacturing; by

Figure 11

LOCATION OF JAPANESE MANUFACTURING PLANTS IN THE U.S., 1989

Total 1989: 1380 plants (1980: 314 plants)

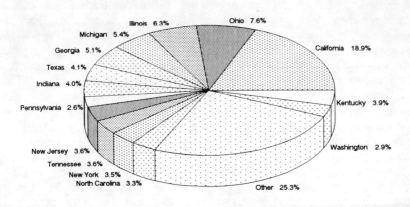

Source: Japan Economic Institute

1990, that figure was up to 13 per cent, including over half of the American companies still involved in consumer electronics.[8]

The statistics are dramatic, but statistics do not by themselves change the public mood. That only happens when trends are encapsulated by dramatic announcements or events. Britain, for example, had long been the leading foreign direct investor in the US, without arousing fears of a British invasion – largely because the British were not seen as formidable competitors. Japanese firms were different. In general, it was the Japanese advance in direct investment (usually by new 'greenfield' factories rather than by acquisition of existing firms) which made the headlines and influenced the political climate.

In general, US public opinion had shrugged off many of the earliest manifestations of Japanese corporate expansion into the USA. Fujitsu's 1972 taking of a 24 per cent stake in Amdahl, the mainframe computer manufacturer, was not seen as particularly drastic. However, by the early 1980s, the picture had changed dramatically.

First, the American electronics industry began to get rattled. Their unease had surfaced in 1976 when Japanese semiconductor manufacturers apparently emerged from nowhere to grab 40 per cent of the world market for 16K random access memory chips. After that, with each quantum leap up the RAM ladder, the Japanese drew further ahead. In 1978, Fujitsu was the first to announce the commercial production of 64K RAM chips, and the Japanese industry took something like 70 per cent of that world market. As US semiconductor manufacturers struggled with this technology, the Japanese moved on to the 256K chips – and so it went on. The US was being challenged at the heart of contemporary (and fashionable) high technology – and it was losing.[9]

This position was reinforced by the news of Japan's Fifth Generation Project computer project (ICOT), which was conceived by MITI and established in 1982 – a development which fostered the rising fear that the Japanese had not only caught up with the USA in computing technology, but were now poised to move ahead through an alliance of Japanese companies, ministries and academics. Incipient American fears about Japanese technology were intensified by the 'Japscam' incident in 1982, when the FBI caught two Hitachi employees red-handed trying to steal the trade secrets of IBM's latest computer series in California.[10] This suggested a ruthlessness on the part of the Japanese competition which went beyond the traditional bounds.

As the trade competition with Japan grew in a number of significant sectors, political attention was directed to the Japanese investment record, even though only 12 per cent of inward direct investment into the United States actually came from Japan in the 1979–85 period.[11] Particularly startling was the 1984 announcement of the NUMMI joint venture between General Motors, the world's largest auto manufacturer, and its leading Japanese competitor, Toyota. The venture signalled that General Motors, so long the bedrock of the US economy, felt that it had to work with the Japanese in order to learn the secret of their success.

This joint venture (in which Toyota took over most of the design and management leadership in a discarded GM plant in Fremont, California) was to demonstrate that the secret of the Japanese success was not a very high degree of automation, but a combination of good product design, factory layout and personnel relations. The Japanese were superb production managers who put their American counterparts in Detroit to shame: the NUMMI workforce, drawn from the same pool of workers employed previously by GM at the Fremont plant, proved to be more productive and quality-oriented in the new venture.

There was an added significance to this venture, in that the Federal Trade Commission actually approved the GM-Toyota deal, despite the fact that it was consenting to a venture between the world's two largest auto companies. However, the Commissioners' logic was simple. They could see how much General Motors had to learn about the Japanese manufacturing system, and so felt that any temporary restraint to competition would more than be compensated by GM's improved knowledge. Naturally, the FTC laid down very strict rules for the ventures (it was only to last for 12 years, for example), but this was one of the earliest cases where the American anti-trust authorities relaxed their guard to take the degree of foreign competition into account.

This venture was an unusual one, in that most Japanese companies either chose the greenfield route (Honda, Nissan etc) or else, in the late 1980s, moved into the more politically sensitive area of purchasing existing American companies.

In the meantime, in 1987, there were a couple of *causes célèbres* further involving the Japanese, both raising different aspects of the security issue. One of these turned on Fujitsu's attempt to buy Fairchild Semiconductor from its French owner, Schlumberger – a deal which might not seem controversial, since it merely swapped one foreign owner for another. However, the times had changed. Where French ownership of this company had been acceptable, Fairchild's move into Japanese ownership was too much for the political system. This case was viewed against the background of a decade-long struggle by the American semiconductor business to protect itself against its new powerful competitors from Japan. It was argued that the US defence effort would increasingly be affected as the American-based semiconductor business fell under predatory Japanese control. Fujitsu read the political signs, and dropped the proposed deal. (Fairchild was acquired two years later by another French company, Matra.)

The second event in 1987 was even more emotive, arising from the export by a Toshiba subsidiary (and a state-owned Norwegian company) of advanced metal milling machines to the USSR, which used them to quieten the propellors of Soviet submarines, thus making them much more difficult to detect. Anti-Japanese feeling converged with outrage at the flouting of COCOM regulations (a coordinating committee of NATO members and Japan, intended to restrict transfer of military-related technology to the Soviet Union and its allies). The political firestorm which erupted in the USA was primarily centred on Toshiba, and the protests included a notorious incident in which Congressmen took a sledgehammer to a Toshiba radio cassette recorder on the steps of the Capitol. Soon afterwards, the Senate voted 92–5 to impose sanctions on the Japanese company. In this single incident, 'Japan-bashing' probably reached its peak, with complaints that Japanese firms were hiring 'Agents of influence', well-connected former legislators or US administration officials, to sway policy in their favour. In fact there was a great deal of lobbying in the Toshiba affair, which clearly indicated the degree to which the US economy was inextricably linked to Japan; governors of states such as Tennessee, (which competed to attract job-creating Japanese investment), and companies such as IBM (which feared interrupted access to vital Japanese components) pressed hard to ensure that punitive sanctions were not imposed on Toshiba.[12]

The sensitivity to Japan's increasing presence in the US sometimes resulted in excessive reactions. Mitsubishi Estates' acquisition of Rockefeller Center in New York in 1989 caused considerable xenophobia (exploited by some American firms in their advertising), while Sony's purchase of Columbia Studios aroused fears of Japanese cultural influence over American entertainment. Only slightly less ridiculous was the row that followed Matsushita's later purchase of Hollywood's MCA, when it was discovered that this meant the Japanese company now owned a catering concession in the Yosemite National Park (which Matsushita promptly sold back to the US National Park Service for a nominal sum). These were, in the cut and thrust of global competition, economically insignificant transactions. However, they symbolized once again just how far the US had lost its place in the sun. Europeans who had once – equally xenophobically – railed against US economic imperialism, could only sit back and smile as the Americans learned the psychic difficulty of having unpopular foreigners buy up one's national heritage.

The Japanese were not the only targets of American hostility to foreign investors. Certainly, British corporate raiders such as Sir James Goldsmith, BTR and Hanson Trust all picked up their share of opprobrium. However, their incursions were not resisted so much because they came from Britain (still the largest investor in the USA at the end of the 1980s), but because they were too close in nature to the 'greenmailers' and other corporate raiders.

In general, the 1980s saw the USA having to come to terms with an influx of multinational investment. This was always going to be a shock to a nation which had come to take its economic predominance for granted. The fact that the most visible investors were Japanese added a touch of racism to a volatile situation.

FRIENDS AND FOES

In the debate which was stirred up in the 1980s, foreign investors had few vocal friends and plenty of enemies.

Amongst the supporters was the Reagan administration of the early-1980s which was entirely welcoming toward inward investment. A typical statement in 1983 ran: 'The United States welcomes foreign direct investment that flows according to market forces . . . A world with strong foreign investment flows is opposite to a zero-sum game. We believe there are only winners, no losers, and all participants gain from it.'[13]

Although the initial welcome became more strained as pressures grew, the Reagan and Bush administrations remained predominantly welcoming.

At the level of individual states, the welcome given to potential inward investors could be positively overwhelming. In fact, critics of the investment wave argue that the states have got into a 'Dutch auction', competing for inward investors by offering ever more generous investment incentives and cutting basic social provisions which might scare off the investors.

Tennessee's former Governor Lamar Alexander illustrates the process well. Like Margaret Thatcher in the UK, he realized the importance of the personal approach in attracting investors. Visits to Japan and sessions with the Japanese prime minister became routine. His state's development officials and state legislators have been equally assiduous, with the result that Tennessee had, by the late 1980s, picked up plants from Nissan, Sharp, Bridgestone and Toshiba – representing in total some 12 per cent of all Japanese investment in the United States.[14]

UNITARY TAXATION: STATES AGAINST THE MULTINATIONALS

However, not all States were concerned with winning inward investment at any cost. For some of them, with long exposure to foreign companies, the issue was to increase their tax yields, and their attempts to achieve this produced a minor, but sharp, diplomatic dispute on the issue known as unitary taxation.

The problem is the thorny one of how companies declare their profits round the world. Using creative accounting by charging subsidiaries in high tax areas with arbitrary costs such as royalties, sales and advertising costs etc. it has proved possible to shift profits to countries or tax havens with less demanding tax regimes. To counter this, a dozen US states enacted unitary tax laws which calculated companies' taxable profits on a formula tied to the percentage of their global sales carried out in the state in question. On the surface, such a formula appears fair, but it ignores the fact that, beneath their transfer pricing activites, companies have genuinely different profitability patterns from state to state and country to country. Under the unitary taxation principle, they would end up paying taxes even where subsidiaries were making genuine losses.

The multinational business community was incensed by the spread of these state laws in the 1980s. Led by the Japanese and British, over 20 nations registered protests with the US authorities. The most affected companies made it very clear to the Californians (who led the field on this issue) that if this method of assessment was not altered, foreign investors would go to other states. States like Oregon gave way first after they lost out to North Carolina in the competition for a high-tech Japanese investment. Finally, in 1986, the California state legislature gave way, producing a compromise bill which offered foreign investors a much more acceptable choice of assessment regimes.[15]

The fact that the states – even including mighty California – gave in to intense lobbying tells us something about the relative power of the multinationals in the US political system. Through the eyes of critics like the Tolchins, this exercise of foreign corporate lobbying power was unfortunate. The companies, they claimed, ignored the right of states to run their own tax policy. '[This] is one of the last bastions of a state's sovereignty. It is significant that one of the blows struck against that sovereignty came from foreign interests. George Washington's warning was forgotten.'[16]

CONTROLLING THE FOREIGNERS

Despite the unease over foreign investment among many Americans, the USA did not have a particularly useful set of institutions with which to fine-tune responses to foreign companies.

One body of potential use was CFIUS, the Committee on Foreign Investment in the United States. This had been set up in 1975 under President Ford to draw some of the anti-foreign fire building up in response to the perceived 'Arab Threat' which emerged in the aftermath of the oil price hikes of 1973–4.

CFIUS was conceived as a loosely-organized interagency committee, with powers and a coherence well below the more formal screening institutions found elsewhere in the industrialized world at that time (Canada's Foreign Investment Review Act was one example). Under the leadership of the Department of the Treasury, it was also to comprise members of the State, Defense and Commerce Departments. It was meant to review investments which might affect national security, and to see that other nations offered reciprocal investment access to US companies.

In practice, its existence has been fairly irrelevant. It barely played a role under President Carter. Under the Reagan administration, it targeted investments involving companies owned by foreign states. In December 1981, it accepted the then controversial $2.5 billion bid by KPC (the Kuwait Petroleum Corp.) for the US energy company Santa Fe, though the Department of Energy had to negotiate a deal which kept some nuclear technology away from the new Kuwaiti purchasers. Otherwise, CFIUS occasionally investigated bids such as one by the state-owned French oil company Elf Aquitaine for Texas Gulf.[17]

In general, CFIUS proved irrelevant because in sensitive cases key departments such as Defense would unilaterally put pressure on foreign companies they wanted to discourage. In 1983 Nippon Steel was thwarted in its attempts to take over a defence-related company, Special Metals Corporation. In March 1987, Commerce Secretary Malcolm Baldridge, acting in conjunction with Defense Secretary Caspar Weinberger, went public with his opposition to Fujitsu's bid for Fairchild, stating: 'We don't want to see the semiconductor industry under Japanese control.'[18] This was enough to scare Fujitsu off.

In fact, cases where foreigners were warned off (or, even, investigated) were extremely rare. Some bids, such as Japan's Minebea for New Hampshire Ball Bearings were given clearance even though the bid would increase the Japanese company's 30 per cent of the US ball-bearings market and would link it to the US defence effort.

However, public unease was growing, and the debates in Congress were growing increasingly emotional, climaxing over 1987–8. This was the period when Michael Dukakis, the Democratic challenger for the Presidency, made one of his themes increasing America's competitiveness in the face of foreign competition. (The hapless Dukakis made a speech on these lines during a factory visit in the 1988 Presidential campaign, only to discover that the plant was Italian-owned.)

At the peak of the debate, the 'Bryant Amendment' to the 1988 trade bill captured a lot of attention. This would have required foreign investors owning as little as 5 per cent of an American company to provide the US authorities with detailed information about their investment. This information would then have been made publicly available, thus giving US firms, working without such stringent reporting requirements, a considerable competitive advantage. This Amendment failed to carry once it was clear that it would have precipitated a veto of the whole bill. However, it had gained a lot of Congressional support.[19]

THE SEARCH FOR SECURITY

Although the rhetoric from the Reagan-Bush administrations was generaly positive toward inward investment, the political environment within which these Republican presidents worked meant that there were limits to their freedom.

For one thing, they had to work against a historical background in which the USA, despite its free-market rhetoric, has practised some discrimination against foreign-located and -owned companies. There has been nothing exceptional about this, since virtually all other countries have done the same thing. However, in the American case, the need to maintain a super-power defence capability has given the anti-foreign arguments an additional respectability as arguments about the need to protect national security have been used as a rationale.

Like most countries, the USA has had a tradition of insisting that government agencies (particularly in the military field) should buy from indigenous companies. The Buy American Act of 1933 laid this down specifically and, by the early 1960s, the price differential the Department of Defense was allowed to accept before it turned to cheaper foreign suppliers was 50 per cent.[20] National security was not cheaply bought. On the other hand, there has never been any blanket ban on foreigners supplying the DOD, though they have been regulated. In general, the US position has been to require foreign investors in important defence firms to leave specific operations on US soil so that they will be available if war breaks out, and to place the administration of the US subsidiary in the hands of American citizens.[21]

Despite these concerns Eisenhower's 'Military-Industrial Complex' was actually in a position of considerable strength. For a long time after 1945, the USA did not have to worry about foreign defence contractors being able to out-compete the Boeings, IBMs or Lockheeds. The more pressing problem was to ensure that the secrets of the US defence establishment did not get sold or otherwise transferred to the Communist world, as its nuclear secrets had been through the activities of atom spies such as Klaus Fuchs and the Rosenbergs. Hence the passing of the Export Control Act of 1949 which gave the USA its first comprehensive and continuing peacetime legislation for export restrictions. Working through COCOM, this Act provided the framework which would allow the US authorities for decades to come to dictate what could, or could not be sold to the Communist powers.[22] It was this Act which underpinned the US position in its disputes with de Gaulle's France in the late 1960s; with both France and the UK over the exports of gas-pipeline technology to the USSR in the early 1980s; and with the Japanese and Norwegians over the Toshiba-Kongsberg exports to the USSR in 1986–87.

In general security concerns have formed only one strand in determining which sectors have been put off bounds for foreigners. There have been tight, nationalistic controls on coastal shipping, the ownership of airlines and the exploration for minerals on federal lands. Security concerns have been involved, but have by no means been predominant. Otherwise, there have been limits on foreign ownership in the communications media (broadcasting in particular) and of federally-chartered banks – restrictions which stem more from worries about national culture than from a sophisticated worry about national security.[23]

In the 1980s the nature of the US debate about 'security', changed from one which focused on military capabilities to an emphasis on economic and industrial security. For the first time, the US defence establishment was faced with a situation in which a complete industrial sector – semiconductors – which was critical to US defence needs was in danger of being drastically weakened by foreign competition. If the US semiconductor companies could not survive in the face of the Japanese, what use were 'Buy American' provisions? What were the consequences if the cutting edge of this key industry had moved decisively to a country, Japan, whose commitment to traditional US security goals was not necessarily absolute and immutable? This debate flared up at the time of Fujitsu's abortive attempt to acquire Fairchild, and also during the FSX fighter decision, which centred on the amount of American technology the USA would transfer to Japan as the latter built a modified version of F-16 fighter plane. Here the concern was that the USA was helping Japan build up its competitive strengths in yet another sector (aerospace) where the USA was currently dominant.

The new twist to the 'security' debate in the 1990s has come precisely from the question about what risks there are in allowing defence-related industries to migrate to competing nations within the industrialized world. Obviously, Japan is not a security threat along the lines of Stalin's or Brezhnev's USSR. However, its attitudes to security issues are not predictable. In the 1990–91 Gulf crisis, Japan was not able to provide military support, and its internal political debate over providing financial aid to the US-led coalition against Iraq was sufficiently ambivalent to worry Americans who could not see why there were any questions at all. In addition, there is a clear strand in Japanese thinking which sympathizes with the polemic of Sony head Akio Morita and rightist politician Shintaro Ishihara, authors of *The Japan that can say 'No'*.[24] In this dialogue (whose publication outside Japan the Japanese establishment desperately tried to prevent, and which eventually appeared in English without Mr Morita's contribution), the authors clearly indicate how American military prowess is increasingly coming to rely on Japanese semiconductors. In the words of Mr Ishihara in the English edition:[25]

If Japan told Washington it would no longer sell computer chips to the United States, the Pentagon would be totally helpless. Furthermore, the global military balance could be completely upset if Japan decides to sell its computer chips to the Soviet Union instead of the United States.

Sympathetic observers of Japan will understand why Morita and Ishihara felt they needed to make the case for a more self-assertive role for Japan. However, to the vast majority of security analysts in the West the way their argument was presented was extremely unsettling. At a time when technology leadership in key sectors seemed to be slipping out of US control, it was disturbing to read a bestselling Japanese analysis of how that leadership might be used to rein in US security ambitions.

Inevitably the US defence establishment had to start to refine its thinking about security in an age of consumer-driven technologies. An appropriate symbol was the purchase by the US of numerous Japanese satellite navigation systems, produced for the leisure yachting market, for use by its troops in the war against Iraq in 1991.

A decade earlier, this concern had not been there. In the announcement of the Strategic Defense Initiative (SDI or Star Wars) the USA assumed that best American technology applied to defence problems would be enough to out-compete the Soviets – which was true. By the late 1980s the Department of Defense was concerned that Japan was taking the lead in a number of defence-related technologies (such as flat-panel displays and composite materials) and that the US was becoming vulnerable through dependence on Japan for vital components and technologies.

The most sophisticated policy response to these new concerns came with the Exon-Florio amendment to the 1988 Omnibus Trade Act which allows the CFIUS to block foreign takeovers and mergers which may undermine national security (though not on the ground that they would affect 'essential commerce', as the sponsors of the amendment originally wanted). In formulating its recommendations, the CFIUS reviews a number of factors including:

- The domestic production needed for projected national defence requirements
- The capability and capacity of domestic industries to meet these requirements, including availability of human resources, technology and materials
- The control of domestic industries and commercial activity by foreign citizens as it affects US ability to meet the requirements of national security
- The past record of the participants in fulfilling export control regulations[26]

CFIUS has had several hundred cases notified to it so far, but has investigated less than a hundred and has blocked only one deal: the acquisition of Mamco (a supplier of metal aircraft components) by the China National Aero-Technology Import and Export Company - [CATIC]. This apparent permissiveness – CFIUS is chaired by the Treasury, rather than the more hawkish Departments of Commerce or Defense – has provoked the criticism that the Exon-Florio procedure is simply a way of dissipating political hostility to inward foreign investment, rather than an attempt to preserve American defence capabilities.

Critics of this permissive approach tend to emphasize 'economic security' – the idea that the transfer of ownership in companies producing sensitive technologies undermines American autonomy. Exon-Florio's more restrictive definition of national security does not take into account the way in which civilian technology has replaced defence-related innovation as the cutting edge. The spread of dual use advanced technologies is significantly increasing the difficulty of defining what constitutes a defence industrial base. What is not clear is whether the concept of economic security is anything other than a sophisticated camouflage for otherwise conventional economic nationalism.

Having said that, there are signs that the Department of Defense has to come to terms with some suppliers falling into sympathetic foreign hands. In 1987, for example, British Aerospace was allowed a stake in Reflectone, a maker of flight simulators and information systems.[27] Despite the threats to its functions caused by the end of the cold war, the Central Intelligence Agency has resisted suggestions that it should turn its surveillance and analytical skills to assessing America's economic competitors and provide commercial intelligence to US firms.

In spite of the argument of Robert Reich and others that ownership is irrelevant, and that what matters is the quality and sophistication of industrial activity being undertaken in the US, this argument about national economic security will continue to be a prominent theme in debates about the American economy during the years to come. As T. J. Rodgers, one of the younger generation semiconductor entrepreneurs building up his company (Cypress Semiconductor) in Silicon Valley, argued:[28]

> The government does need to look at critical technologies and make sure that they are not being bought up cheap by foreign companies. Our national security has much less to do with the export of nuclear triggers than it does with who owns the semiconductor industry.

In some key areas of semiconductor production, such as production of silicon wafers and ceramic packaging, the US is heavily dependent on foreign suppliers (see Figure 12).

THE COMPETITIVENESS DEBATE

If one set of responses to the wave of international competition could be summed up as xenophobic, there was a second set which came over as more thoughtful. Analysts did not set out to argue that this foreign competition was somehow unfair. Instead they focused on the loss of American competitiveness, and looked for solutions to restore it. In a number of cases, the call was along the lines of Magaziner and Reich's demand that:

> US companies and the government develop a coherent and coordinated industrial policy whose aim is to raise the real income of our citizens by improving the pattern of our investments . . .[29]

Such calls grew in number during the 1980s as some of the more dirigiste aspects of the Japanese success story became apparent. It was argued that the USA was falling behind precisely because it did not have bodies like

Figure 12

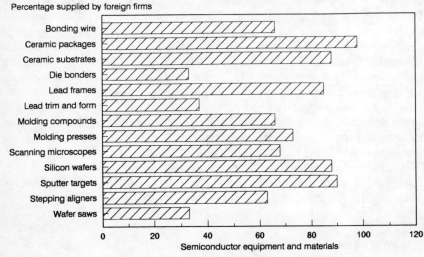

U.S. DEPENDENCE ON
FOREIGN SEMICONDUCTOR EQUIPMENT AND MATERIALS
1989

Percentage supplied by foreign firms

Semiconductor equipment and materials

Source: US General Accounting Office GAO/NSIAD-91-278

Japan's MITI, charged with developing a national strategy for industrial development.

To many observers, the thought of the USA developing an industrial strategy was anathema. The US success story had been built on competition between companies, with the government merely seeking to ensure that such competition followed the rules.

In practice, such arguments were somewhat disingenuous. After all, though the USA has never had a Department of International Trade and Industry, it had certainly had the Department of Defense – and the American defence effort had always had important impacts on the corporate sector. In fact there is some wry humour to be gained from going back to that classic anti-American text of the 1960s, *Le Défi Américain*. In the words of Servan-Schreiber:[30]

> The final handicap European business suffers in competition with its American rivals . . . is the systematic and organized assistance the US government gives to key industries through its contracts and research grants. A good example of this is the American electronics industry, which does *63% of its business* [Servan-Schreiber's emphasis] in the form of government contracts, compared to 12% for European industry

This official assistance was particularly marked in aerospace and electronics. In no way can the mid-century history of firms like IBM, Boeing, McDonnell-Douglas, Lockheed, Motorola, Fairchild or Texas Instruments be written without reference to the American nuclear weapons and missiles programmes, to the voracious needs of the US Air Force, or to NASA's Apollo moonshot programme. The integrated circuit, for instance, was developed in the late 1950s as part of a military programme to cram more electronics into the nose cone of the Minuteman missile.[31] It was such government-funded, Cold War-motivated programmes which carried many American companies to the cutting edge of their particular technologies. Whatever was happening, it was certainly not classic *laisser-faire* (and, in the 1990s, it left many wondering if US high-technology companies would be able to withstand the coming of *détente* and the inevitable winding down of the most specific strand of US industrial policy).

As the loss of US competitiveness became glaringly obvious in the early 1980s, explanations were sought. Japan's policies of industrial targeting were soon identified, and it quite rapidly became intellectually respectable to argue that comparative advantage could be manufactured by an active intelligent government running a very selective industrial policy, with a few well-focused subsidies aimed at increasing the long-term technological strengths of its companies. Under these arguments, comparative advantage can be man-made and does not necessarily flow to those countries with some particular natural advantage. The corollary of these arguments is that some of form of protectionism can be useful, if only to protect infant industries (or those restructuring) at a time of competitive vulnerability. Just as Japan protected its developing high-technology sectors in the 1950s and 1960s so, it is argued by some proponents of managed trade, there is a case for giving special protection to such projects as the High Definition Television market, which may be the forcing ground for the electronic giants of the twenty-first century.[32]

One response to ideas such as this was the sudden acceptance of the value of pre-competitive research collaborations. These have been particularly popular in the electronics industry, where MCC (Microelectronics Computer Corporation) in computers and Sematech in semiconductor manufacturing technology, have tried to lead the way. The latter was created in 1987, with half its funding coming from DARPA (the Pentagon's Defense Advanced Research Projects Agency), a body designed to strengthen American technology in areas deemed crucial to US defence interests.[33] It brought together 14 chip-makers, united in their suspicion of the Japanese, to develop world-leading chip-making technology. NEC wanted to join this consortium, but was excluded on the grounds that the technology is vital to US military and economic security.

It is notoriously difficult to measure the impact of such collaborations. What seems to have happened in Sematech's case is that it, firstly, attracted attention to the crucial role played by those companies which make chip-making equipment. Increasingly it became clear that the traditional atomistic approach of US semi-conductor companies was not enough, that they needed to learn from the way that Japanese companies developed deep, longer-term relationships with the suppliers. Certainly, by the beginning of the 1990s, executives from firms like Intel were conceding that their relationships with equipment producers were far closer than they had been a decade earlier. The atmosphere produced by Sematech seems to have played a role in this, though the consortium has come under attack for being merely a club of the industry establishment, with an annual subscription of between $1–15 million, which effectively keeps the smaller players out. The problem with these collaborations is that they are unlikely to be permitted under US antitrust law to develop into *keiretsu*-style groupings, and no firm is willing to lose whatever individual competitive advantage it possesses: the consortium US Memories Inc., established to compete with Japan in the supply of memory chips, eventually failed in 1990 because several companies withdrew support.

The various attempts to create research consortia in electronics have been attempts to increase the competitiveness of US industry at the supply end of the industry. At the demand end, however, it is probably in the debate over High-Definition Television that the USA has come closest to debating whether targeted intervention could really work within the American environment.

The time has come for the FCC, the agency controlling broadcasting, to choose a new high-technology TV broadcasting technology which will take the USA into the next century. To many, however, this is not just a decision about improving the poor quality of US television pictures (the NTSC system used is known by insiders as 'never the same colour'), but a significant decision for US industrial policy. After all, when David Sarnoff took the decision for NBC to transmit in colour in the 1950s, he was giving the related set manufacturer, RCA, a licence to print money. The fact that both NBC and RCA reported to him allowed him to take a decision which was mutually beneficial to both viewer and manufacturer.

The question this time is whether the move to a distinctive, US-developed HDTV system can deliver the industrial goods once more. The chances are that it can't. Even if an American developed system is chosen, and if the US consumer is willing to pay more to watch better pictures, no one in authority can dictate who will make the sets in question. As American ownership of consumer electronics manufacturing has declined, the chances are that it will be non-American companies like France's Thomson (owner of RCA) and the Japanese consumer electronic giants (Sony, Toshiba and others) who will be the gainers.

The US system is clearly not well designed to produce the kind of industrial policy which Japan managed to run over the years. Certainly the Department of Defense has worried about the need to maintain a secure industrial base and to keep key technologies from migrating abroad. However, the collapse of the Cold War means that this department is simply not going to have the funds to maintain its old clout. Certainly, no other federal department comes close to having the degree of influence in industrial matters that MITI has had in Japan.

The whole American business culture has worked against the kind of symbiotic company-government relationship which allowed effective industrial targeting to take place in Japan. The pre-collaborative research consortia like Sematech were an attempt to mimic Japanese industrial systems, but their influence has not gone particularly deep. Rather, if one is looking at the influence that Japan has had on the USA, then one should probably look at the reactions of the auto manufacturers, who are the companies which have not given up the battle, but have had to reassess their attitudes to quality, inventory control, the design-production-lead time interface and so on. General Motors even went to the lengths of building a new plant in Tennessee in 1985 to produce the Saturn range of cars, using state-of-the-art production systems and Japanese-style work practices; the first cars were marketed in the 1991 model year and were quite favourably received in the press. What was notable about the Saturn launch was that the cars were sold in separate dealerships from the normal GM range, and that all the promotional literature studiously avoided mentioning GM, while stressing that the Saturn Corporation was building American cars based on a study of the best techniques from around the world.

One senses that, in the automobile sector at least, it is going to be the competitive battle between the transplants and established mainstream US corporations which will determine the ultimate vitality of the US industrial culture. What the US authorities can do is not prop up decaying companies that fail to adapt, but to show the kind of flexibility around the edges that the anti-trust authorities showed when they allowed GM to work with – and learn from – Toyota in the NUMMI joint venture. The long-run health of the US economy will be reflected in the health of its companies. Many times these companies may fail, but one of the truths of today's competitive world is that companies may sometimes stumble, and temporarily fall behind best world practice. Sometimes, as with the case of the Detroit giants, such companies can be turned around – at least for a time. One strand, therefore, of an industrial policy must be an ability to bend the competition rules to give companies an occasional breathing space. Once a company goes bust, or it falls into foreign hands, the comparative advantage which comes from being the home base of major corporations is decreased.

LIBERALIZATION AND THE YEARS OF EXCESS

The Japanese incursion into the USA was only one of the two forces which made the 1980s perhaps the most turbulent decade for US industrialists since the 1930s. The second was the liberalization process which produced moderately dramatic results in telecommunications and airlines, but a decade of turmoil in the financial services sector that had a serious knock-on effect on the strategies of US companies. How could they dream of following the long-term strategies of their Japanese competitors, when some opportunistic financial predator, stuffed to the gills with junk bonds, could launch a bid at any time? The 1980s was a decade of managements on the defensive, determined that their companies should not come into play. In the course of ten years, more than a third of the companies in the list of *Fortune*'s 500 leading industrial companies were either swallowed up by other companies or went private.

Some of this restructuring was the result of the normal merger and acquisitions activity one would expect at any period. Since the US economy was in relative decline, its companies were becoming cheaper to foreign predators, so the part played by foreign predators such as Grand Metropolitan, Sir James Goldsmith, Robert Maxwell, Campeau and Sony was not unexpected.

There was, however, a new factor at work. In conjunction with the development of junk bonds, the idea grew that companies could be strengthened by piling debt on themselves so that waste would be ruthlessly stripped out and the entrepreneurial spirit of corporate management would reappear. This was the rationale of the leveraged buyout, one of which (the RJR Nabisco affair) is enjoyably chronicled in all its gory details in Burrough and Helyar's *Barbarians at the Gate*.[34] Simultaneously, new breeds of corporate raider emerged who realized they could use the same financial techniques to launch bids for companies many times their size. Even if the bid failed, they could often come out in profit, hence the development of the 'greenmailing' technique.

So what did all this mean for the US economy?

First, there have been efficiency gains. Entrenched, sleepy managements realized that they had to make assets sweat if they were not to catch the eye of the raiders. Some companies like Exxon with Reliance Electric, and Kraft with Duracell realized that they were over-extended, and could tidy their structures up by selling off relatively autonomous divisions to their managers. Companies which found themselves in the front line of a takeover usually tightened financial controls, and otherwise professionalized their systems, making themselves better run companies.

Against this was the experience of the second half of the 1980s when the 'funny money' took over. Michael Milken, the junk bond specialist with Drexel Burnham Lambert, created a pool of junk bond buyers who were willing to invest in almost anything. This allowed the creation of multibillion dollar blind pools to support notable raiders like T. Boone Pickens. Other financial artists responded, producing two or three years of hysteria on Wall Street and a stream of deals which, on subsequent analysis, were far too financially demanding on the managements concerned. This era came to a fairly clean end in 1989 with the failure of the United Airline buyout and a subsequent collapse of the Dow index.

The LBO phenonemon passed by many of the capital intensive

industries which were in the forefront of the fight against the Japanese (autos, aerospace, computers etc.). The financial manipulators preferred to target the more mundane companies of middle America, where turnarounds could be achieved by a burst of good housekeeping, rather than by product innovation. There is some evidence that LBOs worked well in the manufacturing sector. There is conflicting evidence about whether LBOs led to cutbacks in the research and development needed to maintain long-term corporate effectiveness.

On balance, one should not be too harsh about the excesses of the 1980s. Sure, a number of corporate managements lost their heads, and their companies are now paying for it. However, taking the decade as a whole, the average, perhaps complacent salaried corporate executive was forced to give his (the executives were still nearly all men) company a very thorough check for efficiency gains. Certainly, the LBO craze intensified the short-termism which may be endemic in the US system. On the other hand, it gave a major shakeup to the whole of the American corporate establishment, even where foreign competition was not an issue. Much lip-service is paid to the competitiveness of Japanese industry within Japan. The 'deal decade' was a reminder that US managements are under their own particular form of intense competition. What we will still have to see is where the ideal balance should be struck between the product-driven competition in Japan and the financial-driven competition in the US. The era of global competition we are now entering will probably favour companies which can compete on both axes at once.

Whatever the excesses, no one should underestimate the scale of liberalization which took place in the USA from the mid-1970s. The dismemberment of AT&T, the deregulation of the airlines and the Wall Street 'Big Bang' all, in their way, had a radical impact on at least part of the US economy – and they had a symbolic role in the wider global process of industrial liberalization.

The airline sector was spectacularly shaken up by its deregulation in 1978. Over the course of the next dozen years or so, most of the upstart carriers of the 1970s like People Express, New York Air and Braniff got shaken out. In addition, established industry giants such as Eastern, Pan Am and TWA either went under, or ended up in intensive care. Economists can point to the consumer gains from this deregulation – at least over the initial decade. Airline fares rose far less than the consumer price index. In 1978, 275 million passengers flew on America's airlines; in ten years, this figure increased 60 per cent to 450 million. Although there had been initial worries about small communities losing access to airlines, in practice consumer choice improved.

However, by the late 1980s, the emergence of a new oligopoly had become clear, as the bigger airlines gobbled up their smaller or more faltering competitors (significantly, the antitrust authorities took a back seat during this era). Industry ownership was concentrating quite markedly, with American, United and Delta dominating the skies. In

1978, the majors accounted for 80 per cent of all flights; by 1990, eight airlines controlled around 95 per cent of the US domestic airline market. Certainly, entry barriers to new players were significantly rising as the big players were able to dominate the limited number of airport gates, owned the dominant computer reservations systems, and offered frequent-flyer programmes to increase passenger loyalty. Prices were starting to rise again, particularly around those 'hub' cities which are dominated by one or two airlines.

One possible response by the authorities is to give foreign carriers much greater freedom to compete within the USA. This can be done by allowing foreigners to buy into US airlines, and legislation was put forward in the summer of 1991 to permit this; as a result, KLM was allowed to buy a 20 per cent stake in NorthWest airlines. Again, perhaps as a wider deal with the European Community, foreign carriers might be given much greater freedom to originate flights between US cities, thus injecting a new burst of competition into the system.

Ultimately the airline industry has a clear tendency towards local monopolies and, as long as airport capacity remains restricted, towards continental-wide oligopolies. Inevitably, demands for some form of tightened regulation will increase. This is one sector which, once the full benefits of the initial deregulation have worked their way through the system, will probably see some form of re-regulation emerging. However, if an element of foreign competition can be injected, this would counter the trend toward concentration in the airline industry – though the US airlines would strongly oppose this unless given reciprocal access to the European and Far Eastern regional markets. For that reason it is more likely that the market conduct of US airlines will be governed by regulation rather than foreign competition.

The dynamics of telecommunications are very different. From being a form of natural monopoly, there are now an increasing number of ways in which telephonic business can be carried out. In particular, the old telephone wires are now in competition with microwave transmission (wires are no longer needed), fibre optics (new mega-capacity wires can carry television transmission, multiple phone capacity etc.) and wireless transmission (which starts to give users extreme geographical freedom).

When US District Judge Greene ruled to break-up AT&T in 1982, he was accepting that the benefits of such new technologies would best be brought to consumers by increased competition. He initially concentrated on the long-distance market, barring the resultant Baby Bells from getting into information markets like cable television. This new competition initially led to the lowering of long-distance charges, but also to an increase in local ones where the Baby Bells had few challengers and could no longer subsidize local services from their long-distance profits.

Interestingly, by the early 1990s, there was a healthy debate about unleashing competition at the local or regional level. The new technologies mentioned above, along with new competitors such as the long-distance operators and cable television companies, increasingly called into question whether the century-old system of regulated local phone monopolies still makes any sense. Given that the local market is worth three times as much as all the long-distance business combined, this further burst of deregulation – if it does indeed happen – would add a new innovative burst into the US economy.

On the international front, deregulation's track record has been mixed. On the one hand, the trade balance on telecoms went from a surplus of $1.1 billion in 1978 to a deficit of $2.6 billion a decade later – a deterioration which is quite mild by the standard of other sectors. However, what deregulation did was to make the US telecommunications industry much, much more aware of the international market place. Thus, at the time of divestiture, AT&T had less than 100 employees working overseas. By 1992, the figure was up to 22,000 approaching 10 per cent of the workforce. The goal is to get 25 per cent of AT&T's revenues from overseas by 1995 and 50 per cent by the year 2000. Other telecoms players such as Ameritech, Bell Atlantic, Nynex, Southwestern Bell, Pacific Telesis, US West, Bell South, the US subsidiary of Northern Telecom and Motorola have all signed six-figure (dollar) telecoms deals over the 1988– 1990 period.

By themselves, these deals may or may not be important, but, cumulatively they are consistent with what might almost be called an implicit industrial vision. By liberalizing telecoms early, the US authorities were developing a set of companies which would be reasonably aggressive entrants into the $600 billion global telecommunications industry. It may well be that keeping the pressure on this sector will have much more of a long-term impact on US industrial competitiveness, than a more formal piece of industrial policy such as creating a national High Definition Television policy would have. There are of course still some regulatory nonsenses within the US telecoms scene. Thus Baby Bells like Nynex and US West have had to go to the even more liberalized telecommunications scene in the UK to get involved in cable franchises and personal communications networks (the next generation of cellular phones).

If the seekers after successful industrial policies seek to create competitive industrial sectors, with strong indigenous competitors, then US telecoms liberalization would count as a success. Its world-wide influence has been immense.

It is in financial services that the most serious questions can be raised about whether the liberalizing trends of the 1970s have really worked for the good of the US economy. The savings and loans catastrophe and the decade of junk bond-dominated industrial restructuring are not a good advertisement for the merits of financial liberalization – though one can argue that it is difficult to encourage financial freedom without, at some time, going through a period of excess. If that is the case, the least one can say is that the 1980s were a decade of excess. Out of that degree of mess and confusion, something good must come.

One must question how much of what happened in the 1980s was a result of the conscious deregulation and liberalization. Certainly the world-wide process of deregulating financial services can be said to start with the Wall Street Big Bang of 1975 which loosened up Wall Street practices.

That still left a lot of the American financial services sector handicapped by populist regulations which have stopped the emergence of the kind of universal banks seen in West Europe. Certainly, during the 1970s and 1980s, there was no successful amendment of the Glass-Steagall Act (1933) which blocks commercial banks from entering into the securities business, but does not stop other less-regulated nonbank competitors like General Electric, Sears Roebuck, General Motors or American Express from offering a wide array of bank-like services. Again, although the McFadden Act (1927) which limits inter-state banking has been eroded, the US banking industry is still geographically fragmented by international standards. With 12,230 institutions in early 1991, the USA had more banks per capita than any other country in the world.[35] Given the competition from the Japanese giants who, though hindered by Article 65 (similar to Glass-Steagall), have grown in the unprecedented Japanese economic boom, and from Europe's universal banks, this fragmentation has been a source of competitive weakness for the US system.

The Wall Street Big Bang was a non-Congressional decision which drastically affected the US financial structure. The Savings and Loans debacle was a case where Congress caused much of the problem itself. The Savings and Loans sector was in trouble in the early 1980s. Charged with lending money to the housing sector, they were extremely vulnerable to the high interest rates of the early 1980s since their whole philosophy is based on borrowing short (but interest rates were high) to lend long on mortgages (where they would typically be tied to a 30-year low but fixed-rate deal). By 1983, the whole sector was racking up a $25 billion loss just from this basic interest-rate mismatch.

The whole Savings and Loans sector was in mortal danger. Congress' solution was to broaden the S&Ls' borrowing and investing powers, allowing them to make riskier real estate loans, while simultaneously expanding their deposit insurance. In effect this meant that managers could borrow in new, more risky sectors (such as junk bonds) in the knowledge that the Federal authorities would ultimately bail them out if anything went wrong.

In retrospect this was an invitation to disaster. The mediocre managers which this economic backwater had tended to attract, got carried away and were ensnarled in the whole junk bond hysteria. When property prices fell, a whole raft of extremely dubious loans to Florida condominiums and Texas office blocks were left exposed . . . and then there were the crooks. Criminal opportunists certainly flooded into this sector to take advantage of Congress' unintended generosity. By mid-1990, over 300 individuals were under arraignment for major S&L frauds, and the overall losses sustained by the sector (mostly in non-fraudulent ventures) was between $300–500 billion.

The lessons from this are complex. First, it is a warning to all political and regulatory authorities anywhere – an era of financial liberalization carries very high risks. The S&L saga shows that even the most sober executives can get carried away when faced with a widening of the financial options open to them.

Moreover, it shows the danger of providing financial guarantees without detailed supervision and regulation of the businesses that were granted them.

THE AMERICAN WAY: A NEW ERA OF REGULATION?

Just as the USA was first into deregulation, so it is the country which is discovering just how far it is safe to go down this route. Airlines certainly are showing the continued need for an alert anti-trust policy, which may need to focus on regional, rather than national, concentration. Financial services show the dangers of liberalization without simultaneously increasing the sophistication of the remaining regulatory bodies.

At the same time one can argue that the American political system seems inherently incapable of handling such issues if they involve sacrificing the short-term interests of voters or vocal interest groups to the long-term interests of a sound and internationally competitive economy. The S&L case showed Congress at its most myopic, responding to special interest pleading, without having the vision to sense the need to increase the monitoring the sector needed. The relative fragmentation of the US financial system in an era when global financial concentration seems to be the norm, is a function of a political failure to find the right distance from the populist relics of the New Deal. There may still be a case for stopping banks from dealing in securities, or industrial companies from owning banks, or banks from becoming truly national institutions. On the other hand, there may not – and the failure of Congress in late 1991 to pass a radical reform of banking legislation suggests that the Congressional process may be an impediment to reforms giving American financial institutions the critical mass they are likely to need in the decades ahead. One might argue that, just as the US exported Jeffersonian democracy and Fordist capitalism to the rest of the world, it may have to import Japanese production methods and the German social market economy (capitalism moderated by social consensus arrived at by democratic means) in order to meet the challenges of global competition.

On the other hand, the strengths of America must not be overlooked: it remains the world's most productive economy, it has made greater strides toward creating a diverse and democratic society than any other, and it has pioneered the system of sharing decision-making and regulation between central and local institutions, with the application of (relatively) clear legal rules. As will be seen in the next chapter, the European Community has

borrowed heavily from the American experience in framing its competition laws, and the American legal and regulatory system offers useful
lessons – positive and negative – for other countries. We may have
witnessed the peak of the deregulatory cycle, with increased regulation
and government intervention likely in the years ahead as consensus grows
that the discipline of the market will not necessarily provide public goods
such as a better environment, urban renewal, improved health care access
and better education.

In this respect the USA has an inherent advantage: it is not likely to
swing too far in the direction of excessive intervention in industrial
development, and it has at its disposal a powerful set of myths that can
underpin a process of renewal. The American Dream is couched in almost
exclusively economic terms – a chicken in every pot and a car in every
garage – and few other countries, with the exception of Germany and
Japan, have elevated business executives to the status of national heroes.
Lee Iacocca, who rose from a family hot-dog shop in Allentown, PA to
the chairmanship of Chrysler, is one example, from a line that stretches
back to J. P. Morgan, Andrew Carnegie and Henry Ford. The power of
American capitalist and entrepreneurial ideas should not be underestimated – Disneyland, Madonna and the Big Mac exert a much more
powerful influence around the world (and, indeed, in America itself) than
the Bill of Rights or the Gettysburg Address. The American paranoia
about the Japanese threat and the seemingly inevitable and irreversible
decline of the US is both extravagant and counter-productive; in
comparison with the problems facing the former Communist states, the
task of boosting America's competitiveness looks comparatively modest.

The economic opportunities afforded by America continue to lure
Russians, Mexicans, Ethiopians and Bangladeshis, not to mention
corporate investors from around the world. The North American Free
Trade Area, which is in the process of embracing Mexico as well as the US
and Canada, is an example of the American economy's powers of
attraction and will be a powerful weapon if the US decides to adopt more
aggressive tactics in opening up the European and Japanese markets. In
February 1941 *Life Magazine* proclaimed this to be 'The American
Century'; almost fifty years later a foreign policy adviser to Japan's
former Prime Minister Nakasone reflected on this and concluded 'I think
the twenty-first century will be the American century, too.'[36] Reports of
America's decline are, like those of Mark Twain's death, greatly
exaggerated.

8

WEST EUROPE: A GREAT FUTURE BEHIND IT?

FOR A PEACE-TIME decade, the 1980s were exceptionally eventful for the Europeans. They entered it in deep despair about the alleged 'Eurosclerosis' which was turning Europe into an industrial backwater. By the middle of the decade, they had fashioned the '1992' initiative which in itself was a radical step. But then on top of all this, there was the revolution in Eastern Europe and the Soviet Union, which suddenly produced a series of friendly, if troubled economies on Europe's Eastern periphery. The collapse of communism was welcomed in its own right. However, the unification of the two Germanies was a sign that the reform of the Eastern bloc could be one more positive challenge for West Europe. The Europeans thus exited the decade in a totally different frame of mind from that in which they had entered it.

However, if one puts aside the understandable excitement over the political developments of the decade, there are more lasting questions about global competitiveness which still have not been answered. Within Europe, two industrial cultures have been struggling for dominance. On the one hand, there was the classic Anglo-American capitalism which found a particularly pure form in Mrs Thatcher's Britain during the 1980s. On the other, there is what has been termed the Rhineland or 'Social Market' capitalism of Germany and other Central European economies. In the former, the emphasis is on competition for the sake of competition, and the diminution of the role of the state. In the latter, there is more emphasis on consensus through dialogue between 'social partners' (government, employers and trade unions) and the need for social justice within a capitalist framework. These are two very different concepts of how to run a modern economy, and the battle between them has been fierce. However, what is by no means clear is that either is relevant enough in a world of global competition to allow Europe to pull up its industrial competitiveness whether to American or Japanese levels. The Europeans have become the weakest link of the triad. The question is whether they can strengthen their position relative to the other two poles.

THE EURO-SCLEROSIS YEARS

The Europeans have a long tradition of doubting if they are capable of becoming world-class industrial competitors. In the 1960s, though, there was still an air of optimism when identifying the challenges. Thus Jean-Jacques Servan-Schreiber's *Le Défi Américain*[1] in 1968 was a call for action: if Europe moved fast, by building on its natural creativity, it could turn back the American onslaught, even if the competition was already lost in space exploration and in supersonic aviation (here Servan-Schreiber failed to anticipate the strength of the American environmentalist movement which killed the US supersonic initiatives of the late 1960s stone dead, while the Anglo-French Concorde was a technological, if not financial, success).

During the 1970s this dream went sour. European industrialists did not rise to the challenge, and the American domination of Europe deepened. Certainly, the Europeans backed 'National Champions' such as Fiat and British Leyland in automobiles, or Machines Bull, International Computers and Olivetti in computers. However, these champions were rarely strong enough to count for much in the rest of Europe, let alone on the global scene. Attempts at cross-border alliances were fairly disastrous. There was a totally unproductive attempt to get some of the European computer companies (ICL, Bull and Siemens) to work together in Unidata: there was too much national jockeying for advantage for the collaboration to work. Other ventures such as the link-up of tyre-makers Dunlop and Pirelli were so ill-starred as effectively to mark the end of Dunlop as a world player. The collaborations which did work, such as the Anglo-French Concorde project, only did so because of major government backing, and failed to establish themselves commercially.

Then there was a series of political concerns. The British had joined the European Community but were fighting a series of politically fatiguing budgetary battles to limit their financial contributions to the Community. The Common Agricultural Policy seemed totally out of control, making a travesty of the goals of the Community's founders and diminishing the prospect of developing any new common policies at EC level. There were other rows during the 1970s about proposals for economic and monetary union, the perceived need to protect the steel and textile sectors, and the provision of EC funds for regional development. There were also two oil-induced recessions during this period, and morale was understandably low.

Finally, there came the awareness that the Europeans were not only struggling to keep up with the Americans, but also having to face increasing competition from Japan. In particular, around 1981–2, publicity over the creation of the Fifth Generation Computer project rammed home to the Europeans that their struggling, indigenous computer industry was about to be attacked from a second, totally unexpected source.

Those were dark days for anyone trying to keep the European ideal alive, though the EC itself continued to attract new members (Greece in 1981; Spain and Portugal in 1986); this increased the economic diversity of the Community and made agreement on significant new policies even more difficult.

THE SINGLE MARKET INITIATIVE

The impetus which led to the Community acting forcefully seems to have come from a number of directions. First, despite the difficulties of the late 1970s, the European ideal was not dead, and the drive to take the Community to a new level of integration was already under way. Then, during the late 1970s, there was a particularly forceful Industry Commissioner, Count Etienne Davignon, who was heavily involved in the task of trying to sort out Europe's overcapacity in mature industries such as steel, ship-building and synthetic fibres. Despite the demands of the crisis sectors, he did not neglect tomorrow's industries such as computers and telecommunications.[2] As the Japanese threat became increasingly apparent, so did the political weight of Davignon's recommendations increase. On the political front, the leaders of EC member-states were afraid that they were being marginalized by the two super-powers as they retreated from confrontation towards *détente*, and that America was becoming increasingly Pacific-oriented and less attentive toward Europe.

Simultaneously, European industrialists started to bestir themselves. The key group to emerge was originally named the 'Gyllenhammar Group' after Volvo's chief executive, though it was later to become the European Round Table of Industrialists, backed by heavyweights such as Wisse Dekker of Philips, Gianni Agnelli of Fiat and Antoine Riboud of BSN. This group of top executives were concerned that the momentum had gone out of the European Community, and they worked with Davignon to develop hard proposals which might restore some of the Community's industrial vitality. Their objective was to give European firms the same advantage of a large, integrated home market that their Japanese and American competitors enjoyed: from such a secure domestic base European industry could mount a more credible challenge for global market share.

The fruits of their joint labours were seen throughout 1983 and 1984. Davignon triggered a series of initiatives in key industrial sectors such as telecoms, culminating in the 1984 establishment of Europe's answer to the Fifth Generation Project – the European Strategic Programme for Research and Development in Information Technology (ESPRIT). This was a programme which mimicked what Europe knew of MITI-led programmes, by establishing a set of consortia of firms and academic researchers from different EC countries to carry out pre-competitive research in five basic areas – microelectronics, software, information processing, office systems and computer manufacturing technologies. Of particular importance was the fact that the key companies behind the Gyllenhammar Group played a formal advisory role in ESPRIT, both in defining the programme's goals and in monitoring its progress. The perceived Japanese threat had brought the corporate chieftains together with the officials in Brussels to produce a climate of opinion which insisted that Europe must take positive action to clear away the miasma of Euro-Pessimism.

On the broader economic front, this convergence of political and industrial interests produced the European Commission's celebrated White Paper of 1985, listing 300 measures necessary to complete by the end of 1992 the Community's original goal of a single, borderless internal market embracing twelve countries and 320 million consumers. In order to streamline the sclerotic Community decision-making process, often paralysed by member-states exercizing their power of veto, the Community also passed the Single European Act in 1986. This introduced qualified majority voting on many internal market measures (except for fiscal and social legislation) and gave the Community new competence in such matters as technological collaboration and environmental protection, where it was recognized that national action was no longer sufficient.

The '1992' initiative, as it came to be known, gave the Commission – now headed by the dynamic French socialist Jacques Delors – a renewed and prominent role as the initiator of the package of single market legislation. The objective was to sweep away frontier barriers (which reduced trans-European truck delivery speeds to 22 mph, compared with 38 mph in the unified market of the USA), to enable any EC company to do business in all member-states, and to outlaw discrimination by national governments in favour of home country firms.

The 1992 process was also aimed at attacking the less obvious barriers such as technical standards and regulations protecting national companies from international competition, not by creating homogenized Euro-standards – an approach that had bogged down in the past in the face of member-state opposition – but by the powerful dynamic of mutual recognition of national standards and home country regulation. This 'new approach' was based on a celebrated judgment by the European Court of Justice in the Cassis de Dijon case in 1979–80, when the Court ruled that Germany could not exclude the French blackcurrant liqueur from its market (on the ground that its alcohol content was too low for a liqueur) if the product met the necessary standards established in its home country.

The 1992 process should be seen as Europe's distinctive move toward increased trade liberalization. In areas like banking and insurance it led to radical measures which come close to allowing any financial institution accepted by one EC member state to carry out its business elsewhere within the EC. The Second Banking Coordination Directive, which came into force in January 1991, establishes a single banking passport that enables any bank established in an EC country to sell its services anywhere else in the Community, with primary regulatory responsibility resting with its home government. Similar measures have been enacted for insurance and securities firms, thus permitting universal banks and specialized financial service providers to operate on a pan-EC basis without the need for authorization from each of the twelve EC member-states.

This approach contrasts with the American inability to sweep away the McFadden Act, with its barriers to inter-state banking, and the Glass-Steagall Act, which erects a wall between commercial and investment banking. The restrictions which remain on the freedom of financial institutions to carry out unfettered business throughout the Community are almost solely dictated by the need to protect investors or consumers; nationalistic concerns have been pretty comprehensively side-stepped, although national market differences will take many years to finally wither away.

On a European-wide basis, the 1992 initiative has not led to any deregulatory initiatives which are as radical as those seen in the USA. Airline deregulation remains a patchy affair, with individual nations such as the British or Irish being held back by the footdragging of countries such as France, Italy and even Germany that are seeking to protect their national airlines from the chill winds of international competition. Nonetheless, the pressures of global competition and the dynamic of market liberalization seem to point inexorably toward greater deregulation in civil air transport.

In telecommunications, it was left to the British, once again, to lead the way. The privatization of British Telecom, and the establishment of a domestic duopoly in the UK when Mercury was licensed to compete against BT in providing telephone services, made Britain the most liberal and competitive telecommunications market in Europe. Where the Commission did show initiative was to use the most relevant pre-competitive research collaboration, RACE, to work on standardization. This emphasis reflected the realities of Europe where the problem for consumers was not just a lack of competition within national markets, but that the different national markets tended to be constrained by different standards. Europe's telecommunications equipment market was too fragmented: to produce the latest generation of digital exchange switches requires an eight per cent share of the world market in order to recoup the R&D costs of over $1.2 billion, but no EC member-state market accounts for more than six per cent of world demand. Whereas there are only four US firms in the switchgear sector, and three in Japan, there are five in Europe and room for only half that number if the survivors are to be globally competitive. Thus far the EC Commission has used its substantial powers to ban discriminatory public procurement to open up the market for cross-border sales of both equipment and telecommunications services. This has attracted the 'Baby Bells' from the US, who can provide services in the EC that they cannot yet market in the US under the terms of the AT&T divestiture ruling.

The completion of the EC single market, which now appears both inevitable and irreversible, created added momentum for European integration. Although the single market will happen, it may be a little late and will certainly not eliminate protectionist policies and anti-competitive behaviour overnight. Although Japanese and American fears of 'Fortress Europe' have subsided, there is a danger that the increased competition that promises to deliver most of the benefits of the 1992 exercise will create pressures from beleaguered firms for protection. Since protection against intra-EC competition cannot be provided without undermining the single market, it will be politically tempting to make outsiders pay the cost. The 'voluntary' export restraint negotiated by the EC with Japanese car exporters in 1991 is an example of such a response, even if it is avowedly temporary and is due to be phased out by 1997.

The EC single market has increased the queue of applicants to join the EC: Austria, Sweden, Finland, Turkey, Malta, Cyprus have applied already, although no negotiations will begin until 1993 at the earliest. The six EFTA (European Free Trade Association) countries have negotiated a European Economic Area arrangement with the EC, essentially extending the single market to the 380 million consumers living in the region but not giving the EFTA countries any direct role in EC policymaking. This arrangment clearly is a poor alternative for the EFTA states compared to full EC membership, and firms in the EFTA countries are putting considerable pressure on their home governments to apply for the latter without delay.

The end of the cold war and the collapse of the Soviet Union has reduced the inhibitions that the European neutral countries (Sweden, Switzerland, Austria and Finland) have about the EC membership and there are few economic obstacles to their admission. The same cannot be said about the three East European states, Czechoslovakia, Hungary and Poland, that negotiated Association agreements with the EC in 1991; they (and the former Soviet republics) are unlikely to be economically or politically ready for membership until the early years of the next century, although their economic transformation will depend in substantial measure on resource transfers and investment from the EC and access to the single European market for their exports. As for Turkey, it seems unlikely that it will be able to gain EC membership in the near future, both because of its relatively low level of economic development and because of political obstacles (Greek opposition while the Cyprus dispute remains unresolved and a rather patchy record on civil rights and democratic government).

Further enlargement of the EC will necessitate drastic reform of its decision-making institutions; even with twelve members an initial round of opening statements in the meetings of the Council of Ministers can take two hours or more on each topic. The Maastricht Treaty, signed by the twelve in February 1992 (but still needing ratification as this book went to press), contains an irrevocable commitment to create an economic and monetary union in Europe, with eligible countries (meeting fairly stringent criteria on economic performance and budgetary discipline) participating in a single currency administered by a European Central Bank. Such a single currency would reduce transaction costs and foreign exchange risks for firms doing business across borders in the EC, although the UK has reserved the right to opt out and some countries (including Italy) may not meet the public debt criteria. Maastricht also underlined the commitment of all the members (except Britain, which excluded itself) to increase the amount of EC legislation on worker rights and training – the 'social dimension'.

What may result after Maastricht, therefore, is a 'variable geometry' or multiple-speed Europe, in which not all EC member-states will participate in all EC policy initiatives, and some will be allowed transition periods to adjust to full participation. This is untidy and presents considerable problems for companies; if, for example, some form of worker participation in corporate decision-making becomes mandatory for the 11 participants in EC social welfare legislation, but the UK does not adopt the measure, this will pose particular difficulties for British-based multinationals operating in other EC countries. Jacques Delors has accused the British of opting out of the social dimension so that they can become the 'Hong Kong of Europe' – an extravagant charge, but one that indicates the ways in which the European single market may not necessarily be homogeneous or harmonious in the years ahead.

A EUROPEAN BUSINESS CULTURE?

Viewed from a vantage point in Brussels, the success in passing the single market legislation (even if member-states dragged their feet on implementing some of it) and securing an apparently irrevocable commitment at Maastricht to establish economic and monetary union by the end of the decade seemed to point to the 1990s as a golden era in European integration. The line of potential applicants testifies to the attraction of the single European market, as does the wave of investment in the late 1980s as Japanese and other firms sought to establish a direct presence in Europe. The dramatic widening of the European Economic Space promises faster economic growth. From there it is but one small step to arguing that this extra growth will help restore Europe's general competitiveness in the world.

However, to talk of 'Europe' is to assume that there is a cultural identity – and in particular a business culture – which spans the continent. In practice, there is a considerable diversity of approaches to management and to the governance of economic activity. These differences are far wider than those found, for instance, between the Kansai and Kanto regions in Japan, or between the Rust and Sun Belts in the USA. Within Europe, there are genuinely different concepts of how the capitalist system should be run. It matters greatly to the world whether one of these visions will ultimately become dominant, or whether they will continue to coexist.

BRITAIN AND ATLANTIC LIBERALISM

Certainly, the UK has a system which seems radically different from those found elsewhere on the continent. Even before the Thatcherite 1980s, British companies followed strategies which were clearly more internationalist and American-oriented than those of their continental brethren. During the 1980s they added the ability to tap some of the financial engineering schemes dreamed up by the City of London. So while the Japanese attracted most of the publicity (and hostility) for investing in the US during the 1980s, British companies were on balance even more active.

On top of this relative internationalism, the British system has been kept relatively competitive and focused on the short-term. Its dependence on equity financing is in marked contrast to much of the rest of Europe. In addition, the openness of British financial markets has meant that Britain has been particularly receptive to mergers and acquisitions, and has long been used to dealing with hostile or contested takeover bids. Over the years the British system has evolved to lay down guidelines for matters such as the protection of minority shareholders in bid situations. The nationality of bidders is of decreasing relevance.

What the Thatcherite revolution did to an already relatively open system was to provide a further pro-competitive kick start. Some of the Thatcher government's measures, such as radically reducing the power of the trade union movement, removed some of the countervailing forces to the corporate sector. Others, including the the City of London's Big Bang of 1986, increased the chances of hostile takeover bids by creating financial institutions that stood to gain from managing and advising on such activities. The partial deregulation of telecommunications and airlines were, again, also part of liberalizing the economic process. Similarly, the massive privatization programme which Mrs Thatcher pioneered was also designed with this in mind.

THE GERMAN MODEL: THE SOCIAL MARKET ECONOMY

In contrast is the German model which on a number of fronts has parallels to the Japanese approach; the social market economy, developed by Ludwig Erhard as an integral part of Germany's post-war economic miracle. This is a form of capitalism which gives more weight to social issues and the task of promoting better communication between government, employers and unions than the more ruthless capitalism environment in the UK. Thus the Mitbestimmung (codetermination) system, whereby workforce representatives can sit on German companies' supervisory boards, has no parallel in the UK. Again, the strength of

Germany's Mittelstand, the small to medium sized companies which provide much of Germany's dynamism is distinctive. Often grouped round specific banks (the Hausbanken), they form loose groupings which have some parallels with Japan's *Keiretsu*. Government does not intervene in industry on a day to day basis, but rather sets the rules within which the market operates: this ordnungspolitik (regulatory framework) is then administered in accordance with legal rules rather than the discretionary definition of public interest, which is more subject to change and even political manipulation.

In many ways, Germany's response to global competition has been relatively muted. The Germans have never been as aggressive as the British in investing in the USA, and Volkswagen's retreat was a significant defeat. Neither have they played the trans-Atlantic financial engineering games of a Hanson Trust. There is still a whiff of 'National Champion' thinking as Daimler-Benz created a major automative-cum-aerospace empire in the 1980s when it took over the MBB group, and as failed computer manufacturer, Nixdorf, got swept into the arms of Siemens. German companies have not created aggressive global acquisition strategies, but have tended to put their faith in strategic alliances, mainly with other European competitors.

By British and American standards, the competitive climate in Germany is still a mite cosy. Financially, the German industrial system has turned round the central role of their universal banks, which play a strategic role very alien to the more short-termist banking traditions of the Anglo-American world. The ability to rely on consistent support from the banking sector has been important in allowing German industrial companies to plan long-term without having to worry too much about short-term adverse reactions in equity markets.

The relative unimportance of equity financing to German companies means that the sometimes frenetic, financially-driven corporate restructuring found in the Anglo-American industrial culture is alien to the Germany system. Hostile takeovers are extremely rare between German companies, and it was only with the 1991 Pirelli bid for the faltering Continental Tyre company that Germany faced its first hostile takeover bid from a foreign source. Ultimately, the Italians were forced to retreat, but not before they showed how primitive were German regulations for handling such bids. Germany is one of the main homes of the bearer bond – the financial document which hides the identity of investors from prying eyes (including the tax authorities). It can be argued that the Anglo-American style of corporate governance is not possible in an environment where investors are not willing to shoulder their full share of responsibility. Nonetheless, united Germany is anxious to match and even overtake London as an international financial centre (as is likely if the European Central Bank is established in Frankfurt) and the German authorities are beginning to take a more robust approach to such old German customs as insider trading.

This resistance to the full competitive rigours of the British and American economies was also shown in the deregulation field. While the British made the running in Europe, the Germans have proved relatively slow to respond. In airlines, Lufthansa has been an important force for slowing European airline deregulation down. In telecommunications, the Germans have again moved slowly, and have lost some telecoms-intensive business to more liberalized countries like the UK. They have been held back partly for domestic political reasons, but partly from an instinctive aversion to the social cost of entering a deregulated world in which job losses would be measured in the tens of thousands.

None of this is to decry the underlying achievements of the German political economy. The country has a much vaunted educational and training system which is superbly geared to produce the well-qualified work forces needed for today's competitive world. The respect given to engineering and other industrially-relevant disciplines is high. Industrialists have key roles in areas such as regulation, which is very firmly in the hands of the relevant professional bodies.

All these factors combined to produce a post-1945 economic miracle which has only been outshone by the even more brilliant success of Japan. Both countries have a culture which is oriented toward industrial performance. Both have achieved outstanding success in the post-1945 reconstruction and catch-up period.

There are, though, questions to be asked about the future of the German system. There are signs that its companies have been no better than the Americans in coming to terms with Japanese competition. Leading German companies in the automotive and electronic fields are still powerful players on the global scene, but are no longer setting the strategic pace: Volkswagen's retreat from the USA can be seen as symbolic. Although still powerful on the European scene, it was just not competitive enough to rise from the ranks of the automotive also-rans in North America. Ultimately, this does not bode well for it elsewhere in the world – including Europe. There are real doubts about the ability of German firms to sustain high labour costs and retain export market share, which accounts for the enthusiasm of German executives for investment in East Europe to take advantage of lower-cost labour.

The continued dynamism of the German corporate sector will depend on the precise nature of the global economy we are now in. If one believes that the Japanese-led pace of innovative change is going to slow down, and that export-led corporate strategies are the wave of the future, then the German system will undoubtedly do well. However, if one believes that the pace of change will continue frenetic throughout the industrial system – from the factory floor to long-range strategic thinking – then the German system looks less happy. Unlike the Anglo-Americans who have drastically diminished the veto power of trade unions, the German labour movement is still institutionally strong, with a legally-recognized role in the governance of large German companies. There is clear political resistance to large-scale industrial deregulation, which means that anti-competitive forces are stronger in Germany than the free-market rhetoric one hears there would suggest. There are very few large German companies (the chemical sector aside) which are urgently creating the global investment strategies which seem to be necessary today.

Developments in Eastern Europe may well prove particularly dangerous to the long-term future of German industry. On the one hand, the absorption of the former East Germany into the wider German economy, and emergence of these newly-liberalized economies on Germany's eastern borders has given a major fillip to German industry in general. However, there are worries. There has been a major diversion of German managerial attention towards the immediate region at a time when developing strategies to fight global competitors has never been more urgent. No doubt, the former command economies will produce a burst of demand for relatively unsophisticated, cheap products. What they will not be demanding is state-of-the-art technology or products, which are what will ultimately determine the survival of German companies.

None of this is to argue that the German system is going to collapse. It is, though, to argue that the Social Market Economy may not be suited to the demands of today's global economy.

THE END OF FRENCH DIRIGISME?

The French industrial culture does not fall easily into either of the Atlantic or Rhineland camps. In particular, during the 1980s, when Mrs Thatcher was leading the UK quite markedly towards a *laisser-faire* approach, the socialist President Mitterand was leading France in quite the opposite direction.

Traditionally, since the days of Colbert three centuries ago, there has been a strong *dirigiste* tradition in France, with the state trying to dictate the direction in which the economy should go. In the 1950s and 1960s, when the Commissariat du Plan was at its zenith, France came the closest of all the non-communist powers to putting the economic planners at the heart of its policy-making.

With the coming of the 1980s, and the election of President Mitterand in 1981, France entered a decade in which the country's industrial policies were particularly idiosyncratic. Mitterand started his term by instituting the largest round of nationalizations experienced by any western country since the immediate aftermath of World War Two. These were used to produce a series of national champions across the heights of the French economy. Some, like Usinor-Sacilor in steel, were relatively traditional candidates for nationalization. Others, like Thomson in consumer electronics or Rhone Poulenc in chemicals, were not.

The fascinating point about this massive incursion of state direction into the French economy was that it happened just at the time that the

Reagan-Thatcher revolution was gathering pace elsewhere in the world. A political swing to the right in France during 1986–88 meant that there were some attempts to join the privatization revolution, but this was clearly politically impossible, given how recent the nationalizations had been. In 1988, President Mitterand launched a 'ni-ni' policy, which promised neither ('ni') more nationalization nor ('ni') more privatization. By the autumn of 1991, this policy was being relaxed, and state companies were encouraged to take on private capital, providing this still left the state in overall control. The French were now in the bizarre situation of being in the same camp as the former Soviets and Central/East Europeans, in trying to retreat from the institutions of the command economy. Of course, in the French case, they were merely dealing with some 20 state-dominated companies, but the French had the problem of accepting that the previous policy of mass nationalizations might have been wrong.

Paradoxically, despite this *dirigiste* tendency, France has come close to accepting the tenets of Anglo-American capitalism in the Bourse (France's equity market). By the late 1980s, it had followed the lead of Wall Street and London in abolishing the fixed commission rates which were threatening to turn the Bourse into a backwater. At the same time, the mergers and acquisitions scene also came alive, with hostile acquisition attempts starting to appear – the bitter struggle by M. Bernard Arnault to acquire the luxury goods company LMVH being a good early example. The problem is that what is good for the Bourse will not necessarily be good for classic French industrial policy goals. Once one unleashes the forces of mergers and acquisitions, one cannot guarantee that bidders will be interested in the long-term health of the French economy.

The French establishment has thus accepted that the corporate scale needed to compete in global markets is generally much larger than the French economy can provide. It accepts that it needs foreign investment, and that French companies must have the freedom to find foreign partners to give them the necessary scale. At the same time, where scale dictates, it is determined to pursue its industrial policy visions on the European stage, while ensuring that French companies remain as untainted by foreign investment as far as is possible.

The goals are hard to fault, but history will probably not be too kind to French policy during this period. The sheer scale of industrial reorganization which has taken place during this period has inevitably distracted French management from its pressing goal of finding the right strategy for each company in today's global economy. At the same time, it will probably become clear that the obsessive search for either a French or a European solution to the problem of industrial rejuvenation was a chimera which has blinded French companies to the intensity of change which is now needed to stay competitive. Moreover, as evidenced by a number of clashes between the EC Commission and the French government, the European Community is taking a much less lenient attitude towards state aids to industry, and is looking very closely at state-owned industries to distinguish between legitimate investment and illegal subsidies.

EUROPE'S INDUSTRIAL CULTURES: DIVERSITY RULES

These three industrial cultures are by no means the only significant ones in Europe, and even the advent of the single European market and an enlarged European Community will have little homogenizing effect for the foreseeable future. Other European countries can be fitted roughly into a design which has the UK (equity-driven), Germany (social market-driven) and France (state-driven) on its main axes.

Italy, admittedly, causes a few problems. In some ways, it is like Japan, with a weak central government and correspondingly influential corporate sector – though Italy lacks the compensation of a strong bureaucracy. For a while in the 1960s it looked as though the creation of the state-owned holding company, IRI, might be a key institutional innovation, allowing the state to guide the fortunes of a clutch of state-owned enterprises. In practice, it was captured by both political and sectoral interests, and thus descended into the worst kind of negative industrial policies. It spent far too much of its time seeking solutions for over-capacity in bulk commodities like steel or plastics, and correspondingly had little to contribute in the search for the next generation of successful technologies. Like France, Italy is a candidate for some heavy privatization, but, even more than France, is held back by the political implications.

Within the private sector, Italy is almost feudalistic. Big industrial chieftains like the Agnellis (the force behind Fiat) dominate the landscape, and companies are bound together by a cobweb of cross-shareholdings which make it virtually impossible for foreigners to break into the Italian market by acquisitions (as Ford found to its cost when it sought to buy Alfa Romeo). Italy has by far the smallest equity market as a ratio of GDP of all the major European powers. To correct this position would need a complete reform of accounting practices which are notoriously out-of-line (one might almost say fraudulent) with Anglo-American standards.

This is not to downplay the sheer exuberance of some of the North Italian industrial structures. Michael Porter has written of the dynamism of the Italian design industry. A firm like Benetton has shown precisely how an alert, stylish management could, by using information technology, create a world-beating operation in the very traditional world of woollen clothes. However, too many of Italy's industrial giants (Fiat and Olivetti come to mind) are in the competitive pack, without really challenging the true global players.

No other country in Europe comes as close to the Anglo-American model. At the end of 1988, Britain's stock market capitalization was 87 per cent of GDP, against 46 per cent for the next European player, the Netherlands.[3] For France and Germany, the respective figures were 24 per cent and 21 per cent. Even the Netherlands is a country which is much closer to the Rhineland model than to the Anglo-American one. To some extent, the Dutch government has been captured by big corporate interests. Certainly, the Dutch equity market is one of the most closed in Europe regarding hostile acquisitions (and Europe may have suffered as a result, since the Dutch company Philips was able to delay its reorganization to face global competition for considerably longer than would have been possible in the more competitive equity markets of the Anglo-American world).

Switzerland is another country which is only reluctantly moving toward the Anglo-American end of the spectrum. Like the Germans, the Swiss have traditionally put their faith in bearer bonds and secrecy, in order to help their all-powerful banking industry. At the same time, mainstream companies have been allowed to protect themselves against contested takeovers, with little concern for the rights of minority equity holders. The Swiss are, however, being forced to move. As companies such as Nestlé sought to acquire competitors within the Anglo-Saxon economies (such as Rowntree in the UK), the question of reciprocal access to the Swiss market was increasingly raised. At this point, the leading Swiss companies have had to make a delicate choice. They could maintain their complex defences against hostile bids, but this would be at the expense of their market capitalization (the more unlikely a bid is, the lower the value of the company's equity valuation). If this were lower than it might otherwise be, then Swiss companies would be at a disadvantage when seeking to expand globally, in competition with companies from the Anglo-Saxon economies who would tend to be valued more highly.

ATTITUDES TOWARD JAPAN

One can see some aspects of these different approaches in the way Japanese investors have been treated since they first entered the European scene in the 1970s.

At one end of the spectrum have been the Italians and the French. The Italians were particularly hostile to imports from Japan, using Japanese protectionism of the 1950s to justify holding Japanese auto imports down to 3,500 vehicles right through to the early 1990s.[4] On the surface this was good for Fiat, but it meant that the Italian economy was very slow to come to terms with the true nature of Japanese competition. By the end of 1984, there were only eight Japanese manufacturing ventures in Italy, reflecting the hostile atmosphere they perceived in that country.

France in the early 1980s took some interest in attracting Japanese collaboration to tackle third markets. After President Mitterand's election in 1981, the atmosphere darkened. Economic nationalism grew in intensity, and a potential joint venture between Thomson and JVC was actually blocked for a while. The infamous Poitiers incident, in which all imported video-recorders had to be routed through this inland customs post, was a symbol of how bad things had got. Admittedly, the authorities had positively to encourage Sumitomo Rubber to take over Dunlop's bankrupt French tyre-making facilities when 7,000 jobs were at stake (Sumitomo was taking on Dunlop's British and German facilities). In general, though, French attitudes have been less than welcoming. At the highest level, Prime Minister Kaifu's state visit to France in 1990 prompted French ministerial descriptions of Japan as 'an enemy', with 'an absolute desire to conquer the world'.[5] This was hardly the language designed to convince Japanese investors that they were wanted.

In practice, the French have protected their markets quite heavily, limiting Japanese auto imports to three per cent of their market. Throughout the economy, they have attempted to develop national champions which would be capable of fighting off the Japanese. Jacques Calvet of Peugeot has been so outspoken on the need to restrict Japan's freedom to exploit the European auto market, that the other automotive chieftains have had to create a new trade association which excluded him. Finally, France has been one of the leaders of the campaign not to recognize the output of Japanese plants in Britain as being truly European – a position which the British have been able to capitalize on, by arguing to the Japanese that they provide the one government within the EC which is willing to fight on behalf of Japanese commercial interests.

Since the late 1970s, the British have had the most consistently welcoming policies toward Japanese investment of any major country in the world. On the trade front, there was some protectionism in sectors such as autos and consumer electronics, but the quotas were reasonably generous and, in the case of television manufacturing in the 1970s, was positively used to encourage Japanese companies to invest in the UK. At the very beginning of the 1980s, there was a slight burst of xenophobia as it became clear just how all-conquering the Japanese consumer electronic companies actually were. However, an official working party came up with a strategy for the British television industry which would be based round three poles; the remaining British companies, Philips from the Netherlands and Japanese investors in the UK.[6]

From the late 1970s, through a government change from the Labour Party to Mrs Thatcher's Conservative administration, a consistent policy emerged to encourage inward Japanese investment. The British were one of the first countries to accept that failing national champions might be best served by finding them Japanese partners. The then Austin-Rover Group, the last British attempt to be a mass assembler of automobiles, was allowed to enter a collaboration with Honda which was to deepen over the years. Similarly, the computer company, ICL, entered a collaboration with Fujitsu. In both cases, the British companies were in imminent danger of going bankrupt; in both cases, by working with Japanese collaborators, they survived the 1980s. As a result ICL was the only profitable European computer manufacturer in the early 1990s.

The British believe that their open attitude to inward investment and their willingness to fight in Brussels to gain access to the rest of the EC for UK-based Japanese car export production will pay dividends in making the UK the preferred location for both Japanese and American investment. The British position will almost inevitably be eroded during the 1990s, as other EC countries compete more vigorously to attract inward investment, and as the Japanese diversify their locations for investment to serve the dynamic central and North European markets and diversify their sources of political support within the European Community.

THE BATTLE FOR BRUSSELS

It is in Brussels – the heart of the European Community – that one can see the conflict between these competing views of industrial culture at their clearest.

The Treaty of Rome was a 'fair-weather' treaty, aimed at producing a flourishing and expanded economic system, with relatively little government intervention.[7] Apart from the creation of the Common Agricultural Policy, the Treaty created a customs union and had few articles to encourage interventionist industrial policies or measures of positive distribution. The drafters felt it was safest to avoid too much controversy, so put their faith in the market and hoped that continued economic growth would sweep aside problems of regional or sectoral inequalities.[8] Sections of the Treaty resound with words which would keep any liberal-market supporter happy. Thus one of the earliest Articles (3(f)) talks of the 'institution of a system ensuring that competition in the Common Market is not distorted.'

Naturally the founding fathers of the European Economic Community had political goals which went far beyond the mere creation of a customs union. As Jacques Delors was to say much later, 'It is hard to fall in love with a single market'[9] and the founders saw the original 'Common Market' as a stepping stone to much deeper eventual European political integration. It is therefore difficult to pigeon-hole them as extreme proponents of free markets, even though it was via the liberalization of markets that they hoped to achieve their wider goals.

In any case, whatever the liberal market rhetoric of the Treaty of Rome, it has to be put in a wider context. The Treaty of Rome was part of a package which included three sectoral interventions. The creation of the European Coal and Steel Community gave the EC Commission fairly comprehensive powers to supervise the pricing, production and investment programmes of the industries in question. Similarly, the creation of Euratom was an attempt to build a major European presence in the nuclear industry which was at that time seen as one of the new commanding heights of the world economy. Finally, within the Treaty of Rome, the Common Agricultural Policy was created which, in its motivation and workings, has been about as far from the liberal market ideal as it is possible to get.

The easiest way of looking at the Community is, therefore, to view it as having emerged from a deeply schizophrenic background. In some ways the Treaty of Rome reflected the liberal market ideals which, over the previous decade, had been embodied in these archetypical Anglo-American institutions, the International Monetary Fund, the World Bank and the GATT. Some provisions, such as the anti-trust ones, were fairly directly modelled on the American experience.[10] At the same time, whether one takes the Common Agricultural Policy as definitive evidence, or looks for the more subtle evidence within the Treaty of Rome which points to an interventionist tendency among the founding fathers, there are clear signs of an interventionist, non-Anglo-American streak in the original Treaties, which ran side by side with the liberal market tendency.

This initial schizophrenia has survived over the decades. Once the Customs Union was created, there was positive resistance to attempts to put teeth into the competition policy which the Treaty of Rome had envisaged. Simultaneously, attempts to harmonize non-tariff barriers such as standards got bogged down in a tedious case-by-case exercise which progressed very little during the 1960s and 1970s.

Then, as the economic boom, which had made the Treaty of Rome seem so costless, collapsed dramatically in the 1970s in response to the worldwide inflationary boom climaxing in the 1973 oil shock, the interventionists made ground. In particular, there was a concern with how growth was distributed within the European Community, and there was an increasing attention to the need for Community-wide industrial policies.[11]

For most of the 1970s, these fledgling industrial policies were concerned with propping up troubled sectors such as steel, shipbuilding and synthetic fibres. The emphasis was on the creation of crisis cartels, and the Commission worked to produce enough inter-company co-operation to smooth away that excess capacity. In the 1980s (as we have described earlier), the Industry Directorate looked more to tomorrow's industries such as computers. However if one added the economic nonsenses of the Common Agricultural Policy to the defensive industrial policies of the 1970s and the failure of pro-competitive initiatives to gain ground in the anti-trust and standards-reduction areas, then the picture of a Community run by people unconvinced of the virtues of the free market would not be far from the truth.

On top of this, the late 1970s and early 1980s saw the launch of a number of initiatives aimed at the multinational business community. There was the 1980 Vredeling initiative from the Commission which would have demanded that key corporate decisions should be discussed in advance with the trade union movement. There was the 'seventh' directive which would have forced multinationals with significant business in

Europe to consolidate their account worldwide. There was also some initial thinking about creating a common Company statute across Europe, which raised the interesting problem of whether non-German companies might be forced to accept some form of supervisory board, involving, amongst others, workers representatives. (Alternatively, the Germans were worried that a less demanding European-wide statute would allow German companies to slide out of the supervisory board structure they now face in Germany.)

By the end of the 1980s, the balance was swinging back toward the pro-competition forces, despite the fact that the decades's greatest European proponent of free-trade (Mrs Thatcher) was a relatively negative contributor to the debate. As the Treaty of Rome had done, the Single European Act of 1985 combined a number of visions. Para-doxically, it was British insistence that Europe should concentrate pragmatically on completing its common market which led to the preparation of a list of 280 laws and measures needed to produce the desired-for single market, which would be at the heart of the Single European Act. In turn, this Act was then used by federalists like Jacques Delors to forward longer-term European ideals such as European Monetary Union.

Cumulatively, the 1992 process gave a major fillip to Anglo-American view of a competitive world of free markets in which failure must pay the price. In particular, the European Merger Control Regulation of 1990 is a

Figure 13

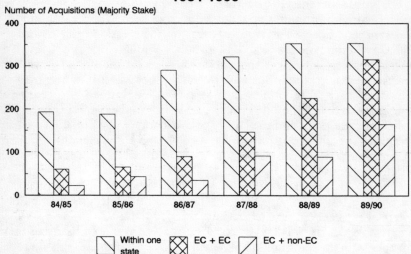

TAKEOVERS OF FIRMS IN THE EC
1984-1990

Number of Acquisitions (Majority Stake)

Within one state   EC + EC   EC + non-EC

Source: Commission of the European Communities,
15th-20th Report on Competition Policies

remarkably liberal piece of regulation which, in the words of Sir Leon Brittan, the responsible commissioner, enshrines competition as 'the guiding force of economic life'.[12] Although the regulation only covers mergers above a certain size, it was bound to push the Commission into conflict with countries like France which judge mergers on a wider public interest basis. One of the earliest of such cases came when the Commission turned down a takeover of Canada's De Havilland aircraft company by two state-owned European companies, Aerospatiale of France and Alenia of Italy. The Commission's objections turned on a fairly narrow measurement of market dominance, while the French industry minister talked of the chance for a European group to acquire world stature. In her words, 'if Europe applies a competition policy which only takes the immediate or short-term into consideration, it condemns itself into becoming an industrial no man's land.'[13]

Similar disputes have occurred in the area of state aids, where the Commission has increasingly given hostile rulings against European governments which subsidize national champions in the interests of 'industrial policy'. The British were caught when a deal which found a home for the Rover automotive group with British Aerospace was sweetened by undeclared subsidies. The French have been more publicly aggrieved by attacks on its subsidies to Renault.

On paper, then, Community policies seem well to the Anglo-American end of the industrial policy spectrum . . . but the doubts persist.

For one thing, the new Community competition policy has yet seriously to inconvenience one of the giant players on the European scene, despite the fact that strategic alliances abound – and some of them can be interpreted either as anti-competitive or as contributing to long-term industrial policy goals.

Secondly, the Commission has been very much less adventurous than its UK counterparts in pushing liberalization and deregulation in state-dominated sectors such as airlines. Whereas the Americans have been reasonably relaxed about the disappearance of a large number of uncompetitive airlines, the Europeans are still clearly unable to face the fact that giant national champions like Air France can only survive with major subsidies, while seeming reluctant to come to terms with the full logic of the competitive world which would benefit consumers.

On top of this, there is a degree of corporatist thinking in Brussels which grates on the more radical free-marketeers in the Anglo-American world. Certainly, Mrs Thatcher spent a great deal of effort to eject the principle that government had a duty to consult with both trade union confederations and representatives of employers before major policy initiatives. There can therefore be no surprise if her successors are worried by the way that the EC Commission gives both UNICE (the European employers' federation) and the ETUC (the Trade Union equivalent) the right to see early versions of the social initiatives, which Commission President Jacques Delors sees as a necessary counterbalance to the rigours of the market. The commitment of eleven of the EC member-states at Maastricht in December 1991 to create a body of European social legislation (Britain excluded itself), is further evidence of this.

The post-Maastricht European Union, however, has a lot to commend it to the free-marketeer. The commitment to completing the internal market; the strong anti-trust mechanism and the drive against unjustified state subsidies to industry are all developments which fit in well with the Anglo-American philosophy.

On the other hand, it is far from clear that the industrial cultures of the average European state have yet adjusted to the kind of competitive market which the European Union increasingly assumes. Cross-border mergers and acquisitions have certainly been increasing, but they rarely involve major companies. Except in Britain, the industrial giants are still effectively off limits to predators – however sub-optimally they may perform.

Moreover, there is very little evidence of the industrial dynamism needed to catapult Europe back into the world industrial leadership. In automobiles, key players like Volkswagen, Fiat and Peugeot are increasingly becoming regional, rather than global players. In information technology, European companies are becoming also-rans: Philips has slipped out of the top ten of the world's semiconductor manufacturers; Olivetti and Bull barely register in the top ten of computer makers and have actively sought links with American and Japanese players; only in telecommunications do firms like Alcatel and Siemens genuinely rank among the world leaders. Amongst other mainstream manufacturing industries, Europe fares well in chemicals; in natural resources, Britain's oil companies shape up well; in food, drink and tobacco, firms like Nestlé, BAT and Grand Metropolitan hold their own. However, at the heart of this analysis is the deadly weakness in high technology industries, where Europe undoubtedly lags in adjusting to the post-Ford world.

The European dilemma thus resolves itself like this. Institutionally, the European Union has been heavily influenced by the Anglo-American view of the world. This has been despite, not because of, the views of the average European bureaucrat or industrialist, which tend more towards the welfare capitalism of Central Europe than the Anglo-American capitalism found offshore in the UK. The tension between these two cultural approaches will continue. At the moment, though, neither seem to have the solution regarding global competition. The Thatcherite experiment in the UK may have produced somewhat slimmer companies by the end of the 1980s, but few apart from the oil and the food, drink and tobacco companies were particularly impressive world leaders. On the continent, a less frenetic approach to competition has not really produced convincing results either. Only time will tell how the post-'1992' pressures for more competitive behaviour affect Europe.

Finally, to round off the 1980s, there was the spectacular collapse of the command economies of East Europe and the USSR. This did not come about because of EC pressure, but it was effectively a further extension of market-driven forces within the European arena. In the initial euphoria over these events, hope grew that the new Eastern and Central European economies could become a magnet for wider East European development. As the old command economies responded to market forces with faster growth, they should impart new dynamic force to a revitalized EC economy, if the EC can marshal sufficient resources to underpin economic and political stabilization and change in its Eastern neighbours. In a time of slow economic growth this may be difficult, and European unity may at times be rather fragile: as de Gaulle noted, 'In war you fight your enemy, but in peace you fight your friends.'

9

DEATH OF THE COMMAND ECONOMY

'We are going to do something terrible to you – you will no longer have an enemy.' Georgi Arbatov, once adviser to President Gorbachev.[1]

THE WEST MAY indeed have lost a super-power competitor. However, the flip side of the death of communism is that over 400 million people who have lived in command economies where the state dictated all economic policy, are now faced with the challenge of coming to terms with the market economy. In entering the world of global competition, they have taken on a world of potential competitors. One of the most important questions of the coming decades is how well the former Eastern bloc will be able to respond.

The collapse of the command economy as an economic model is one of the great turning points in recent world history. Marx's teachings had their moderate victories in the later nineteenth century, but, with the triumph of the Bolsheviks in Russia, the command economy became a real political competitor to capitalism. In fact there were times during the 1950s, particularly when the Soviet space programme seemed to have moved into a lead, that one could have been excused for half-believing Krushchev's threat in 1956 to Western diplomats that 'History is on our side. We will bury you.'

At that time many people thought that there was a chance that the new information technology could offer a new life to the central planners. With enough computer power, they could genuinely model and thus understand the intricate workings of national economies. By such understanding, they could control economies with a precision which had never before been possible.

Ironically, such technologies did not prove to be the saviour of the command economies, but ultimately speeded their downfall. To start with, the complexity of modern-day advanced economies proved to be beyond the modelling capability of the computing community – and there was nothing an economic modeller could do about crucial economic variables such as lack of entrepreneurial motivation.

Because the overall system was under-performing, the Soviet system was unable to generate the intellectual originality and the financial resources necessary to keep up with the escalating demands of the technological race at the heart of the Cold War. Superpower status demanded Soviet parity with the USA in all areas of military prowess. Although the Soviets showed they could compete with less technologically sophisticated weapons, the rivalry ultimately turned on the escalating costs of the electronic infrastructure. When President Reagan launched the Star Wars initiative in 1983 the stakes were raised yet again. By the mid-1980s, it was clear to the circle around President Gorbachev that the Soviet Union could not simultaneously maintain a military parity with the USA while also raising living standards for the Soviet citizenry. Ultimately, *glasnost* became an economic imperative. The Soviets had fallen foul of the economics of technological intensification. To stay in the race, development spending has to rise disproportionally. Once you slip behind the leaders, you have probably lost your place in the race for good.

The Soviet leadership's confidence in its ability to apply high technology to the overall economy was further destroyed by the Chernobyl nuclear disaster in 1986. Although censorship could be used to stop a full public analysis of the scale of the disaster, the incident was clearly a major psychological shock to the Kremlin leadership. In yet another area, Soviet technological leadership was being graphically demonstrated as being over.[2]

But although the Soviets were outspent at the level of defence technology, they and their client states were simultaneously being undermined by the liberalizing impact of information technology developments. To the west, quite simple machines such as photocopiers were viewed as devices for increasing office productivity. To the Soviets they were potentially subversive in that they undermined the central control of the KGB and its minions of the flow of information. No wonder that users of photocopiers had to have a permit from the state. Despite that, through the use of typewriters, duplicating and copier machines the underground flow of *samizdat* publications increased, helping the ideas of dissidents such as Andrey Sakharov to get clandestine distribution. By the late 1980s, transmission by fax was becoming a factor. During the abortive coup of August 1991, Yeltsin's supporters were able to communicate with much of the rest of the USSR both by phone and by fax, thus putting steel into the resistance to the coup in centres beyond Moscow.

Radio had always been a medium which had attracted special attention from the thought police. Within the USSR, sophisticated jamming techniques had long been used to block channels like the Voice of America and the BBC World Service from the airways. Until very recently, television, with its much more limited footprint was much less of a problem. However, within the border states of Central and East Europe, the position was more complex, because television transmissions from countries such as West Germany and Austria inevitably carried across the borders into countries such as East Germany, Czechoslovakia and Hungary. Politically, it became increasingly difficult for the Eastern bloc leaders to stop their citizens watching western television and in East Germany, certainly, there was an unspoken agreement that the East German leadership would buy compliance from its citizens in return for not hindering access to West German television signals. Inevitably, this meant that the citizens of these border states could compare their life styles with those of westerners – and such comparisons were damning, preparing the ground for political change at whatever time the political log-jam started to break up.

When change did come, the new potential of television started to bear fruit. Within Eastern Europe, it was impossible to stop the images from first Poland and then Hungary, East Germany and so on from flooding into the countries in which the communist system had yet to fall. It was no accident that some of the most dramatic (and bloodiest) moments of the whole saga took place around the television stations in countries such as Romania and Lithuania. At the same time, the growing ease with which pictures could be beamed out of these countries was of almost equal importance. The world had already had a taste of this from China, where the camera crews which had originally gone to cover a visit from President Gorbachev stayed to cover events in Tiananmen Square, and recorded events which the Chinese authorities could have otherwise have swept under the carpet. Similarly, in Eastern Europe, the live transmission of the pictures of the breaching of the Berlin Wall, or of the battles round the television station in Bucharest sent messages round the globe. Within the USSR the presence of the world's television teams gave incidents such as Yeltsin's speech of defiance from the top of a tank an impact which will reverberate down the ages.

Ultimately, then, the technologies which have created a world of global competition were powerful enough to unleash the forces for change which had built up within the former communist bloc. The technologies themselves may be ideologically neutral. However, they have permitted the free competition between ideologies which was not possible in the Stalinist era when the forces of repression were faced with a much simpler world ... And in this era of ideological competition, the communist model of the state-led, command economy was swept aside ... but, for what?

It will take a decade or so before it becomes clear what model of industrial organization will eventually win out in the former Soviet empire. The pessimists argue that weak central governments, faced with almost insuperable problems of economic transition, will end up buying political survival by resort to the monetary printing press and the attendant hyper-inflation. The model pointed to by the pessimists is post-1945 Latin America. Optimists can point to other models which may offer more hope.

However, what was striking about the collapse of the communist model was the role played by a global élite of economists who had been pushing a very austere version of the market economy. Taking their cue from techniques developed by the International Monetary Fund in handling the rescue of stretcher-case economies in Latin America, they have argued for a 'Big Bang' approach in which the necessary political and economic changes are made in one fell swoop. So, it is argued, the currency should be made convertible, subsidies should be stripped away from the entire economy, state-owned enterprises should be privatized and the monetary printing presses should be stopped. If such measures lead to 30 per cent or 50 per cent falls in production, so be it. By taking such measures together, there is a reasonable chance that the workings of market forces will become apparent before the political will calling for economic change evaporates.

The classic exponent of this approach has been the widely influential Professor Jeffrey Sachs who was called in to advise Solidarity in Poland in the summer of 1989, when initial attempts to reform the Polish system had run into the sand and inflation was running at 600 per cent. Although only 35 years old, he had been involved in drawing up a survival plan for Bolivia whose economy was in such a mess that it was running a 24,000 per cent inflation rate before the IMF team moved in. In Poland, he was advising a political movement which, through a decade of hard political resistance to the old communist system, had a political legitimacy which most other post-communist parties elsewhere in the old Soviet system did not have. The resultant Balcerowicz plan (named after the finance minister – significantly an ex-academic economist – who implemented it) was put into force in December 1989 to general approval from the international community – particularly from the World Bank and the IMF which came up with crucial financial support.

The impact on the Polish economy was dramatic. Production collapsed in 1990. Unemployment was still rising (to at least 12 per cent of the labour force) in 1991. Queues disappeared from the shops. 300,000 new businesses were created over the first two years. Political resistance to the pain became significant and, at the time we write, no one can confidently predict that market forces will start delivering such clear economic gains over the short-term future that the reforms will become an accepted part of the Polish political landscape. The trouble is that Poland is not really the country with which the radical reformers would have liked to start. Both Hungary and Czechoslovakia had more promising entrepreneurial traditions. But Poland was the country where the political forces first admitted the possibility of a rapid transition to a market economy.

During the transition years of 1989–1992 it has been western-oriented, market-driven economists who have taken the initial intellectual lead in defining what kind of economic model should be put in place of the old command economies. Some of these economists have come from centres like Harvard, the LSE and so on; many were educated under the old system but came away with a respect for market forces (Yigor Gaider, Yavlinsky, Primakov and Shatalin). The bulk of these influentials speak English, and they have generally found it easy to work with western academic colleagues who are currently advising widely within the old Soviet empire. There are disagreements about how fast the reform process can go, but the basic principles of currency convertibility, the abolition of subsidies, and the importance of privatization (Mrs Thatcher's legacy) tend to be common to them all. They are a cosmopolitan group, fully aware of economic experiments from all over the place. Some talk historically of the lessons from Gladstone (the nineteenth century liberal leader) and Adenauer (who master-minded the post-1945 West German economic recovery); others of the lessons to be learned from restructuring programmes in countries like Bolivia or Chile. Most have views on the relevance of the Thatcherite privatization experience in the UK (generally favourable, though the social cost is noted).

What is far from clear is whether these exponents of free-market ideology will maintain their political influence. In Poland, there is a growing revulsion against the scale of the unemployment which may be necessary if the full range of state-owned companies are to be privatized and thus exposed to the cold blast of market forces. In Hungary and Czechoslovakia, the political leadership has been careful not to reform too fast, which may reflect more a lack of political courage than a greater economic sophistication. Romania, Bulgaria and many of the post-Soviet republics have hardly started the reform process yet. In Yeltsin's Russia, it was significant that the radical price reforms of January 1992 immediately triggered a serious amount of political dissent. Market ideology is still a very fragile bloom within the old Soviet Empire. There is no guarantee that the influence of the IMF-oriented market economists will survive.

THE ROLE FOR FOREIGN INVESTMENT

The freeing of prices and the cutting of subsidies are only part of what will be needed to revolutionize the economies of the old Soviet bloc. A fairly serious contribution of western managerial and technological expertise is also necessary. Whether the problem is a food distribution system which is whole decades behind best western practice, or an oil and gas sector which is under-performing at a time when it is the Russian and Kazakhs' best chance of earning significant foreign currency, deals with western multinationals clearly have an enormous potential. However, the problems are legion.

In a large part of the newly-liberalizing bloc it is still far from clear with whom the multinationals should be dealing. In Eastern Europe, for instance, there can still be claims from the original owners of properties which were confiscated in the post-1945 era. At the other extreme, within the former USSR, there are valid questions about the legal rights of allegedly autonomous regions to sign deals. Some analysts even suggest that the situation in Russia during the early 1990s has parallels with the Wild West era of US expansionism in the nineteenth century. There is a large legal vacuum, and companies may well be signing contracts which will be invalidated in years to come.

Secondly, however beneficial the contribution of the multinationals, there will almost inevitably be some form of xenophobic backlash against them at some stage. After all, these are countries which have been cut off from the outside world for decades. In virtually all industries one cares to mention the competitive position of indigenous economic organizations is dire. Therefore, wherever they do have some potential, they will, unless politically protected, be sitting ducks for acquisition by western competitors. So, almost before the liberalization era has got under way, famous names like Skoda (the Czechoslovak auto company) and less famous ones like VAZ (the Russian manufacturer of the Lada auto) and FSM (the Polish car manufacturer) have either been acquired by foreign companies, or are taking them on as part-owners. Other famous names such as the Czechoslovak beer companies Pilsner Urquell and the original Budweiser could, if not protected, be bought without a second thought by any of the world's major alcohol companies. Should the ex-Soviet energy sector be fully opened to foreign investors, there is little doubt that the world's energy community would pile in, for the simple reason that this is the largest set of energy provinces which has not yet worked out its relationship with the international oil and gas industry.

At the crudest level, however committed the economists are to encouraging foreign direct investment, public opinion is just not going to be prepared for seeing the commanding heights of their reformed economies falling into the hands of foreign multinationals. If the Americans find it demeaning that the Japanese have acquired the Rockefeller Center, how much more demeaning is it going to be for, say, Russia, the inheritor of a super-power's mantle, to accept that large swathes of its economy will be under foreign control?

There is also the problem that negotiators within these new economies have virtually no experience of negotiating with western companies about investment issues. Thus almost inevitably there will be cases where negotiators make unrealistic demands on the multinationals, not realizing some of the constraints under which such companies work. On the other hand, some negotiators will be far too generous to foreign companies, thus triggering a popular backlash against the relevant deals.

At the time of writing, there have been few such *causes célèbres*. Many joint ventures may be dormant, but it is possible to point to a series of deals within the ex-Soviet bloc which are working after a fashion. However, one can illustrate some of the potential problems with a couple of cases. In the case of Tambrands (the American manufacturer of Tampax) which invested $10 million in a factory near Kiev in Ukraine, the problem was how much freedom they had to dispose of the cotton through which they are due to earn their profits. The idea was that

Tambrands would earn its hard currency by exporting some of this cotton, but it immediately fell foul of a concept left over from the old Soviet system which dictates that an enterprise cannot export products it does not produce itself. There does seem to be a solution in the fact that Tambrands actually processes and bleaches the cotton in question. (McDonald's in Moscow had to find its way around the same restriction.) This is one of the surmountable problems, but it illustrates the kind of issues which can complicate otherwise quite attractive deals.[3]

A second case showing some of the problems is Chevron in Kazakhstan. For over four years Chevron has tried to put a deal together under which it would invest several billion dollars over a decade in order to recover hundreds of thousands of barrels per day from a couple of known oilfields. Originally the delays were caused by the Republic and the central Soviet authorities arguing over the legal rights of foreign companies to the ownership of resources, and over the terms of any deal involving the export of oil for dollars. As we write, the sticking point is that Chevron wants to own half the oil coming out of the ground, while the Kazakhs are offering less. Natural resources are emotional areas in which feelings run high and where a political backlash against allegedly too generous deals is possible.

Hungary shows that, even where a country is seen as being politically stable and reasonably friendly to foreign investors, there can be knee-jerk xenophobic reactions. For instance, in 1990, the flotation of the Ibusz, the national travel agency, triggered a major public row when the government criticized the involvement of the Vienna Stock Exchange. Perhaps less seriously, the managing director of the Hungaraton record company was sacked by the government the day before he was due to finalize a joint venture arrangement with a British company. Each such case is an irritant to would-be foreign investors, but is probably fairly typical of the era into which we are moving. Governments will try to find the happy mean in their policies towards inward investment. Inevitably, there will be inconsistencies in policies over time.

Despite such problems, the terms under which foreign direct investment will be allowed are slowly being put into place. At the time of writing, Russia has announced a policy (still to be enacted) which would allow foreigners to buy shares in Russian companies, even to the extent of being offered full ownership of loss-making enterprises and unfinished construction projects. The larger privatizations and ventures in oil and gas exploitation would still need government permission. Thought was clearly being given to public opinion because workers were to be given 25 per cent of the shares of privatized enterprises, or 10 per cent of the price of a company bought outright.

Polish policy toward foreign investment has not been seriously tested, since the Polish economy is not seen by outsiders as having the comparative advantages of the ex-Soviet Union (all that gas and oil), Hungary (a better entrepreneurial tradition) and Czechoslovakia (a more productive labour force). All the same, there is enough stability in the Polish system to allow Unilever to take control of the country's biggest detergents producer, while both Pepsi-Cola and Coca-Cola are investing in bottling plants as part of the global battle between these soft drinks giants.

In Hungary, there is a slightly more complex message. On the one hand, formal policies give foreign companies unlimited investment rights in the service sector, while permitting full repatriation of profits. There are also quite significant tax breaks for certain joint ventures in manufacturing and tourism. In late 1990 a government package narrowed the number of sensitive areas in which foreigners need a licence. Although there has been a certain amount of economic nationalism in the ranks of the ruling Forum party, some of the largest investment deals in East/Central Europe have taken place in Hungary. General Electric paved the way in 1989, buying 51 per cent of the Tungsram lighting company for $150 million. Other significant companies have also moved in, such as Guardian Industries (the US glass company), Allianz AG (German insurance giant), General Motors, Suzuki and Ford.

WHAT DO THE MULTINATIONALS WANT?

The first point to make is that the multinational community is, in general, extremely cautious in its approach to Eastern Europe and the ex-Soviet

Figure 14

Major Multinational Company Investments in Eastern Europe and the Former Soviet Union

Investor	Partner (if any)	Industry	Value mn	% Stake
Volkswagen (Germany)	SKODA, BAZ (Czechoslovakia)	Cars	$ 6630	70%
Coca-Cola (USA)	Treuhandanstalt (ex-GDR)	Beverages	DM 660 *	N/A
Philip Morris (USA)	Tabak (Czechoslovakia)	Tobacco	$ 395.8	100%
Allianz (Germany)	Deutsche Versicherung (ex-GDR)	Insurance	$ 278.4	100%
Suzuki (Japan)	New Factory (Hungary)	Cars	$ 235	40%
Mercedes-Benz (Germany)	Avia (Czechoslovakia)	Trucks	DM 450	31%
Siemens (Germany)	SkodaKoncern (Czechoslovakia)	Power Generation	$ 170	67%
General Electric (USA)	Tungsram (Hungary)	Lighting	$ 150	75%
Asea Brown Boveri (Sweden/Switzerland)	Treuhandanstalt (ex-GDR)	Engineering	DM 112 *	N/A
Asea Brown Boveri (Sweden/Switzerland)	Zamech (Poland)	Turbines	$ 50	76%
Pilkington (UK)	HSO Sandomierz (Poland)	Glass	$ 140	40%
Nestle and BSN (Switzerland, France)	Cokoladovny (Czechoslovakia)	Food	$ 95.5 **	43%

Sources: The Financial Times, The Economist, Business International, Bureau of National Affairs "East European Reporter"
* Total Investment Commitment; ** Proposed.

Union. Partly for political reasons, there are only a handful of Japanese investments in these countries – though there is a natural interest in the Russian Far East around the Japan Sea Basin.

In the early days after the breaching of the Berlin Wall, attitudes were more optimistic. There was talk of the East Europeans becoming West Europe's Korea – i.e. a nearby source of cheap, well-disciplined labour. The Germans, in particular, with their very high labour costs and their cultural closeness to these newly opening economies, were attracted by the fact that, say, the well-educated Czechoslovak labour force is available for roughly one tenth the German wage cost.

Obviously, the cheap-labour potential does exist, but investors have generally been holding back – though the exceptions are interesting. Four automotive companies are taking the region reasonably seriously. The first of these is the Italian company, Fiat, which is clearly gambling that an extension of its East European interests will help strengthen its general competitive position within Europe as its market share starts to slip in the face of intensified competition from Japanese newcomers and the enforced opening of the protected Italian auto market. To some extent, the company is building on a particularly intense past relationship with the USSR and other parts of the Soviet Empire. It was Fiat which built in the early 1970s a giant 600,000 car per annum plant in what was then named Togliattigrad after the veteran Italian communist leader. Within Yugoslavia, it has been involved with the automotive scene since the mid-1950s, linking with Crvena Zastava (Red Star) to produce some of the smaller Fiat models which were no longer viable within Italy, and also exported some components back to Italy.

By 1992, the Yugoslav venture was enmired in that country's nasty little civil war, but its ambitions elsewhere in the old communist bloc remained substantial. In Poland, it hopes to take over the Polish manufacturer, FSM, to produce 160,000 Cinquecentos per annum. Within Russia, it is negotiating hard to take a 30 per cent stake in VAZ, whose Togliattigrad plant Fiat first built on a turnkey basis some twenty years previously. The aim would be to produce a vehicle which would be both suitable for the Russian market and competitive in West European export markets. Significantly, though, at the time of writing, there is a dispute about whether the plant should be valued at $2 billion or $4 billion – the kind of difference which is inevitable in an economy with an extremely primitive market structure, but which is absolutely critical to the success or failure of such deals. On top of that, it has visions of producing a further 600,000 automobiles at another Russian site at Yelabuga (though these plans are very tentative).

General Motors is the leading American manufacturing company with stakes in the new Eastern Europe. As befits a company with very well established production facilities in the old West Germany, it is clearly driving eastwards to lower production costs and to give itself marketing credibility in these new markets. It is investing DM 1 billion in a plant in

Eisenach in Eastern Germany; has a stake in a Hungarian venture at Szentgotthard to produce 30,000 autos and 200,000 engines, and is negotiating a smallish joint venture in Poland. None of these investments is massively ambitious, and GM is clearly putting its toe in the competitive water of the new East Europe to gain experience.

Volkswagen is following a similar strategy to GM. It too is investing in the former East Germany, by building a 250,000 car per annum plant in Mosel, the former production base of the late-unlamented Trabant. More interestingly, it won the international auction to buy Skoda, the Czechoslovak auto company: a DM 9 billion investment programme is designed to double production to 400,000 per annum by the turn of the century, with a further 300,000 gearboxes to come from a plant in Bratislava. (One of the factors which won VW this auction was the conviction that it would behave more humanely to its workforce than some of the other bidders.)

Finally, the only Japanese involvement so far is a small venture in Hungary involving Suzuki, one of the smaller Japanese players. The larger players such as Toyota[4] and Nissan may well sell in this area, but have no manufacturing plans.

From the above analysis of the automotive sector it is clear that few of these companies are acting as if they believe that East Europe will become an important export platform. Fiat clearly feels that this might be possible, but most observers would question if Russia really is the most likely location for such a platform. Volkswagen, with its deal with Skoda, may be best placed to demonstrate if such a strategy is viable. In acquiring this company, VW has at least picked up a company with some kind of track record in the West, and this also gives VW a base in one of the two economies in the region with the best reputation for cheap, skilled labour-forces. This may well allow VW to build up for Europe the kind of peripheral low-cost supply base which it has developed in Mexico, at least in part for supplying the US market.

As one looks at other sectors, a not very encouraging pattern emerges. Sure, there are a handful of old-timers like Rank-Xerox, Pepsi-Cola, ICI and, of course, Fiat which are seeking to build on their long-established relationships in the region. Amongst the newcomers, it seems to be consumer-oriented companies which are most visible. The ubiquitous Marlboro brand has of course already established itself (in fact, in the Soviet black markets of the late 1980s, this cigarette brand established itself as a prime alternative currency). Throughout the region, advertisements for products such as Marlboro, Camel and Persil (the Unilever soap powder) were amongst the dominant early attempts to build brand loyalty. McDonald's was one of the earliest food chains to take advantage of the liberalization of Soviet markets. Gillette has struck a deal to have its razor blades made in St Petersburg. As mentioned earlier, Unilever has established a plant in Poland to get into detergent manufacturing.

In general, though, the picture is of the multinational business community holding back. It sees an uncertain political future for many of these states in transition – and companies like stability. It sees labour forces which have forgotten the pressures of hard, disciplined, unbroken spells of work. It sees an era of falling demand and, potentially, high inflation. None of this makes the region attractive in the short to medium term.

In the long run, perhaps, things will be different. The closing of the productivity gap between East and West should speed development and boost domestic demand. The magnet of the European Community should ensure that political and economic evolution in the East will not take place in a vacuum. One or two of the countries in question may do particularly well (Hungary? Czechoslovakia?). The problem for the multinationals, though, is deciding how much to gamble in the short run in the hope of reaping eventual long-term gains. For sectors such as ex-Soviet energy, clear short-term hard currency earning deals can start building relations which could pay off magnificently in the long run (the same may become true of some parts of the agricultural and food-chain sectors). In branded goods, the multinationals will play their oligopolistic games, investing enough to build quick brand recognition, thus raising the stakes for late entrants into this game.

It is for the classic manufacturing companies that the dilemma runs deepest. For them, there are no quick-fix solutions. When VW acquired Skoda, it was entering a long-term commitment which will drain VW of precious managerial resources. This commitment will only pay off if the Skoda workforce and management can be turned around to produce much more effectively – and some of the wider political factors which will affect their productivity are well outside VW's control. Perhaps the Skodas of the world can be turned into major export-platforms, but this still has to be demonstrated. It is the VWs, GMs and Fiats which are the real pioneers. They are gambling that the former Eastern bloc will enter a 'catch-up' phase equivalent to what has already happened in large parts of the Third World. By getting in early, they hope to steal a march on their competitors. If they get their gamble wrong, they may rue the diversion of executive attention from other more crucial parts of the global competitive jungle.

THE FUTURE

The former Eastern bloc is clearly entering a period of considerable turmoil. On the one hand, some sectors of their economies will go through a period of substantial productivity growth, as apparently simple Western technologies are applied to processes which have got stuck in a time-warp. Stories abound of factories utilizing equipment which is twenty or thirty years out of date. One can still find pre-1939 phone systems in existence, the replacement of which will bring huge improvements in general efficiency. All parts of the food chain, from methods of pest control, to packaging, distribution and retail methods can be drastically improved by the application of fairly basic western expertise. (A good part of what McDonald's has been up to round Moscow has been simply improving the quality and flows of the produce needed for a modern burger bar.)

Again, there will be an unleashing of trade gains as neighbouring ex-Republics create intra-regional trade flows after decades of being forced by planners in Moscow to trade primarily with the centre.

On the other hand, all such gains will be against the background of a massive amount of disruption in sectors which are no longer relevant to the new world. The massive industrial infrastructure underpinning the old Military-Industrial Complex will inevitably be devastated. Some of it may be converted to more productive civilian uses, but for much of it this will prove impossible. So, very slowly, new economic tasks will have to be found for labour forces (and, often, whole communities) which have devoted themselves to activities which are no longer needed.

Another drag on economic improvement will be the time it will take the managers of enterprises to build up marketing and supply relationships without relying on central planners. This problem should not be underestimated. Many of the flows of components and intermediate products in the old Soviet Empire were planned on an inter-continental scale. Factories in the Baltic Republics could supply products for enterprises in Central Asia – often on an exclusive basis. With the breakdown of trade between the former Soviet Republics (and between them and the East and Central Europeans) there is an enormous void. Not only are managers having to re-think the very nature of their enterprises (often extremely large and out-of-date), but they are having to create from scratch a whole set of commerical relationships without any sense of who is going to be any good as a partner.

This final outcome, when the simple productivity gains from the 'catch-up' process are set against the losses from industrial destruction as the debris of the old command economy system is swept away, has political consequences. The political roots of the free-market economists guiding this economic transition are very shallow indeed. Of course it is important that the top economists in, say, Slovenia, Mongolia, Russia and Poland are slotted in to the same networks of international advisers. For the moment this will ensure that the general direction of economic reform will point in roughly the same (market-driven) direction. The existence of these global networks also gives important psychological reassurance to top politicans and their closest advisers as they try to battle their ways through the political complexities of price liberalization.

On the other hand, as one looks more closely into these societies, the intellectual hold of the 'Harvard Boys' looks much less sure. Even in Poland, there is hesitation about how best to handle the privatization and/or closure of the largest state-run companies. Elsewhere in the Eastern bloc, the acceptance of mass lay-offs running into tens of thousand employees still has to be tested. It is when market forces start dictating this kind of sacrifice that one can predict that the intellectual hold of free-market enthusiasts will decline – often quite drastically. There is absolutely no guarantee that the free-market momentum of the 1989–1992 period will be maintained. The interesting question is what alternative models might emerge in its place.

There could be a complete relapse into the kind of hyper-inflationary nightmares of Weimar Germany or of the bad old Latin America. This is not implausible, since there are few governments in the old Eastern bloc which have the genuine democratic authority to impose austerity on their populace for the years which may be necessary to get the reform process off to a convincing start. Even leaders like Walesa in Poland, Havel in Czechoslovakia, Yeltsin in Russia or Landsbergis in Lithuania, who have heroically picked up the right credentials in the political reform process, generally head administrations which are politically much less authoritative. In these circumstances, the political commitment to a full conversion to the market economy tends to get increasingly equivocal the further one moves down it. In particular, the Russians are in the classic Latin American situation of needing to keep a disgruntled military apparatus happy. This is important since the destruction of the baleful economic influence of the Military-Industrial Complex is one of the central needs of the post-Soviet economic planners.

This pessimistic scenario assumes that weak central governments, often concerned about the possibility of coups, will be unable to take the really tough decisions needed to sustain the switch to market-oriented economies. They will, for instance, be frightened of cutting subsidies and closing unwanted enterprises or plants. Instead, it is argued, they will resort to the classic response of weak governments and will turn to the printing presses. By printing money they will buy themselves out of short-run political unpopularity, albeit at the expense of triggering hyper-inflation further down the line.

For at least parts of the former Eastern bloc, such a scenario is depressingly plausible. However, there are reasons why the pessimists may be wrong. For one thing, the hyper-inflation of past eras took place at times when economic counter-examples were weak. In the case of Weimar's Germany, the chaos caused by the first world war had created a world in which former liberal trade models counted for little. Again, in Latin America, traditional anti-Americanism meant that it was extremely difficult to point to US-style capitalism as an alternative model.

Within the ex-Soviet-bloc, however, the picture is different. First, the winning of political freedom from the USSR has generally entailed a fairly firm pro-Western orientation. There is thus no parallel within East and Central Europe to the anti-Americanism of the Latin Americans. The European Community may have its faults, but it is serving as a magnet to many of the newly-free states. Similarly, other market-oriented international institutions like the IMF and World Bank have been playing an important role in providing support to the market-oriented mafia who are so thin on the ground. All this means is that, while the political resistance to economic rationality will remain strong, the champions of market forces will have plenty of outside allies. It may be possible to bad-mouth the insensitively hard-line role that the IMF has sometimes played in the Third World; but it beomes increasingly difficult to reject advice which is coming in much the same form from the IMF, World Bank, European Community, the OECD, the European Bank for Reconstruction and Development, the Scandinavian governments and a variety of peripatetic professors from Harvard, the London School of Economics and elsewhere. Compared with ten or twenty years ago, there are very few intellectual or political centres of equivalent weight calling for serious alternative strategies. Economists arguing about the need for relatively autarchic economic policies to overcome international dependency are currently out of fashion. There is thus a formidable international network in place to stiffen the backbones of anyone who might feel tempted to slide into the hyper-inflationary spiral.

Having conceded this point, it still remains implausible that more than one or two of these newly liberated states will succeed in the short run in turning themselves into classic Anglo-American style market economies. The chances are that none of them will make this transition. In addition, democratic traditions will remain weak in many of these countries, adding to their problem of winning international acceptance. Also most of the politicians and technocrats responsible for new measures have come up through the old education system which for generations has systematically attacked the whole concept of the social benefits from entrepreneurship.

If such countries do stick to the capitalist route, therefore, it is likely that they will be happiest with 'Rhineland' or 'Social Market' capitalism – the form of industrial organization most associated with Germany. The former East Germany has already been directly absorbed into a greater Germany, and German traders and investors are the dominant outside force within the former socialist bloc. Already one can point to areas in which the emerging industrial systems are moving in a Germanic direction. In particular, in most of the privatization initiatives, there is a conscious concern to give the existing work forces a significant stake in the resulting enterprise. This immediately brings to mind the post-1945 creation of the 'Mitbestimmung' principle in West Germany, whereby workers' representatives were given statutory rights to representation on the supervisory boards of larger firms. Although none of the ex-Eastern bloc have got as far as creating a similar system, there is still a paternalism toward workers which is totally understandable, given the political ethos which has governed such countries for so long. Already, in the case of VW's acquisition of Skoda, the preferred western company has been chosen at least in part because it promised a more paternalistic approach to the indigenous work force than other candidates.

But the 'Social Market' model is still one in which market forces determine the ultimate direction of the national economy and there are real doubts about whether such a *laisser-faire* approach will be ultimately accepted. Yes, it may be seen to work quite fast at the level of food distribution and small-scale entrepreneurship. However, can the first-generation entrepreneurs really be found to take on the problems of converting and otherwise redirecting the giant state enterprises which have, throughout the Eastern bloc, to be found a new role in life?

The heavy weather which much more experienced market-oriented executives are making of, say, restructuring the Detroit auto makers, or the West European steel industry (let alone its agricultural sector) makes it very difficult to feel confident that such paragons are going to emerge spontaneously in sufficient numbers to do more than scratch at the surface. One can in fact go further to argue that the first generations of would-be entrepreneurs will make some pretty ghastly mistakes.

Is there, therefore, a third way which may be politically more acceptable to the leaderships of some of these countries?

Increasingly one toys with the model of 'Developmental Capitalism' seen in Newly Industrializing Economies (NIEs) such as South Korea, Singapore (and to some extent in Japan in an earlier stage). In all such cases, democratic traditions have been less than flourishing and some political force has moved into the vacuum to steer the country's economic development. Generally, this has been a set of ministries or planning agencies working within a political environment in which the political rights of workers have been downplayed at the expense of the primacy of management.

This is not suggesting a return to the dead days of Gosplan and the Stalinist model of the command economy. The officials in such countries have accepted the importance of market principles and have understood the need to use success in international markets as an indicator as to whether a planning direction is wise or not.

It is, though, to accept that the politics of many of these countries is likely to be more authoritarian than not, and that the interventionist tendency will be strong – particularly given the scale of readjustment which is called for. The Japanese model of indicative governmental leadership will be tempting.

The trouble is that the industrial and political culture of these countries is relatively unpromising. On the political front, there are serious questions about the legitimacy of many of the governments which have come to power. There are also serious questions about the positions of ethnic minorities in many of these countries. The example of the bloody fragmentation of Yugoslavia hangs in front of them all. The situation is far removed from the political and social cohesion enjoyed by the Japanese (with a bit of help from the US occupation authorities) even in the post-1945 period.

All-in-all, these countries remain unpromising material to become model IMF-style market economies. An entrepreneurial culture remains very weak, and governments will include high proportions of wistful planners – people who have only half accepted that the concept of centralized planning cannot be made to work in today's economic climate. Such people will grasp at the Japanese model because it seems to give a new role for planners, while they will grasp at the more welfare-oriented parts of the German model which do things like enshrining workers' rights. In the wrong hands, this combination of indicative planning and concern with the social market will be a recipe for stagnation. In many cases, the old apparatchiks remain too close to power. One cannot be particularly optimistic.

The main hope remains that some combination of the lure of the European Community, steady market-oriented pressure from bodies like the International Monetary Fund and courageous leadership from the limited number of sophisticated market economists may keep the crude interventionists at bay. However, in countries like Russia, the scale of the transformation required is so great that it will be a miracle if the first wave of market economists survive politically. Their successors are likely to be much more pragmatic, perhaps much more concerned with political crises with ethnic minorities or neighbouring powers than with the virtues of market forces.

All-in-all, the intellectual legacy of the Command Economy will remain, making it difficult to establish market disciplines. It will be like planting a tree on rocky ground. If the roots have to fight to get established in a hostile environment, the tree may not live, or, if it does survive, it will be stunted.

The latter is the most likely future for the liberal market model in the former Soviet bloc. At best the tree will be stunted. At worst, they may need several attempts to get any version of the market model to survive.

The cultural and political soil is very unpromising.

10

THE NEW THIRD WORLD
ENVIRONMENT

THE 1980s WERE a particularly unpleasant decade for much of the Third World. The aftermath of the oil price rises of the late 1970s was a massive debt crisis, which in particular bedevilled relations between Latin America and the industrialized world.

Towards the end of the decade, the attention of many executives and economists who were otherwise sympathetic to the Third World was diverted toward developments in Eastern Europe and the collapsing Soviet Union. Investment in the Third World by multinational companies actually fell during the 1980s. However, while their attention was diverted, a fair amount of political change was actually taking place in the Third World. In particular, the acceptance of market principles made a major advance in the latter half of the 1980s.

The signs of this changed environment could be seen at a variety of levels. For instance, at the most general level, the eighth conference of UNCTAD (the UN Conference on Trade and Development) which met in early 1992 marked a major step away from classic Third World demands for special, trade-distorting privileges. Instead it called for the successful conclusion of the Uruguay Round of the GATT, making clear that it wanted the protection offered by unambigous multilateral rules.

At the level of national economies, the picture was even clearer. Just as the former Soviet bloc has rejected classic forms of state intervention, so did a number of hitherto-interventionist governments turn towards more liberal economic models in the late 1980s. This was certainly true for Africa: Tanzania, once the home of African socialism, turned to private investors to invigorate its tourist industry; newly independent Namibia, whose leadership had a long history of calls for nationalization of mines and other industries, came to independence asking for a business partnership in a mixed economy. By mid-1990, more than 30 African countries had adopted programmes to privatize numerous state-run businesses.

In Latin America, the change has been equally dramatic, and perhaps of more significance, since it was this continent which, in the late 1940s and early 1950s, gave the then emerging Third World a model of import-substitution as a counter to the dependent development which they could see all around them. For instance by early 1992, Brazil had launched a programme of two-a-month privatizations. The programme was started in September 1991 (to some controversy) with the sale of Usiminas, the continent's largest steel mill. Once that went ahead smoothly, passions cooled and, by the turn of the year, the government was issuing weekly decrees expanding this programme. During 1992, it is intended to sell (amongst numerous other companies) Embraer and Lloyd Brasileiro, the state aerospace and shipping companies. There was even mention of the possible sale of Petrobras, the state oil company, though this would be issuing the ultimate challenge to the economic nationalists.

The experiences of Mexico have been even more dramatic. Since the election of President Salinas in 1988, the country has been on an even greater privatization drive. By 1992, three-quarters of Mexico's state-owned companies had been privatized, and the intention is to finish the programme in 1993. To show the openness with which this programme has proceeded, the tactics for the privatization of the steel industry were masterminded by Sir Ian McGregor who, under Mrs Thatcher, had been involved in the privatization of British Steel (and the British merchant bank S. G. Warburg was chosen as the relevant investment bank). Given the enthusiasm of the Mexican government for the expansion of the North American Free Trade Area to include Mexico, there has been a revolution in Mexican thinking since the early 1980s when Mexico was one of the last major Third World players to reject membership of the GATT because this might compromise its freedom to run protectionist, nationalistic economic policies.

Elsewhere in Latin America, Argentina and Venezuela were following a similar path. Peru has settled a long-standing dispute with Southern Peru Copper Corporation, its principle foreign investor. Free trade agreements have either been signed or are being negotiated involving various combinations of the Latin American economies. Market principles have never been so acceptable south of the Rio Grande.

With variations, this new openness is echoed by evidence from the rest of the Third World. Even Vietnam, a long-time supporter of the command economy, is now talking of opening the doors needed to attract foreign investment, and has taken back offshore oil tracts controlled by a joint Soviet and Vietnamese company in order to offer them to western oil giants such as BP, Total, Statoil and Royal Dutch/Shell. India, long a byword amongst the multinational business community for stifling bureaucracy and fairly tight controls on inward investment, is allowing foreign trademarks back into the country and, in late 1991, was negotiating with both Coca-Cola and IBM – the two main multinationals driven out of the country by the previous investment regime – about re-entering the Indian market.

All these developments make up a political revolution which, though not as startling as what occurred in the old Soviet empire, still remains of considerable economic significance. In many ways, the spread of economic liberalization within the Third World is analogous to what had started earlier in the decade in the industrialized world. What were the forces at work?

To some extent the Latin American developments were a response to the debt crisis of the 1980s, which delivered them into the grasp of bodies such as the IMF and into schemes such as the Brady Plan. However, this does not explain much, since previous generations of Latin American leaders have never been overly hesitant about attacking the ruthlessness of the IMR free-market solutions. This time round though, a new generation of leaders is in power. In particular, Harvard-educated President Salinas is a US-educated free-market economist, very much in tune with the equivalent figures who have risen to influence in Eastern Europe.

In particular, as the 1970s rolled into the 1980s, it became increasingly clear that the interventionist economic policies of socialist regimes as far afield as Cuba, Tanzania, the whole of the Soviet bloc and sympathetic east Asian regimes such as Vietnam and North Korea just were not delivering the results that the more export-orientated Third World capitalist states such as South Korea, Singapore and Taiwan were capable of. In particular, whereas it was always relatively easy to play up populist anti-American sentiments to reduce the psychological attraction of free-market capitalism, the rapid economic progress of Japan meant that an alternative model of capitalism emerged which could not easily be explained away in crude political terms.

EAST ASIA

In particular, the steady growth of the East Asian economies within the emerging Yen-zone was a phenomenon which no economic analysts – be they in the Third or First Worlds – could ignore. The success of the original 'Newly Industrializing Economies' (Taiwan, South Korea, Hong Kong and Singapore) continued, but there were signs that a new wave of economies in the region (Thailand, Malaysia, even parts of China itself) was starting to show some of the dynamism which had turned the 'Four Dragons' into significant economic competitors even within moderately sophisticated industrial sectors such as automobiles and personal computers.

It would be wrong to overstress developments in China, but one cannot ignore the fact that it was growing ten per cent per annum throughout the 1980s and looks set to be the fastest growing economy in Asia during the first half of the 1990s. Despite the Tiananmen Square massacre it became possible in February 1992 to trade (admittedly only a single stock – Shanghai Vacuum Electron Device Co., a maker of black and white television tubes) on the Shanghai Stock Exchange, and shares of ten other companies will become available by the end of the year. By 1990, China had a $10.4 billion trade surplus with the USA, and was running into inevitable disputes about the copying of software, the alleged use of prisoners to manufacture for export, the use of protectionist barriers and so on.

What virtually all the economies of the region have learned from Japan is how to move fast into labour-intensive export-orientated sectors, and how to target the world's biggest unprotected consumer market (that of the USA). Thailand, Malaysia, Indonesia and the Pearl River Delta (which takes in Hong Kong and Guangzhou, a.k.a. Canton, and has averaged a 15 per cent per annum growth rate from the early 1980s) all have economies which look as if they will remain dynamic for a long time to come.

The Asian success stories, starting with that of Japan, are very much a result of the information-rich global economy in which we all increasingly work. Obviously, there are some cultural factors at work, such as Confucian traditions, but this is a part of the world which values education highly, and has learned from the Japanese model what economists now call 'the new interventionism' – government intervention which works to augment the impact of market forces and thus channel the animal spirits of increasingly entrepreneurial cultures into sectors which have the potential to become globally competitive.

The information and transport barriers between Asia and the American market are also falling year by year, with the result that the region's

Figure 15

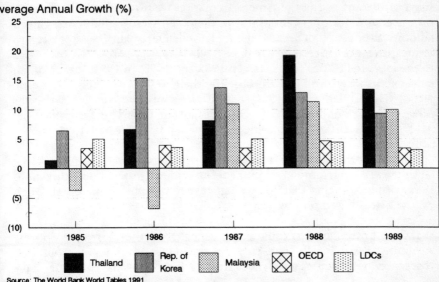

Growth in Gross National Income, 1985-1989
Comparison of Growth in Income of 3 NIEs with
High Income OECD Members and LDCs

Source: The World Bank World Tables 1991

exporters are able to penetrate the US (and other) markets steadily more effectively. While western firms like Procter & Gamble (Head and Shoulders shampoo), Avon and Pabst Beer are muscling their way into South China, local factories are producing products such as 100,000 Ninja Turtles a day – vivid testimony to the efficiency with which turn of the century global capitalism is matching markets to production facilities across the globe – even where that means finding them in politically complex societies such as post-Tiananmen China.[1]

Although the catch-up phenomenon now being unleashed throughout the Third World is of undoubted economic and (given the scale of the phenomenon) ecological importance, we should not automatically assume that the application of disciplined cheap labour will inevitably sweep upwards through the world's manufacturing processes. There is a point at which the application of increasingly sophisticated, flexible, high-quality (and cheap) manufacturing systems will hold the cheap labour phenomenon at bay. If one adds to that the creative ability of First World companies to generate successive waves of new products to meet the emerging needs of a fast growing world economy, then it is possible to argue that 'catch-up' economies at about the relative position of South Korea today may find their competitive environment suddenly getting very much harsher.

It is far too soon to tell whether the growing defensive power of cheapening flexible production technology really will redefine the boundaries at which the cheap labour phenomenon can be effective. There are signs, though, from South Korea that this point has been reached.

Item: South Korea was the first non-OECD producer of automobiles to become a world force, particularly through the efforts of Hyundai whose Excel model (based heavily on licences from Mitsubishi) showed signs in 1986 of taking the American market by storm. By 1988, Korean producers had four per cent of it. But then their strategy fell apart. Cheap labour was not enough because it could not deliver quality close enough to best Japanese practice and, when auto workers' wages rose, Korean sales to the USA fell 50 per cent between 1988 and 1990. In 1991, total Korean auto exports were still one third below their peak 1988 levels. Domestic wages had tripled since 1986, and Korea's productivity growth was nowhere near good enough to compensate for this. The authors of the MIT study on the world automotive industry take this case to argue:[2]

> . . . the world economy, in a short period, has changed in remarkable ways. . . . the triumph of lean production has created a new threshold for product quality that no producer can hope to offset merely through low prices based on low wages.

If one probes into the underlying health of the Korean corporate structure, these beliefs can only be strengthened. The *Chaebol* (the Korean conglomerates modelled after Japan's pre-war *Zaibatsu*) have followed a scatter-gun corporate strategy, particularly focusing on industries where sheer scale economies of production have brought them export gains in the past. These companies remain family-run concerns, as against the professional managements of today's Japanese competitors. Korean companies are still woefully weak on research spending, which means that they have great difficulty in closing the quality gap with Japan. In 1991, Hyundai's Excel was selling in the US at only $215 cheaper than the better quality Toyota Tercel model. All attempts to narrow the trade deficit with Japan have floundered because product quality was just not good enough to satisfy the discerning Japanese consumer (the Koreans are not the only would-be exporters to Japan who have that problem).

The jury, though, must remain out on this question of where the international dividing line will fall in the competition between disciplined cheap labour and best quality flexible automation. For all the advances in automation, the Japanese have found it difficult to hold on to the cheaper ends of the video-recorder market (the Japanese share of the US VCR market is falling fast – admittedly from very high levels). There are clear economic limits to how far one can push the automation process.

On the other hand, the political tensions in Korea between, first, the work force and the *Chaebol* and, second, between *Chaebol* management and the politicians have been marked and, often, quite bitter (as we write in February 1992, the founder of Hyundai is launching a new political party to oppose President Roh Tae Woo). Clearly, the Japanese model of dominant bureaucrats, relatively submissive industrialists, and a totally emasculated labour force is not one which will be replicated automatically in other countries of the region. It may yet prove that the Japanese model is *sui generis*, at least at the level of development where countries have come close to catching up with the west – but where further relative progress depends on innovation, rather than replication of existing products.

'THE NEW INTERVENTIONISM'

If the import-substituting, command economy model has lost its influence in the Third World, it is still unclear what dominant model will take its place.

The classic IMF or World Bank approach stresses the pre-eminent role that free-markets must play in economic development. In one sense this model has won out, as the more *dirigiste* approaches have lost out.

. . . but are we merely seeing a subtler form of *dirigisme* coming to the surface?

Clearly, the success of Japan has been a victory not for classic *laisser-faire* capitalism, but for a form of developmental capitalism (Chalmers Johnson's term) in which government played a subtle role in guiding the development of market forces, by steering companies and their investments towards those sectors in which Japan needed to become globally competitive.

As one considers Japan's successors in the coming generation of Third World competitors, one sees a number of points in which they are mimicking Japan in essence, if not in every detail. Perhaps with the exception of Hong Kong, what is striking is the way interventionism (industrial policy and some protectionism) is combined with small governments, relatively open trade regimes and an emphasis on competitive exchange rates.

The supporters of this approach call it the 'new interventionism'[3] in which governments seek to guide, and not substitute for the market. Such governments use relatively subtle guidance to steer investment into productive sectors, encourage the development of technological strengths and develop links with the multinational business community.

Obviously, the subtlety with which governments manage this new interventionism will vary from case to case. What is significant is that, again with the probable exception of Hong Kong (which is perhaps the closest any economy will get to the IMF ideal of a totally free-market economy), all the leading East Asian Newly Industrializing Economies have a significant element of interventionism in their system, albeit in a relatively subtle form.

The subtlety of the new interventionism is important because it marks the difference between it and the import-substituting strategies of, say, the Latin American economists such as Raul Prebisch who dominated Third World economic thinking in the 1950s and 1960s. In the latter case, imports were seen as evil, to be kept out by quantitative restrictions or high tariffs; investments which substituted for imports were almost bound to be beneficial to the developing economy.

In tody's new interventionism, imports are seen as a challenge. In the case of an economy like Taiwan, there will be a mechanism for approving imports, which can be used to block or delay imports where it is felt local competitors are potentially able to supply at roughly equivalent prices and quality. If local producers fail to come up to international standards fairly promptly, then the licensing authorities are now quite likely to let imports rise both to keep costs down for local users, and also to keep competitive pressures on the would-be local suppliers of the relevant intermediate goods. In such a case, market forces are not being ignored. The search is always to encourage local companies to become globally competitive as fast as possible. Imports are seen as an important competitive pressure to be used to speed the local response.

One of the subtler political questions is whether Japan will fight within international agencies for this 'new interventionism', which is so close to its own approach to economic management. After all, Japan is now second only to the USA in providing funds to the World Bank, and in 1989 that country became the world's leading aid donor.

Leading Japanese officials are starting to question the extreme *laisser-faire* emphasis which is dogma for so many top officials in both the IMF and the World Bank. The Japanese are starting to compare the mess which the Anglo-Americans seem to be making of their economies, with the dynamism of many of the economies which have developed under some form of 'new interventionism'. There are warnings that the Anglo-American way of seeing political economy has outlived its usefulness.[4]

The likelihood is that the new interventionism will indeed win out as the dominant model in the Third World – if one assumes that the crash transitions to market economy in Eastern Europe and the former Soviet Union have only partial success. It would need the overwhelming success of the Anglo-American model in such new areas to outweigh the steady increase in the influence of the Japanese model of 'developmental capitalism', and the related new interventionists in East Asia.

The emphasis will still remain, though, on equipping one's economies and companies to compete on international markets. Government interventionism will win approval, but only in so far as it aims to strengthen the workings of the market economy in the medium term.

TECHNOLOGICAL DIFFUSION AND THE THIRD WORLD

The message of this chapter is that technology is now being diffused very fast to Third World countries. Brazil has an aircraft industry. Malaysia exports cars. The Koreans are a significant force in micro-electronics. The Taiwanese export computers.

The mechanisms used to develop these industries are increasingly varied. The old, classic route of multinational investments certainly plays its part – and Japanese multinationals are now joining the Americans and Europeans in forming joint ventures or putting down greenfield investments to take full advantage of the comparative advantages of the more productive parts of the Third World. Sometimes the multinationals merely source key components from the Third World – and this is important as intra-industry trade increases. Thus Singapore is a major source of hard-disk drives for the world's computer industry. But then Singapore may do its own sourcing elsewhere in the Third World, taking, for instance, head stacks for computer hard disks from an Indian company in Bombay.

Governments are using a variety of mechanisms to speed the development of new technologies in their countries. Export Processing Zones remain one classic route, designed to provide export platforms for the world's multinationals. These are proving important in China; they have been held back by red tape in India (but still, as in the Santacruz Electronics Export Processing Zone near Bombay, have had their role to play). Each Third World country will, as it seeks to enter world markets, create such zones, as Vietnam did in early 1992 when it opened its first Export Processing Zone on the outskirts of Ho Chi Minh City.

Today the leading Third World countries know that they must increase the knowledge bases of their economies. Increasingly, they are creating science-based industrial parks like Taiwan's Hsinchu science park, which by late 1991 had attracted 133 companies ranging from Acer, Taiwan's largest personal computer manufacturer, to AT&T. The aim of this park is to move the Taiwanese economy upstream into higher value-added activities such as computers and peripherals, ics, telecommunications, optoelectronics, automated systems, bioenginering, and environmental and energy science.

Observers from the older industrial powers must accept that such parks are no longer unusual, and that one like Hsinchu will now involve 22,000 people of whom around a third are university graduates, with around 170 holding doctorates. Growth is being built on high-calibre human capital. Competition is not just coming from cheap, disciplined assembly operatives, but from workforces who are now capable of innovating around the edges of the key industrial sectors of today.

What all this means is that the west's monopoly on technology has now been thoroughly broken. A worrying example of this is the way that Iraq – not one of the scientific power houses of the Third World – was able to develop an effective nuclear weapons programme despite international bans on the transfer of much of this technology. Some of the lessons they learned by the simple device of attaching a brilliant Iraqi scientist to one of the nuclear enrichment consortia in Europe. In the course of his work there, he observed and questioned and came away with most of the process firmly lodged in his head.

For some parts of the separation and enrichment process, they reverted to slightly out of date technologies which may have been inefficient, but called on local manufacturing or easily acquired technologies. For the more complex processes they launched an extremely well camouflaged world-wide buying programme for the components and materials which would be needed. In many cases, the technologies were dual-use ones which did not arouse too much suspicion. Since countries like Pakistan were helping in this process, they were also able to spread the financial transactions through a web of financial institutions which did not have to know all the details.

The United Nations inspectors who went into Iraq after the Gulf War are convinced that Iraq was within eighteen months of producing a regular supply of the enriched uranium which would be needed for a military programme. . . . And this was despite a Nuclear Non-Proliferation Regime which is designed to stop this kind of surreptitious development of nuclear weapons, and despite the very active attention of the Israelis.

The lesson from Iraq is that it is impossible to stop motivated Third World countries from acquiring advanced technological capabilities if they are so determined. They may not necessarily make optimum use of their knowledge, but where they have other comparative advantages which can be allied to precocious knowledge, they will be formidable competitors.

As argued earlier, the new forms of flexible manufacturing systems may mean that the industrialized world will be able to fight off the Third World challenge for the forseeable future. However, it is clear that the competence of the challenge from the Third World will continue to increase. This does not mean that the Third World will overrun the older industrial powers. What it does mean, though, is that the industrialized world cannot focus just on competition from Japan. Beyond Japan there will be a continuous series of new industrial powers, many of whom are run very capably indeed.

The leading countries of the Third World are yet one more force pushing for a Global Shakeout.

11

REGULATION REVISITED

THE 1980s SAW a significant jump in industrial liberalization and deregulation. However, as we moved into the 1990s, it was unclear just how far this process could safely go. It was almost as though the withdrawal of Mrs Thatcher and President Reagan had left an ideological vacuum. They had helped push the industrialized world in a more liberal direction – but economic liberalism has its dark side. Would the regulators have to be brought back to stage centre to mop up some of the excesses which were triggered in the liberal decade of the 1980s?

Certainly there were enough *causes célèbres to* justify alarm. In the USA, there was the Savings and Loans disaster, along with the prosecutions of financial shooting stars such as Ivan Boesky and Michael Milken (and lesser luminaries such as Dennis Levine). Major financial institutions such as Drexel Burnham & Co. and Salomon Brothers got sucked in to scandals such as these.

Internationally, the raping of the Bank of Credit and Commerce International by its top management was uncovered in 1991, and turned out to be the largest bank fraud in history. In this case, the worries were not just about the fraud itself, but about the fact that BCCI had, for a number of years, been monitored quite closely by authorities such as the Bank of England. Yet, by judicious shifting of funds from one jurisdiction to another, it had managed to stave off collapse for years.

Later on in 1991, the mysterious death by drowning of Robert Maxwell led to the unravelling of yet another transatlantic set of frauds whereby he had plundered both his British and American holdings in order to try to bolster the price of his tottering empire.

In Japan, the steady stream of scandals from the Recruit affair onwards sapped the reputations of the political class in general, but were not specifically caused by financial deregulation *per se*. However, the collapse of the bubble economy in the early 1990s put consistent, worrying pressures on Japanese banks and the property market. The failure of prices to rise on the Tokyo Stock Exchange from the lows of 1991 merely increased a general sense of malaise. In retrospect, the bubble economy was unsoundly based on inflated property values and risky banking practices. Once again, there was an increased awareness of the risks of too much market freedom.

Such unease was felt throughout the industrialized world. It was the relatively liberalized Anglo-Saxon economies (Britain, the USA and Australia) which went into the 1991–2 slow-down first, and then found it very difficult to pull themselves out of the slump. In Britain consumers had borrowed too much in the aftermath of financial deregulation, and thus behaved much more cautiously when faced with an incipient economic recovery. This was the down-side of the greater economic freedom which consumers had been given.

In addition, the problem of industrial over-concentration was raising its head. The American airline industry, having benefited from substantial liberalization in the late 1970s, was now starting to become oligopolistic again, as major players like Pan Am were driven from the scene. Elsewhere, there were worries about the behaviour of privatized companies such as the telecommunications giants. Had privatization merely replaced publicly-owned monopolies with privately-owned ones? Should the relevant authorities step in to create a better competitive balance?

At the same time, new problems called for increased government intervention. The problem of dumping toxic waste was highlighted by the voyage of the *Karin B*, during which this ship was turned away by a number of countries because she was carrying a cargo of flammable solvents and PCBs which had originally been dumped in Nigeria. Environmental issues have become politically more central. California continues to lead the way in keeping the pressure on automotive pollution. The growing acceptance of the link between climate warming and the use of fossil fuels meant that governments took on the obligation to arrest emissions of carbon dioxide. Earlier in the 1980s, governments had regulated use of CFC in items such as refrigerators because these compounds were linked to the damage of the ozone layer. Again, the sale of military hardware and other sensitive dual-use technologies to the likes of President Saddam Hussein moved to the fore in the aftermath of the war against Iraq. Could companies trading in such products be left unregulated? Then there was the growing health-driven attack on products such as cigarettes and alcohol.

In all these cases, some kind of governmental regulation was clearly needed and, in most cases, such regulation did in fact increase during the last decade. This clearly ran counter to the deregulatory trend in other parts of the international economy. The question, then, has to be asked: to what extent are we seeing a form of re-regulation taking place to protect the globe from the excesses of an overly deregulated system?

THE FORCES AT WORK

The answer is that there are a number of forces at work which will not necessarily roll back the liberalization which has taken place over the last decade or so. What they will do, though, is ensure that governmental regulation will remain a force to be reckoned with. The new balance of international regulation will be much less xenophobic than in the past and generally much lighter in its application.

RE-REGULATION

There will certainly be some re-regulation where deregulation is felt to have gone too far. The US airline industry is one candidate for such a step, given the degree of industrial concentration at the local level. Intervention, though, need not be in the form of a return to price controls. The authorities first have the option of allowing much greater foreign competition; if this does not overcome local problems, a more active anti-trust policy towards the airline industry would be the logical next step. Only if it then appears that airlines naturally tend toward oligopolies at the local level would some rebuilding of the regulatory framework be necessary.

In other sectors, such as financial services, where unease about deregulatory excesses runs deep, the response may well be more one of slowing deregulation, rather than reversing it. Thus it is explicable that Congress ultimately refused to vote through the 1991 proposed banking reform measures which sought to loosen the controls on inter-state banking, and to break down the barriers between banking and other financial sectors such as insurance. Given the S&L disaster and the various scandals in Wall Street, refusing to take the next steps in deregulation is understandable. It does not preclude moving on down that route sometime in the future.

In Tokyo, there has been a similar loss of enthusiasm for further experiments. This also is explicable, given the weight of the problems which have been bearing down on Japanese property and equity markets.

In general, though, there is little pressure for a reversal of the deregulatory trend of the 1980s. Caution may be the watchword; not scrapping the whole principle of liberalization.

THE INTERNATIONALIZATION OF REGULATION

Of much more significance is the way that regulation is becoming more international – reflecting the fact that industries to be regulated increasingly operate on a global basis.

Sometimes this is a case of regulators in two or more countries consulting with each other to check that their actions at a national level are mutually consistent, or do not unnecessarily harm the interests of other countries. A routine example of this is the network of bilateral relationships which the US futures industry regulators had, by the late 1980s, built up with their opposite numbers in the UK, Australia, Canada and Singapore. In the case of the UK, it is agreed that the US agency is the primary agency for US futures companies working in London, and there is a clear understanding about the kind of information on these companies which the two sets of regulators will pass on to each other.

Increasingly, though, this type of understanding needs a more comprehensive approach. In financial services, the coordinating role has been played by the Bank for International Settlements – the Swiss-based organization which brings together the world's central bankers. Its key committee is the Committee on Banking Supervision (often known as the Cooke Committee) which has grown in importance since the 1970s when a series of banking crises (Herstatt, Ambrosiano et al) showed that regulators were unclear as to who should be regulating the operations of banks as they went abroad (should it be regulators in the parent or host country?). In 1988, this committee took the major step of introducing common standards for the capital ratios which banks are expected to maintain (the Basle ratios). It is these ratios which are causing Japanese banks so much grief as equity and property prices remain low in Tokyo – thus making it very difficult for them to build their capital ratios to the levels required by the BIS.

This is the most notable case of the world's regulators coming together to hammer out common guidelines for their chosen sector. Given the intangible nature of international financial transactions, it is no accident that progress has gone furthest in the field of financial services. Past crises such as the Banco Ambrosiano affair (the Vatican's Bank of God) showed how easy it was for a country like Luxembourg to deny responsibility for losses racked up on its territory by financial institutions owned elsewhere. However, after more than 15 years of the Cooke Committee's work, the BCCI affair showed how easy it still is for unscrupulous financiers to play London off against the Cayman Islands, Luxembourg and New York. The regulators have to keep moving to stay in touch with the financial sharks.

A more comprehensive attempt to shift regulation up from a national to a supranational centre is that of the European Community. As part of the 1992 process, a range of regulatory activities will be increasingly carried out within Brussels, rather than at the national level. One of the most obvious cases is competition policy, where Brussels now has preemptive rights to rule on mergers above a certain size. This does not mean that national competition policies are dead, but it does mark the beginning of an era in which competition policy starts to be tackled at a supranational level. Over recent years, there has been a certain amount of transatlantic consultation in this area. However, there is growing US concern to ensure that the Japanese start to apply their anti-trust rules with more vigour. The US position is that an arrangement such as the *Keiretsu* company groupings is ultimately anti-competitive, particularly regarding the aspirations of foreign companies seeking to break into Japanese markets. Such issues are already showing up in the Structural Impediments Initiative (SII) dialogue between Japan and the USA. Clearly, in an age of global competition, the tolerance of cosy oligopolies in one part of the triad world is now of major political importance in other triad centres. Inevitably, this issue is filtering upwards into the transnational dimension.

This is one area where different kinds of institutions will make the running in different areas. Where strong supranational bodies like the European Community evolve, they will clearly be of major importance for the constituent countries in a number of sectors. Sometimes, though, there are pre-existing functional international institutions like the Bank for International Settlements in financial sevices or the World Health Organization for medical issues which will become important for their particular sectors. Ad hoc bilateral consultations also have a role to play, particularly between continents in areas without any existing supranational framework.

WILL THE AMERICANS SET THE AGENDA?

Almost inevitably it will be the Americans who drive much of the global regulatory debate in the next couple of decades.

Partly this is because only the USA has developed an active, legally-based approach to regulatory issues. In most of the rest of the triad world, the emphasis is on a collusively corporate approach in which companies are nudged in the right direction by forms of administrative guidance of varying subtlety. The first trouble with this 'clubman's' approach to regulation is that it often (in American eyes) comes far too close to corruption for comfort. For instance, Americans find it very difficult to accept the Japanese regulatory system which produced the selective kickbacks from the big securities houses to their major clients. The Americans are equally appalled by the tolerance shown by such collusive regulators to practices such as insider trading which, often, are barely investigated, let alone punished with any vigour.

The second trouble with the collusive approach to regulation is that it relies on regulator and regulated having a common set of values. As the business world becomes increasingly multinational, this is less and less true. A wonderful example of the incongruities of today's world is the BCCI case. Here, for various reasons, the Bank of England was the key supervisor – an organization which has long been used to working in a culture where an Englishman's word is his bond. In the case of the BCCI, it was up against a global bank which was run by a tight mafia of Pakistani Shia Muslims, led by one Agha Hasan Abedi, who would occasionally describe to senior colleagues the conversations he had with God in the corridor outside.[1] This produced a corporate culture which was wholly alien to that of the Bank of England's mandarins. It is probable that no regulatory system would have stopped the alleged financial rape of BCCI, but it is certain that the British approach was out of place.

In a world of increasingly complex cultural mixes, there is really no alternative to adopting a legalistic approach to international regulatory issues – and that means it will be the American approach which dominates, since only the US has the necessary legal culture (and the battalions of hungry lawyers supporting it) ready in place.

The Americans have always had a crusading side to their legal character. Working on the basis of the doctrine of effects (i.e. if some action in the outside world affects the USA, then that action should fall subject to US law), they have long argued that measures such as their anti-trust or strategic export control policies should be observed wherever US interests are affected.

More recently, one can see the way that the US authorities (particularly the Securities and Exchange Commission) have been fighting overseas authorities to get insider trading offences treated seriously. Switzerland, with its famed banking secrecy, was one of the first targets. By the mid-1980s, it had been persuaded that its banks had to open their books in cases such as that of Drexel Burnham Lambert's Dennis Levine who was using Bank Leu as a conduit for his insider trading on Wall Street. Again, it was the SEC which pushed the French authorities when it found evidence of unusual advance trading as the French steel-maker, Pechiney, bid for the American company Triangle in 1988. Partly as a result of this affair, the French have been tightening up their definitions of insider trading.

Other countries have similarly been tightening up their own procedures. The British system does now occasionally jail financial operators who operate illegally. The Japanese brought in quite tough insider trading laws in 1988, though there was some initial reluctance to use them aggressively.

Effectively, the rest of the industrialized world is following (sometimes reluctantly) the American lead on transparency in financial dealings.

What has happened in Switzerland is a good example of the forces at work. In 1986, when the authorities cooperated with the SEC over Dennis Levine, insider trading was not a crime under Swiss law. However, the Swiss authorities were simultaneously embarrassed by the fact that they were offering a haven to the ill-gotten gains of two corrupt (but recently deposed) Presidents, Marcos of the Philippines and Duvalier of Haiti. The Swiss froze the relevant assets. In 1988, the SEC pressure paid off and the Swiss made insider trading a crime. US attention then turned to money laundering by criminals, an action which was made illegal in 1990, with banks having to certify that deposits are not the proceeds of criminal activities. In 1991 the Swiss were persuaded to abolish their secret accounts (Form B accounts). In all cases, the names of account holders must be made known to a bank employee.

It may be possible to read too much into the Swiss case but it seems to indicate a trend. Secret bank accounts and unaccountable tax havens are an incitement to fraud in a world in which the healthy functioning of international financial transactions is crucial to the health of the world economy itself. The smooth functioning of this system will inevitably require the lightening of too onerous national regulations, and thus will play into the hands of the unscrupulous. However, it is equally plain that the major financial centres of the world cannot condone such behaviour. Hence the pressure on countries like Switzerland which have asked no questions when taking money. Criminals – be they insider traders or drugs barons – have to be tracked down on a global basis. Banking secrecy can no longer be tolerated when it interferes with this process.

The final reason why the US will tend to act as the ethical trend-setter of the global business system, is that only in this country is there a set of political and judicial institutions which is totally independent of the governmental process.

For instance, despite protests from overseas, the US judicial system concerns itself with the behaviour of both foreign companies in the USA and American companies overseas. In the former case, it is Japanese companies which have had most to worry about. Unused to managing culturally diverse labour forces, various Japanese companies have run foul of suits by women who feel they have been denied promotion, and there is a constant undercurrent of accusations that these companies have also been cautious about employing racial minorities. Where Japanese managers get themselves into trouble, there is a clear tension between the American tendency to prosecute and the Japanese preference to maintain face. Mitsubishi Bank of California got into this dilemma in 1987, when the US authorities wanted to extradite a former senior executive back to the USA to face embezzlement charges. The former executive remained in Japan and was never formally charged.

The American position is equally interesting. Here the question is whether US anti-bias laws should be applied in American companies overseas. One case which was winding its way through the judicial process in 1991 was against Aramco (the American-owned oil joint venture in Saudi Arabia) alleging discrimination when American citizens were laid off during a 'Saudi-ization' drive in the Aramco ranks.

There are also increasing problems with issues such as whether an American firm should respect Japanese unease about dealing with women executives, or Arab unwillingness to work with Jews. In an era when career paths are increasingly international, should bias in important overseas commercial centres be respected, when it could blight the career prospects of otherwise well-qualified personnel? Even if it is decided that US anti-bias laws do not apply in such cases (and a number of foreign governments argue that they should not), the problems will not go away. All companies have to respect the aspirations of their employees. So, whatever the legal position, American companies are going to come under strong internal pressure from women and ethnic minorities to ensure that corporate employment practices overseas are as bias-free as they are in the USA.

On the legal front, the speed (and relative effectiveness) with which prosecutions for financially-linked offences are carried out, will inevitably have its effect on the rest of the world. For instance the US authorities had completed legal proceedings against the Bank of Credit and Commerce International before the British had even completed an official inquiry into how things had gone wrong. Inevitably, this speed puts pressure on authorities elsewhere which drag their feet.

And then, there are the Congressional hearings. . . . Few other countries have this tradition of no-holds-barred legislator-driven public hearings. As they demonstrated during the international corruption scandals of the late 1960s and early 1970s, they are a potent force for uncovering corporate wrong-doing. The hearings may not always be fair to corporate executives, but it would be a very stupid executive who thought he/she could afford to ignore Congressional opinion. Whether through formal hearings, or less traditional methods such as smashing Japanese products in front of the television cameras, the US Congressional process publicly magnifies issues, not just within the US but around the globe.

Having said all this, the legal-driven US system will not always win out. For instance, in the 1970s, the USA went out on a limb with its Foreign Corrupt Practices Act. This was a response to the headline-making overseas payments scandals of the Watergate era, and the act was an attempt to ensure that US executives were squeaky-clean in their dealings with the outside world. So tough was this act that executives in Moscow would even have to detail payments to taxi-drivers, since these were officially state employees – and payments to such employees had to be logged. Significantly, although other western countries did tighten controls somewhat, none of them went anywhere as far as the American legislation. Inevitably, this raised the complaint that American companies were being undercut by competitors able to offer more generous bribes. Under the 1988 Omnibus Trade Act, therefore, the corrupt payments provisions were watered down. An example of the difficulties facing unilateral attempts to impose ethical standards on the rest of the world.

THE NEW ISSUES

Regulatory levels are ultimately determined by levels of public concern. During the 1980s, new political issues emerged which have dictated some regulatory response.

Green issues are foremost among those which have won their way onto the political agenda.

The CFC (Chlorofluorocarbons) issue is the leading example of how scientific agreement about the ecological damage being caused by a group of chemicals has led to a global campaign to control their usage and then to phase them out. Implicated in the destruction of the ozone layer, these gases came under international control through the 1987 Montreal Protocol which initially laid down a timetable for cutting their production by 50 per cent over ten years, but was subsequently amended to call for the total end of their production by the year 2000.

Similar concerns about the 'greenhouse effect' means that there are calls for international regulation of gases such as nitrous oxide, carbon dioxide and methane. At the very least, we will be seeing the creation of carbon taxes in various parts of the world. More widely, industry is going to have to face environmental charges on polluting activities, tax incentives to reduce pollution, and controls designed to encourage the recycling of disposable items such as bottles and containers. The mechanisms used to regulate the polluting activities will vary from country to country, but there can be little doubt that government intervention to control the environmental impact of industry will rise substantially over the coming couple of decades. This will be a major increase in the regulatory burden on industry.

Certain other industries are sure to come under increasing scientific attack. Prime among these are the tobacco and alcohol industries, which are already coming under pressure in areas such as freedom to advertise. Other scientifically sensitive industries will include the pharmaceutical industry (particularly as it moves towards bio-engineering). It is extremely unlikely that the regulation of the pharmaceutical industry will be relaxed. The most which will happen is that regulatory authorities will collaborate more in accepting evidence of testing in one another's territories.

There some other less obvious issues which are starting to demand increased government intervention.

One of these is the fight against international crime – particularly the international drugs trade. At the moment, the increased regulatory pressures are being placed on banks which are seen as playing a major role in the identification of the financial flows which are the first step in laundering the profits from criminal activities.

The fight against international terrorism and the spread of dangerous technology to potential aggressors such as President Saddam Hussein has also been steadily creeping up the political agenda. The ending of the Cold War has reduced one major source of danger, but the awareness of how close Saddam has come to producing his own nuclear devices served to alert us to the need for a new war to control the proliferation of unfriendly technology to unstable regimes and outright terrorists.

The message of this book is that this dirty war will be with our readers for the rest of their lifetimes, because technological maturity in certain areas and the increasing problem of miniaturization means that the technological balance is swinging in favour of the terrorist and the regional aggressor.

This is a terrifying prospect, and it will inevitably mean that the

Figure 16

Reregulatory Milestones

Year	Sector	Country	Comments
1985	Automotives	Canada	Motor Vehicle Safety Act: imposes safety standards on production, import and export of motor vehicles and components
1988	Finance	Japan, EC, US	Basle Accord: sets an international standard of minimum capital adequacy ratios for international banks
1989	Finance	US	Financial Institutions Reform, Recovery and Enforcement Act (FIRREA): imposes capital standards on solvent thrifts
1989	Television Broadcasting	EC	Broadcast Directive: imposes requirements regarding distribution, including an EC content requirement; the production of TV programs; TV advertising and sponsorship; and the protection of minors
1990	Competition	EC	Merger Control Directive: EC Commission gets power to screen mergers of firms with combined global assets of Ecu 5 bn + and Ecu 250 mn + turnover in the EC
1990	Environment	US	Clean Air Act: introduces changes to existing environmental controls on US industry and provides for further cuts in emissions
1991	Environment	EC	Urban Waste Water Treatment Directive: regulates and sets standards concerning the collection, treatment and discharge of waste water
1992	Finance	Germany	Introduction of new Insider Trading Law (in progress): provides for legal sanctions against offenders with the possibility of confiscating any financial gains

Source: Financial Times

multinational business community will be caught up in the attempts to limit the damage. Undoubtedly, the old Cocom mechanisms which were used to slow the spread of sensitive technology to the former Soviet bloc will be revised to target a much wider range of potentially unfriendly regimes, and to include a much wider range of 'dual-use' technologies (that is, commercially-driven technologies which also have a military or terrorist use). Even to start to be effective, any such control regime will have to include companies from all the main industrial centres in the world. It may, however, take a major regional or terrorist catastrophe (the first successful chemical or nuclear attack by some international renegade?) for a true global consensus to emerge on this issue. In the meantime, there will be constant pressures to extend controls on the relevant technology transfers. In our judgement, these pressures will steadily increase in intensity. Any company or government which assumes that they will go away will be very stupid (and irresponsible) indeed.

THE LIMITS TO REGULATION

Despite all the arguments in this chapter, the pressures to reduce regulation will remain strong. There will of course be areas (such as capital adequacy ratios for the world's banks) where economic self-interest ensures that governments work together. There will also be rare cases (such as with CFCs or global warming) where governments become sufficiently frightened to band together to create a new set of regulations designed to help the planet.

In general, though, competition between nations means that countries offering relatively light regulation will pick up investment from more restrictive economies. This shows at the level of direct investment where 'Trojan horses' such as the UK or Tennessee have benefited at the expense of less open investment sites. It has also shown in the financial services sector where, over the post-1945 period, it has been the lightly-regulated financial centres which have tended to flourish (Tokyo being the exception in that it owes its central place to the strength of the Japanese economy despite an unhelpful regulatory regime).

This is not to say that the pressures are for no regulation at all. All responsible players in the international economic community know that a totally unregulated system would be a recipe for disaster. The pressures are, rather, on competing business centres to produce systems which offer effective regulatory floors, but with the mimimum of taxation and other financial burdens. In general, companies do not fight regulations which are clearly designed to stop companies cheating each other – or the citizen at large. They do try to draw the line when reporting burdens become excessive or where information is demanded which is not for the use of the regulators, but to help a wider political debate. The multinationals are always going to fight initiatives which ask them to lay out their overall investment plans. Hence initiatives such as the abortive EC Vredeling proposal for worker participation in European company decision-making or the USA's Bryant Amendment will always stir a hornet's nest of corporate resistance.

What the multinationals want is cheap, effective, carefully-focused, minimal regulation. Regulators in the world's most powerful economies may be able to resist these corporate pressures to some extent. However, the more they try to increase their tax-take or the complexity of industrial supervision, the more vulnerable they are to investment strikes by the multinational business community.

The pressures are on governments to get involved in a 'Dutch auction'[3] whereby they steadily reduce their regulatory standards to attract an increasingly footloose global business community. As this chapter has shown, there are some counters to this trend. A great deal, however, depends on governments determining together that they will not allow themselves to be played off against each other in this way. On a continental basis, this may be possible – though it is still undecided whether the European Community can control the Dutch auction process within Europe. On an inter-continental basis, this consensus-building will be much more difficult.

Ultimately, where the regulatory line is drawn will depend on how vexed global public opinion becomes over any particular issue. At one level, it is clear that international storms of protest will continue to be raised by ecological *causes célèbres* such as Bhopal, Chernobyl, Exxon Valdez, Karin B, Minimata, or (more difficult to dramatize) the destruction of the tropical rain forests.

There will be more diffuse anger against major financial skulduggery at the level of the Recruit, Milken/Boesky, BCCI or the Maxwell scandals. However, while public opinion is more confused by the technicalities, the international financial community generally has an interest in ensuring that such affairs are minimized. Hence, there is still an alliance supporting some form of regulation.

Where the Dutch auction operates effectively is in areas where losses to the public welfare cannot be illuminated by clear-cut scandals. The pressure to erode the tax-take from the corporate sector is an example of this. Lowering corporate tax rates is a classic Dutch auction ploy in attracting foreign investment – but its effects are very difficult to illustrate.

Similarly, the Dutch auction will work in areas where labour forces in different nations or regions can be set against each other. This is why an assault on trade union power is one of the devices used by authorities trying to attract international investment. Whether people worry about this aspect of the Dutch auction depends on their political sympathies. However there can be no denying that levels of union influence are steadily being eroded wherever the attraction of footloose investment is a priority.

Each country will have to decide where it will draw the political dividing line on this question of regulatory priorities. There are areas in which there is a global consensus for action. There are, however, a far greater number of areas where such consensus does not exist. It is in these areas where competitive deregulation will continue to take place.

On balance, the global pressures will remain for less regulation, rather than more.

12

NEW CHALLENGES FOR THE CORPORATE WORLD

SOMETIME IN THE past, management could actually be fun. Competition was primarily at level of the nation state. Changes in competitive status would take time to achieve. Often, one would know one's competitors, and the chances of building a form of more or less disguised oligopoly were quite high. One would compete, but not to the extent of driving the competition to the wall at all costs. The salaries would be relatively high.

Today, the salaries of top executives in large parts of the western world remain (often outrageously) high – but the fun has largely disappeared. Under the impact of the Information Technology revolution all aspects of management are simultaneously being forced to evolve. On the one hand, the IT revolution is directly affecting the way managerial hierarchies are structured. As organizations are down-sized and flattened, whole layers of management have been made redundant, and the executives who survive are continuously having to justify the existence of the roles not only of friends and colleagues but their own as well. Again, technology has become something far more than what goes on in research labs and factories; information technology has become the very sinews of the managerial function. Building new structures around the capabilities of IT has become one of the continuing tasks of today's executive. The classic hierarchical management charts from the days of Henry Ford have been thrown away. Each day becomes an experiment in looking for the right organizational structure for tomorrow's world.

Simultaneously, the role that the IT revolution is playing in speeding up competitive change between companies and the very continents themselves cannot be overestimated. As development times are consistently lowered, the world's marketers are increasingly discovering the competitive importance of 'time to market'. The company which gets to a new product or technology first gets in at the top of the learning curve. Each successive imitator will find that the pioneers are hard to dislodge because they are further down that learning curve, thus benefiting from rapidly falling production and marketing costs, which will allow them to out-compete the latecomers. On the technological front, the world has become immensely more unforgiving. To be late into a market is to risk competitive death. The competition can come from most parts of the globe, and it is pitiless in its ferocity.

At the same time, the need to speed the development of products and processes which are becoming much more complex systems means that the relative cost of staying in the competitive pack is steadily rising. This is increasingly forcing firms 'to bet the company' or, if that is too frightening, to find partners with whom the risks can be shared . . . and the pace of development is not just increasing as far as products are concerned, it is also rising for the production process itself. The message from the MIT study on lean production systems is that the rethinking of the relationship between the social structures of factories and their ever-more flexible production technology is another task for executives which can never end.

On top of this process of continuous technological and organizational churning, there is another quickening challenge of geographical expansion. Once again, this is a function of the IT revolution in its role as destroyer of distance and national boundaries. On the one hand, this has unlocked the competitive challenge from companies which, in many industries, can be located half the globe away. On the other, to get the scale economies to support the intensified technological effort needed to stay in the game, companies must increasingly be competitive throughout the triad world (or whatever combination of countries may matter for a particular industry). All other things being equal, a technologically-driven industry which is globally successful will overrun a competitor which is only continentally successful. For technologically-sophisticated products, national strategies are now completely suicidal.

The pressures on brand-driven companies are slightly less, in that successful brands are rarely destroyed overnight by competition. However, with the exception of some premium brands (yes, you can pay $1,000 for a presentation bottle of whisky) where production costs bear no real relationship to the price charged, product quality and production costs do matter. Hence the revolution that IT is bringing about in research labs and on the factory floor affects the branders too.

However, at the level of geographical expansion, the branders are being driven into global strategies just as dramatically as the more high-tech companies. With the branders, the drive is on to establish their brands as one of the leading handfuls in each key market segment in each key market. With brands, the importance of establishing an early dominance is crucial, because this gives the company preferential access to the vital distribution channels. Once again, the urgency comes from the way that the importance of national boundaries has been falling away. Although the branding battles are relatively mature within USA and West Europe, they are still very fluid elsewhere in the world (including Japan). What the branders are involved in is an oligopolistic race to see who will be the top three or four companies in each relevant market. The fact that the telecommunications revolution makes the establishment of global brands an easier job than was once true is a benefit. However, global brands are only one tool to be used where relevant. Currently, what is much more important for the brand-driven companies is an active mergers and acquisitions policy to snap up the more interesting under-exploited brands as a prelude to rolling them out across the globe. Currently it looks as though industrial concentration is taking place in most brand-led sectors. Companies which cannot get themselves into the top division of their industry (say, the top five companies globally) should probably find themselves a good, defensive niche strategy very fast.

There are many industries which do not fit neatly into either the technologically- or brand-driven categories. However, in most cases, they too will have come to terms with the IT revolution. Financial servies are a case in point. Long a somewhat gentlemanly part of the international economy ('bankers' hours' is a derogatory term for a maximum five hour day), the industry is being ripped apart by the IT revolution just as surely as manufacturing is. The very concept of a bank is under attack as IT networks bring all kinds of non-bank financial institutions into competitive play. And at the international level, the competitive health of complete financial service industries in specific cities is dependent on how effectively they can link their activities into the 24-hour financial market. Within Europe, for instance, there is a very real battle between London, Paris, Frankfurt and Zurich in this sector. The effectiveness of financial deregulation will partially determine which cities survive as leading financial centres, but the quality of their technological response will be equally important. Then, of course, there is the competition from the commercial networks such as those of Reuters and Telerate. As financial services 'de-materialize' (i.e. terminal will communicate with terminal, demanding no paperwork, and the people concerned being under no obligation ever to see each other), will geographical concentrations of financial institutions be needed any longer?

And now we are seeing the emergence of the 'tekkies' – computer-driven strategists of financial service companies who compete on financial markets purely on the strength of their computer analysis of increasingly obscure trends and ratios – and fleeting arbitrage opportunities thrown up by their ability to predict the decisions of competitors' computer programmes a moment before those decisions are made.

So even an apparently low-tech industry like financial services is becoming technologically-intensive. So far, this is an industry which remains remarkably fragmented, but this is likely to change. Power will presumably pass into the hands of those companies which master the arts of developing the increasingly powerful national and international electronic networks needed in this industry. There is already evidence that few companies which invested heavily in IT systems after the various financial Big Bangs of recent years have made adequate profits to support them. This points to the fact that the competitive use of IT is becoming as crucial in this industry as any other.

Analysing the problems is easy enough. Providing solutions is more presumptuous – and pointless since solutions will quite often be specific to particular industrial sectors. All one can say is that the first step on the path to survival is the conscious awareness of the all-pervasiveness of competition in today's world and the multiple sources from which it comes. Any solutions which focus on just one competitive source are almost bound to fail. Also, solutions which involve slowing the competitive response down (for whatever kind-hearted reasons) will also almost certainly fail.

There are, though, a couple of cautions.

First, it is fully understandable that many western companies have taken the 'total quality' message on board as a way of catching up with Japan. The simple justification for this is that, during the 1970s and 1980s, Japanese management moved so significantly ahead of average practice in North America and Europe that a catching up process was inevitable. However, as western quality standards do catch up with Japan, some diminishing returns will set in.

Secondly, one can overestimate the importance of simple technological solutions. For one thing, the lesson from 'Lean Production' is that getting the technology right has only been part of the process. Equally important is getting the overall system right, which can include keeping the workforce motivated, and also involves the creative coordination of designers, production engineers, marketers and all those others involved with the product design process. Within the office, this lesson is equally important. Purely technological solutions such as putting computer terminals on everyone's desks will only work where the managerial structures within which information must flow are shaken up as well.

There are some interesting questions about whether one can push ahead too fast with technological development. It can be argued that in some sectors such as semiconductors, particularly intense competitive rivalry is pushing companies into the expensive development of new generations of chips long before chip-users have properly started exploiting the current generation. Similarly, some of the developments in consumer electronics and HDTV seem to be pushing companies and countries into price ranges and new levels of technological complexity to which the consumer does not want to respond. It is relevant that, in early 1992, Japanese companies were, under financial duress, starting to cut back on the numbers of products they maintained. Matsushita was, for instance, due to cut its domestic range from 50,000 products to nearer 30,000. MITI was even calling upon electrical appliance manufacturers to lengthen product cycles.

Another controversial area is that of the optimum relationship of research effort to total sales. Technological intensity is undoubtedly increasing, but should one plan (as some Japanese companies were certainly doing up to a year or so ago) for a steady proportional increase in the importance of research spending for the next decade or so? Given the competitive pressures on all companies, can one spend too much on research and development as well as too little? For instance, the world famous Bell Laboratories – the birthplace of the transistor – takes 7.8 per cent of AT&T's sales revenue, while Japan's NTT spends just over 4 per cent and British Telecom just under 2 per cent.[2] Such a wide disparity of research effort suggests that only one of these companies has got the balance right – but which one is it?

At the end of a book which has spent a lot of time pushing the message about the intensification of global competition, this may seem a paradoxical note of caution. However, one can point to a company like Philips which has, over the years, had a superb reputation for its research activities. This did not prevent it from making massive commercial losses at the beginning of the 1990s. Quite clearly, the company's balance between long-term research strengths and more short-term commercial considerations had gone awry. Somewhere a balance has to be struck. It is by no means clear where that balance should actually be.

A third reflection on this new world leads one to ask how well Japanese companies will come to terms with its total complexity. Now it is quite clear that these companies are masters of the interplay between technology and general management systems with Japan itself. The Lean Production system is a lasting tribute to the multi-faceted strengths of their industrial system. In so far as products are technology-based, and global market penetration is extremely dependent on the speed of new product development, then Japanese industry will undoubtedly perform well. There is plenty of evidence that they can repeat their productivity performance as they go overseas. What is less clear is how successful they are going to be at integrating non-Japanese management, experience and culture into their overall planning routine. Despite all the talk of 'global localization' there is little current evidence to show that this actually goes very deep. The transplant stage of the investment process is the easy part; what has to come now is the development of global investment strategies which allow national or regional subsidiaries to develop their own distinctive strengths within the company.

When one gets into politically and culturally complex areas such as branding strategy, international property and mergers and acquisition policy, the evidence is even less convincing. In the latter area, it looks as if Japanese companies are tending to pay too generously for companies which may prove difficult to manage. In property, the Japanese companies which moved overseas in the 1980s have generally performed disastrously.

In all fairness, one has to add that Japanese companies are relative newcomers to the overseas investment game, and so there is not a lot of hard evidence to support this cautious view. All the same, the further one moves from the export strategies of technology-driven sectors such as automobiles and electronics the more doubts come to the fore. For the moment, the big Hollywood deals of Sony, Matsushita et al will serve as a good test. If these deals can be made to work, then a great deal of our sceptism will be swept away. If they fail, then it will be legitimate to question Japan's global competitiveness in a number of industries where hardware prowess counts for little – financial services; oil and gas extraction; international property; food, drink and tobacco; hotels and tourism which cater for others than the Japanese; perhaps also any industry such as aerospace where global systems integration is the key.

On balance, though, Japanese companies will remain potent competitors. They have come through past crises with aplomb. When the domestic economy has slowed, they have always proved able to step up exports via the development of new products.

There are some apparently convincing counter-arguments. As noted above, there are significant industrial sectors in which Japanese management has no observable comparative advantage. One can, in fact, argue that the world economy's steady swing toward the tertiary sector (i.e. financial services, tourism etc.) is moving into areas in which Japanese supremacy is in serious doubt.

In addition, the collapse of Tokyo financial markets over 1990–92 indicates that Japan needs to enter a period of substantial institutional and political reform. Inevitably, this has to call into question the political stability which has underpinned so much of the post-1945 industrial success story. There is a real possibility that the pro-industrial consensus in Japan will break down, dragging Japanese companies back to the kind of growth rates seen elsewhere in the industrialized world.

With the one proviso that few Japanese companies seem to be revising their organizational structures to adjust to the changed environment created by the information technology revolution, such pessimism is unconvincing. The message of this book is that the Japanese managerial classes are highly competent and dedicated by Western standards and, whatever medium-term political turmoil there may be in Tokyo, these managers will maintain most of the dynamism their companies have possessed over the last three or four decades. The gap between best Japanese practice and that of western competitors may well narrow because of developments in Japan. However, Japanese companies will not self-destruct. They will remain formidable competitors.

TOMORROW'S WORLD

The challenges described in this chapter are clearly serious enough to stretch any practising executive to the full. However the management world is becoming even more complex.

The IT revolution which has brought us global brands has also brought into being an international public opinion from which corporate executives cannot hide. This probably first made itself felt in the early 1970s when ITT's attempts to interfere in Chile's political process were exposed: years later recruiters for this company were still having to fight the belief that ITT had been involved in the overthrow and death of President Allende (an unjustified charge: ITT's skulduggery was aimed at stopping Allende's original election). The key point here is that the vilification of ITT took place on a world-wide basis.

Since then it has become even more obvious that corporate disasters will increasingly become global. The lethal chemical discharge from Union Carbide's plant in Bhopal became world news, as did the environmental disaster caused by the *Exxon Valdez* oil discharge. The image of both companies was badly damaged. In a different way, Perrier suffered round the globe when traces of benzene were detected in its fashionable water. On a more political level, Toshiba triggered a heavy backlash in the USA when one of its subsidiaries (along with the much less well known Norwegian company, Kongsberg) was discovered to have been providing sensitive technology to the Soviet military machine.

There is now no hiding place if a company is involved in an environmental catastrophe, or is caught in a piece of political skulduggery. All one can do is engage in very active damage limitation. The classic example of how to handle such an incident is Johnson & Johnson's handling of the malicious poisoning of one of its products, Tylenol. The basic lesson is not to bluster or obfuscate, but to act fast to take whatever (perhaps costly) immediate steps are needed to provide immediate reassurance, and for top executives to talk openly about what is or is not known of the problem. Companies need to rehearse how they will handle a global incident. With the world's media involved, no company can afford to take two or three days to decide how to handle such an incident. Nor can it afford to underestimate the seriousness of a crisis, along the lines of Perrier's original reaction in France to the benzene scare, when it continued to serve its bottled water to the initial press conference (which was, anyway, being held five days after the story had broken).[3]

Executives almost have to assume that they are permanently on the record. John Akers, IBM's chief executive, discovered this in May 1991 when he reportedly told some of his middle managers that the company's tension level was not high enough, and that 'everyone is too damn comfortable when the business is in crisis'. One of those present prepared a résumé for close colleagues but inadvertently distributed the summary on the internal electronic mailing system to employees throughout the company – with all the resultant damage to corporate morale.

Akio Morita, the chairman of Sony, also demonstrated the way top executives now perform in a goldfish bowl where all their activities are subject to scrutiny. He took part in a dialogue with a right-wing Japanese politician Shintaro Ishihara about the circumstances in which Japan might take a more assertive role in the world political scene. The exercise was understandable, though his choice of partner was unfortunately extreme in his views. It must have been obvious from the start that US public opinion would be outraged by some of the views expressed (mostly by Ishihara), but it was felt that a debate in Japanese would somehow or other not attract attention. When this proved wrong, there was then the somewhat unedifying and unsuccessful scramble to prevent the resulting booklet being translated into English.

Today any executive, on any occasion, speaking in any language has to assume that his/her views will leak. Executives increasingly have to think of themselves as diplomats. It is true that Akers' experience was unusual: in most cases, messages to the corporate family will stay off the record. However, what it does mean is that executives can no longer afford the throwaway sexist or racist comment. There are almost certain to leak and do damage.

Although attitudes on such issues will evolve at different speeds in different cultures, any company seeking to be a world player should set standards which are at least defensible in the minorities-conscious American culture, and inoffensive to the somewhat over-sensitive Japanese. Sexism and racism have to be avoided as far as US culture is concerned. Given the growing economic tensions stemming from systemic US decline, executives (and politicians) from other countries must be very cautious in seeking to explain why this decline is taking place. At the moment, a number of public figures in East Asia continue to get into unnecessary controversy by arguing from contentious scientific data about relative IQ levels of different ethnic groups in the USA or the impact of American ethnic diversity. Inevitably, the statement of such views is seen in the USA as evidence of racism in Japan. That is one belief which Japanese companies can do without as they seek to penetrate western markets.

In the reverse direction, anti-Japanese sentiments are relatively widely held among western executives, and are expressed by many including Lee Iacocca in the USA or ex-premier Edith Cresson in France. Any western executive who allows such sentiments to go unchecked is doing his/her company no good at all. The success of Japan is real. There are solid reasons for it. Serious companies should be seeking to break into Japanese markets or perhaps collaborate with the Japanese. Indiscriminate Japan-bashing will hinder executives' comprehension of the Japanese phenomenon, and can damage cooperation with Japanese executives at a time when this may matter.

This is not a call for all our readers to become life members of the so-called Chrysanthemum Club – westerners who cannot admit that there is anything wrong in Japan at all. What is needed is a respect for Japan (and the USA), but allied to an intellectual honesty which can identify areas where either country can improve itself. Debates about the Japanese distribution or *Keiretsu* systems are just as legitimate as a discussion of the strengths and weaknesses of the American education and financial systems.

THE ENVIRONMENT

The one issue which can now be guaranteed to produce a popular reaction round the globe is the protection of the environment.

As each year goes by, this issue has grown in potency. Twenty years ago, the chemical industry was viewed relatively neutrally; now, all round the world, it is seen as a source of pollution which needs ever tighter controls. Already CFCs are to be phased out globally to protect the ozone layer. Now the 'greenhouse' gases (carbon dioxide to the fore) are increasingly coming under control too. The environmentalist agenda is continually widening, and now includes the issues of air pollution, the greenhouse effect, protection of the ozone layer, acid rain, toxic wastes, marine pollution, the preservation of Antartica, whaling and wildlife conservation in general.

These issues will remain a minefield for executives.

First, there are the 'time bombs' such as the growth of mega-lawsuits against companies whose actions years ago are still doing damage today. The world insurance industry, for instance is still having to meet claims for deaths caused by long ago exposure to asbestos. Chemical dumping is another activity capable of producing time-bomb lawsuits, but at the same time societies are becoming more sensitive to how chemicals (and other noxious products) are being dumped today.

Second, manufacturing companies all round the globe are having to work within increasingly tough regulations about factory emissions, the chemical content of processes and the possibility of recycling the product or its packaging. In energy consuming industries, there are a growing number of regulations and taxes designed to reduce the ecological damage from over-use of hydrocarbons (primarily oil and gas).

As concern grows for wildlife conservation, a new set of problems emerge. The issue of the use of animals for testing the safety of products has led to a wave of terrorist attacks by animal-rights activists on scientists, their labs, and executives with wider responsibilities. Growing concern for the preservation of the tropical rain forests has embroiled a range of companies from oil exploration companies, to hamburger chains, to the providers of disposable wooden chopsticks in Japan and elsewhere. Then there are bouts of almost total cultural incomprehension when western activists target the preservation of whales, dolphins or seals which countries such as Japan, Iceland or Norway may view as fair game. 'Wall of death' fishing practices in the Pacific are now causing clashes between cultures which may value animal life in noticeably different ways.

So what is the sensitive executive to do in such a complex area?

First, there is an absolute obligation to obey the relevant laws. This has to be stated, since executives may often have doubts about the scientific rationality of certain regulations designed to protect the environment. Companies are on a public relations hiding to nothing if they play games with the law in this area.

Second, they should try to ensure that their plants worldwide follow international best practice and are not notably more polluting in countries with slacker rules. Crusading journalists and politicians will inevitably whip up a storm where, say, a company slips standards in the Third World. The Union Carbide disaster at Bhopal illustrates the publicity a disaster now gets. A company which knowingly sets up a dangerous operation anywhere in the world will not be able to hide behind the excuse that local laws were lax. In fact, a number of companies now have a policy of applying environmental best-practice technology throughout the world. The bigger the company, the more such a policy makes tactical sense (assuming the ethical case is not otherwise conclusive).

Third, the company should of course feel free to enter the scientific and political debate leading to the creation of relevant international laws and regulations. Although environmental activists may be unhappy, corporate lobbying is a legitimate activity, and this is a classic area where companies may be able to steer the debate (which increasingly takes place in international fora) in directions which are least damaging to business.

Finally, companies should be aware that they are dealing with global sensitivities – and with issues which are becoming steadily more sensitive. On the latter point, companies should be flowing with the tide; there is absolutely no point in fighting the whole principle of tightening environmental controls. It is more difficult to know how to respond to sensitivities of people which may be very culture specific. For instance, even very sophisticated Japanese find it difficult to comprehend the value put by many westerners on preserving species. The issue of whaling is not particularly tied up with multinational companies, but the treatment of tropical rainforests increasingly is. The nub of some of these issues is simply how companies want to be perceived round the world. Any company has the freedom to ignore the views of international activists – but the larger the company, the more stupid such a strategy becomes.

All these suggestions have been negative ones, but environmental concerns offer commercial opportunities too. Sometimes these will be cynically exploited and it is remarkable how many companies have proudly discovered 'green' credentials. In a large number of cases, it is the marketing department who has led the discoveries. Conviction further down the line may be slightly less impressive.

On the other hand, there are cases like Britain's Body Shop, an international cosmetic manufacturer and retailer, using environmentally acceptable ingredients, but with no marketing department or advertising. The chain had sales of $238 million in 1991 and 78 outlets in the USA; its charismatic founder, Anita Roddick, who first developed many of her products from Third World sources, runs campaigns on behalf of institutions such as Amnesty International and issues such as saving the rain forests. Using franchising techniques, it has been growing fast over the last 16 years, but is now running into copycat operations run by Estee Lauder (Origins) and the Limited.

There are not many 'New Age' entrepreneurs with Roddick's credentials (Steve Jobs, one of Apple's founders, and Richard Branson the founder of Virgin Records and Virgin Airlines are two others with more of a counter-cultural background than most). However the bigger multinationals are moving into green areas with gusto.

To take one example: environmental services have now become a major sector in their own right, worth $130 billion in the USA alone. Companies in California, which is the world capital for the environmentalists, are learning how to hone their wares in this demanding state, so that they can be rolled out to other parts of the USA (or the world) as regulations move in the Californian direction. The state leads in the production of electricity from the wind and sun; by 2003, one in every ten autos sold in the state must be emission free, so General Motors is spending $1.3 billion to commercialize electric cars there. Major engineering companies such as Bechtel, Fluor, Daniel and Parsons are using their Californian experience to bid for projects like chemical waste treatment plants worldwide. Even defence giants like Lockheed and Hughes are seeking to diversify into environmental businesses.[4]

CORPORATE END-GAMES

Switches in public opinion may be of moderate importance to most industries, but they can be crucial in certain sectors.

Tobacco is a case in point where the medical evidence is damning, and the political pressures are steadily tightening all round the world – though outright bans on the manufacture of cigarettes still seem a long way off.

In such an industry, we are seeing an 'end-game' – that is a strategy designed to keep income up for as long as possible from the threatened product, while finding new businesses into which to diversify. The explains the thoroughness with which Philip Morris (the company behind Marlboro) has diversified into food since its acquisition of General Food in the mid 1980s, Kraft in 1988 and the Swiss chocolate company, Suchard, in 1990. Its British competitor, BAT, has diversified into financial services. Part of their strategy has been to maximize the global coverage of existing cigarette brands, which leads to ethical anxieties about the extent to which Third World countries are giving these companies an easier regulatory time than they get in the USA and parts of Western Europe.

A similar situation can be seen in alcohol. Here the health worries are less, though public attitudes toward this sector have been hardening. Certainly, growth prospects for products like whisky in the USA look increasingly problematic. This is one other reason why this is one industry which is particularly globalizing its brands.

And then there is the defence industry throughout the industrialized world. No US Surgeon General will declare this an industry injurious to health. However, the ending of the Cold War has left a number of companies in the USA, the UK and elsewhere with the major problem of converting a significant proportion of their activities to peaceful uses. This will be easier said than done. For one thing, the defence colossi are generally poor marketers, in that they have traditionally done most of their selling to bureaucrats in place likes the Pentagon. Secondly, their whole attitude to production tends to be wrong for a fast-moving world in which production costs matter greatly. Typically, the defence industries have over-engineered products, since reliability in extreme conditions is what has traditionally mattered to them. In consumer goods, reliability clearly matters, but products do not have to be designed to, say, withstand the radiation from a nuclear explosion.

FROM COLD WAR TO GLOBAL COMPETITION

Those of us with decent-paying jobs will find that the emerging world is going to favour us as consumers. As such, we will be able to choose products from anywhere in the world, and we will be offered a plethora of models, with ranges of functions which will increase significantly year by year. Progress in electronic projects will continue to amaze. In a whole range of other products, such as automobiles, we will increasingly be able to buy models which are virtually personalized. In so far as we are socially conscious, the technologies used to produce these products will become cleaner and generally more environmentally friendly.

If, however, one is one of the executives charged with achieving this consumer's nirvana, then the world will look very different. The technology to achieve what consumers want will be available, but the pace of competitive change is going to remain horrendous, and may yet become even faster. Part of the competitive pressure will come from a steady stream of foreign competitors, often based in countries with considerable lower wage rates. Many of the pressures for change will come from the way that the IT revolution is changing every aspect of the executive's job. Add to that, the need to come to terms with an increasing range of national cultures as one's company is forced to go global to survive, while social attitudes require even greater social and environmental sensitivity.

In competitive terms, there will be a battle for survival in which competition can come from virtually any direction, and in a number of different forms. The successful executive will be technically aware, socially sensitive, geographically cosmopolitan and must have the competitive instincts of a ravening beast. Of the would-be global players, only the very fittest will survive. We are entering an era of corporate decimation.

13

LIFE IN A WORLD OF SUPER-COMPETITION: THE NEW CHALLENGES

IN THE LATE 1960s, the Canadian sociologist Marshall McLuhan was one of the earliest people to write about the impact of electronics on society. He looked back fondly to the pre-Gutenberg (i.e. pre-printing press) world, when life was lived amidst vibrant and close-knit communities. With the coming of electronics, he saw an end to the relative isolation which a book-driven culture imposed on people. He saw and approved of the revolutionary capability of electronics to allow citizens to interact in the 'global village', returning people to a sense of community – in this case a global one – which had been lost so many centuries ago.[1] While many people scoffed at McLuhan's ideas, today they do not seem so far-fetched.

Over two decades later, the shelves of airport bookshops are stacked with titles of which he would have approved: *The Borderless World* (Ohmae), *The End of Geography* (O'Brien), *The Global Factory* (Grunwald and Flamm (eds)), even one proclaiming *The End of History* (Fukuyama). If he could browse the shelves, the former guru would be chuckling to himself. He might not have approved of all the social attitudes expressed in these tomes. However, he would have recognized the world that they are analysing.

The electronic revolution he identified is now fundamentally reshaping the nature of the world system. In this book, we have emphasized its impact on the nature of corporate competition, because that is one of the most dramatic ways in which the revolution is affecting world society. But this aspect of technology-induced change is part of a broader revolution that will affect virtually every aspect of our lives.

What, then, are the challenges this revolution is posing?

THE TRIPLE CHALLENGE

We are all facing a triple challenge to the way we live now – to our economies, our cultures and our political systems. There is no part of our lives today that is immune from the sweeping influence of the super-competitive world.

The first challenge is that we all have to survive the economic battle now raging round the world. The pace of competitive change is quickening. It is not just companies which are being tested to the limit by this intensified competition. It is the economies of proudly independent nations which are now clashing. They may not be vulnerable to bankruptcy as companies are, but they can be severely dented. In a super-competitive world, to respond too slowly is to lose ground. We have shown that classic *dirigiste* industrial policies may not be the answer: bureaucrats are not well-equipped to second-guess the market or to pick winners. However, no politician can afford to stop thinking of how the competitiveness of his/her national economy can be strengthened – this will be Item One on every electoral agenda.

The second challenge is for the world of nations to come to terms with the cultural impact of an emergent, globalized mongrel culture on traditional national cultures. This 'cosmo-culture' is partly driven by the needs of the international business élite – the businessman with the Louis Vuitton luggage, Mitsubishi cellular telephone and Hertz #1 Club car rental card. Global corporations have a vested interest in developing a core culture – however mongrelized it may be – around the world's big spenders. To these companies' marketers, distinctive ethnic cultures may have a role in adding novelty and richness to the cosmo-culture – as long as this is confined to style rather than substance. True cultural differences add to the costs of selling globally: they are diseconomies of scale. However much they may protest, the global corporate giants are deeply subversive institutions as far as national cultures are concerned.

The third, less obvious, challenge is to comprehend how the electronic revolution, which has already triggered radical new approaches to corporate management, is ultimately going to affect the political management of the new world order. Competitive pressures mean that technological change makes its impact most swiftly on the corporate sector – and these effects have only been felt in their full intensity over the last decade or so – and its full impact on the international political scene may not be felt until sometime in the next century.

COPING WITH SUPER-COMPETITION: THE ECONOMIC CHALLENGE

There are some economic developments which the world's politicians, business executives and workers will just have to accept.

The first is that the economic ascent of Japan and some of surrounding East Asia relative to the rest of the world is firmly based and will not evaporate – though the countries in this region will find that catching up with best western practice will prove easier than moving ahead of the *gaijin*.

A second element is that the line demarcating the international comparative advantage of the average Third World country *vis-à-vis* a given advanced industrial country over the coming decades will depend on the outcome of a fascinating battle between the expansion of a disciplined, educated, cheap labour force in the former, and the continued application of sophisticated, flexible technologies to the production methods of the latter. It is not inconceivable that the threat of cheap labour will be rolled back on several fronts by the application of 'Post-Ford', Lean Production techniques. However, this will only be achieved in conjunction with continued organizational turmoil as the western industrial system is adapted to the needs of this new era.

Third, there will be no competitive hiding place for any economy – anywhere in the world. Maintaining one's relative competitive position in the global economy will require a continuous fine-tuning of the relationship between management, government and the work force, with increasing emphasis paid to the educational and training systems which determine how productive and adaptable a country's human capital actually is.

East Asia and parts of Latin America are going to contribute the shock troops of the New Industrial Competitors. The end of the Cold War and the collapse of the old Soviet empire is more likely to produce an area of economic and political turbulence than a major new source of economic competition. There is very little evidence that the citizens of the former Soviet bloc have the mind-sets needed to develop the industrial dynamism found in other parts of the world, and they do not start with a clean slate: they have inherited an antiquated industrial structure and a poisoned environment.

JAPAN IS HERE TO STAY

One uncomfortable fact which 'western' public opinion has got to accept is that the competitive pressures from Japan are just not going to go away. The current difficulties Japan is facing in reforming its political, financial and property systems in the aftermath of the collapse of the 'bubble economy' of the 1980s, are far outweighed by the internal dynamism of its manufacturing sector. As long as trade in manufactured goods provides the dynamic core of the international trading system, either exports from Japan or goods produced overseas by Japanese companies will be at the heart of the world economy. There is nothing that the west can do about this.

This success will not be universally welcomed. For one thing, the Japanese political culture is badly equipped for steering it through the coming diplomatic minefields. A cultural unwillingness to take strong, controversial positions is one disadvantage. The country's history of relative isolation means that it lacks the depth of geopolitical awareness that one finds in powers with a longer internationalist history, such as the USA, France and the UK. Finally, Japan's tradition of viewing the world from an economic standpoint will frequently get it into trouble in an era when the rise of nationalist sentiment in the former Soviet empire and, perhaps, some parts of the Third World (now that Yugoslavia has been allowed to unbundle, how long will Africa be satisfied with its mostly artificial colonial boundaries?) is of growing importance.

There is sufficient xenophobia in the west and within Japan itself to make the acceptance of the latter as an economic super power an ill-tempered affair.

Japan clearly evinces a degree of contempt about the inability of western competitors to get their act together. This shows itself in the regular journalistic coups that quote senior Japanese politicians and industrialists bad-mouthing the educational standards, intellectual capabilities and (particularly counter-productive) the racial hetero-geneity of western competitors.

Such attitudes clearly run deeply in Japanese society. One of the authors vividly remembers being harangued for an hour in the early 1980s by a very senior Japanese electronics executive about the sheer stupidity of the Europeans trying to preserve small, uncompetitive electronics plants. The economic logic of his argument was impeccable. What was fascinating, though, was that he clearly could not begin to comprehend how the Europeans would be appalled at the short-term human cost of industrial restructuring, and the lost chances for industrial policy. Equally fascinating was the sheer intensity of his argument. He could not see why economic rationality should be resisted in any way whatsoever – and such western resistance obviously angered him. This economic logic, however, is not applied to the continuing Japanese protection of their marginal and inefficient rice-growers!

In examples like this, cultural insensitivity on the side of the economic-ally victorious Japanese gives them an image of arrogance. This image is irritating to foreigners but ultimately irrelevant, since the super-competitivity of the Japanese industrial juggernaut will remain a crucial factor in the future. Nevertheless, this streak of insensitivity will undoubtedly hinder the effective globalization of Japanese companies.

Much more important is the time-lag that will occur before the once-dominant economic powers – particularly, the USA – come to terms with the fact that Japanese super-competitivity is not going to go away.

The reason this is important is that there is going to be considerable psychological resistance to acceptance of this fact. Just as it has taken the more xenophobic Europeans at least thirty years to accept that they can live with the American industrial challenge, it is going to take decades for mainstream European and American public opinion to come to terms with the Japanese challenge and view it in rational and relatively dispassionate terms. We use the adjective 'mainstream' advisedly, because there are countries like the United Kingdom which have accepted relative industrial decline reasonably gracefully, and have extended to Japanese industrialists the relatively warm welcome which it offered the earlier wave of American inward investment. Some parts of the older industrialized world will find it easier to come to terms with the super-competitive world than others.

In general, though, we are in the midst of an unpleasant era where 'Japan-bashing' has a racist element which was missing in Europe's early resistance to the Americans (though some of the anti-American sentiments ran very deep indeed and also inspired a form of industrial paranoia). However, it is essential that the western powers come to terms with Japan's super-competition as fast as possible, because a new competitive balance will not emerge until they undertake an unemotional analysis of the strategies needed for survival in the Post-Fordist world.

What the older industrialized powers have to accept is that they have entered an era in which there will be absolutely no respite from the competitive pressure which will be applied from Japan and the other East Asian tigers. Putting protectionist barriers up will not slow Japan's competitive advance. Its companies will continue to progress in third markets, wiping out the export markets of their protected western competitors. Direct investment by Japanese firms within the protected home markets of its competitors – as with the establishment of 'transplant' production in the US after so-called 'voluntary' export restraints were imposed in the early 1980s – will simply intensify the Japanese competitive challenge. On the other hand, what evidence there is suggests that protection slows down the adaptive response of protected companies. Protectionism will thus probably undercut the return to competitiveness of western companies. It will not slow the Japanese down, but it will slow western responses.

If protectionism is ruled out, attention should focus instead on strategies which may at least start to give the older industrial powers a chance to hold their own.

Mimicking the Japanese system is not the way forward. The time is long past when the creation of super industry ministries like MITI makes any sense. The guiding role played in Japan by the likes of MITI owed a great deal to the precise way in which company-government relations evolved in the immediate post-1945 period in Japan. MITI's targeted intervention was also relatively easy while Japan was tracking and catching the USA. Now that Japan has caught up with the west, it is far from clear that MITI's visions of the future are any better than those of any other intelligent planner contemplating a world of turbulence and uncertainty.

Similarly, we are not convinced that there is much the west can or should do about its allegedly short-sighted financial markets. It was easy for Japanese planners to think long-term when their economy was in its long, successful catch-up mode – and when the Japanese financial system was quite consciously biased in favour of the corporate sector at the expense of individual savers. With the collapse of the bubble economy, the Japanese economy is moving into a new financial era. We predict that coming decades will show the planning horizons of Japanese companies receding quit rapidly towards those of the more far-sighted 'old' capitalists like Germany.

What does make some sense is that western executives and policy-makers should openly accept that Japanese management systems moved ahead of those of the west in key areas during the 1970s and 1980s. It is only after this is acknowledged that western companies can get down to the long-drawn out task of adopting those parts of the 'Lean Management' armoury of techniques which can be exported into non-Japanese cultures. These will include devices such as Just-in-time inventory systems, parallel engineering, and the deepening of relations with favoured component suppliers. Although there is a current belief (which we do not share) that the *Keiretsu* system gives Japanese companies a competitive advantage, there is clearly no point in trying to transfer that to western business cultures. Even if anti-trust authorities would tolerate the attempt, *Keiretsu* are far too culture-specific for export to the west. What can be adopted profitably from the system, though, is the long-term relation-ships between component suppliers and end-assemblers which, if developed constructively, clearly can bring competitive advantages, particularly at the product development stage. The collaboration can even be extended – in a way that it has not been in Japan – to create a meaningful partnership between management and the workforce.

Basically the challenge to the west is a managerial one, and the best strategy home country governments can follow is to ram home to their companies that they have entered a world of intercontinental, super-competition – and that there is no hiding place. Either they turn themselves around, or they go under. This is a message which has been slow to filter through to many giant companies. The problem with firms like Philips and General Motors in the 1980s had little to do with short-termism (the Dutch electronics companies had some of the best long-term research in the world); rather, they failed to accept that their managerial performance had fallen well behind Japanese standards. It is only because they have each now gone through a managerial crisis and have recognized the scale of the new challenge that they have a chance for survival.

Arguably, the first contribution governments can make is to insist that they are not going to give protection to their national champions against world competition – from wherever it may come. The German govern-ment takes German performance in export markets as a criterion of success, and, under Mrs Thatcher, the UK took this stance for at least a decade. In both cases, it is arguable that the competitiveness of their respective companies has been enhanced in the international arena.

Less controversially, governments have an indispensable role to play in creating the infrastructure needed to support competitive businesses. Partly, this means concentrating on the competitiveness of sectors such as telecommunications, underlying financial markets and air transport – hence the competitive importance of the relative early liberalization and deregulation of such sectors. The cheap and flexible provision of such services is now just as important as providing traditional infrastructures like effective road, rail, electricity or postal systems.

Increasingly, though, improving infrastructure means improving the quality of educational systems. One of the lessons for western policy-makers is that competition coming out of East Asia is based on a very effective educational system. The proportion of Japanese in higher education is roughly equivalent to the (high) rates of the USA, and well above the proportions found in West Europe. When one considers performance in particularly functional areas such as mathematical skills, the Japanese look even better. Many western countries are therefore trying to speed techno-logical and competitive change on inadequate educational foundations. This is a recipe for continued relative decline. One of the reasons the Japanese can manage so well is that they have an alert, numerate, well-educated work-force below them. As the 'Post-Ford' factory floor becomes a place demanding intellect more than brute force or mere dexterity, a country's educational levels become a major item in its competitive armoury. It is in areas like this that the 'long-termism' issue should really focus. Educational systems take decades to reform or expand – and this is one area where only governments can move.

THE INTERNATIONAL DIVISION OF LABOUR: THE FLUCTUATING BATTLE FRONT

Our message about the need for western societies to respond to the era of super-competitivity would be the same even if Japan were taken out of the frame.

Japan's success has shown the way for a subsequent generation of fledgling industrial powers – the Four Tigers and their imitators in East Asia; the leading Latin Americans and so on. The west is deceiving itself if it thinks that it only has to cope with competition from Japan. Even this super-competitor is having to react extremely fast in order to stay ahead of cheaper-labour competitors such as South Korea and Taiwan. The pressures from this next wave of super-competitors will not die away in the lifetime of any of our readers.

Admittedly, few of these economies start with such a favourable mix of circumstances as Japan did, but, even so, these new competitors are mostly led by well-educated, increasingly market-oriented élites who will make the most of their competititve opportunities. Their work-forces are young, ambitious and, once again, much better educated than their relatively short industrial history would suggest. All these countries have learned a lot from Japan on how to play the catch-up game.

Once again, protectionism is not the answer. The general rise in Third World competitive capabilities will defeat the purposes of the protectionists. Protection can do nothing to save the export markets of beleaguered First World companies. Companies which can only sell in protected home markets have no future in today's super-competitive global markets.

What can be done is to see how far the application of Lean Production techniques can be used to offset the competition from disciplined, literate, cheap labour from the new Third World export platforms, which are increasingly integrated into world markets through the steady improvement of global information systems. Quite clearly, the competition between flexible manufacturing systems and Third World aspirations is only in its infancy. The electronic revolution is working to help both sides of the international division of labour . . . and no one can yet foresee how this competition will ultimately end.

One senses that it will probably be possible for the older industrial powers to hold on to some key industries for several decades longer than seemed possible some ten or fifteen years ago. However, the older powers are going to have to work long and continuously to defend their competitiveness. The executives of all key companies must accept that they cannot relax the pressure for productivity improvements for a moment. In the background, home governments must equally accept the need for continued improvements. Without this commitment to continuous acceptance of change from top to bottom of the industrial chain, the older powers will steadily lose ground. However, with such a commitment, they at least have a chance of maintaining their competitive ground.

COPING WITH SUPER-COMPETITION: THE CULTURAL IMPACT

This competitive world bodes well for a considerable part of the globe. For those who can get their feet on the 'catch-up' tread-mill, life will continue hard-working, but should promise steady progression in material well-being. Few will be able to emulate the peculiar success of Japan, but there should be nothing to stop a number of countries emulating the success of, say, South Korea which has, over a couple of generations of fast growth, hauled itself up to a level of prosperity equal to that of the poorer parts of Europe. The catch-up phenomenon may get harder as existing industrialized powers become more adept at applying labour-saving technologies and at developing fast-moving, highly targeted marketing strategies. On the other hand, the information revolution means that productivity growth will remain healthy within the Third World as a whole.

This does not necessarily guarantee increased prosperity throughout the Third World. There are limits, for instance, to the extent that high productivity in parts of a partially-traditional economy can do to counter the effects of a population explosion. Nor can it do much in places like the

Horn of Africa where political confusion and ecological disaster walk hand in hand. Finally, there is always the danger within parts of the Third World (and within the ex-Soviet empire) of a vicious circle of hyperinflation and weak central governments; if countries get drawn into this classic 'Latin American' quagmire, one is more likely to see relative economic decline than a steady 'catching-up' with the west.

The future for the citizens of mature economies is less certain. As far as Japan is concerned, continued relative economic progress should be possible, as long as its workforce remains productive. There are signs, though, that demands are growing for a life-style which is based on more than work-for-the-sake-of-work. Japanese executives who serve abroad return home knowing that there are countries where people take three or more week vacations each year, where weekends are relatively sacrosanct and where employees can generally expect to get home to their families in the early evening – not near midnight. At the same time, company recruiters are discovering a growing resistance among graduate engineers to what they call '5K' careers. These are jobs which are *'kiken'* (dangerous), *'kitani'* (dirty), *'kitsui'* (demanding), *'kurai'* (dark) and *'kakkowarui'* (unbecoming).

This revulsion against industrial life will take time to work its way through a system which remains heavily skewed towards the company and work. One would expect top Japanese executives to bemoan the trend away from the work ethic, but it is unlikely to slow the Japanese economy significantly for some years to come.

Rather, one suspects that the pressures will fall on North America and West Europe, two continents which had hoped that they were moving toward a 'post-industrial' society in which a steady shift toward services and knowledge-work would provide enough well-paid, pleasant work to compensate for the loss of all those dirty blue-collar jobs.

The early evidence is that this transition is going to be very selective, and that there may well be as many losers as winners in the process. Adjustment to the quickening tempo of global competition means that the massive shakeout of middle management from bloated corporate bureaucracies will continue, and that the qualities needed on the shop-floor increasingly include serious intellectual capabilities. The core companies which make such adjustments in time will continue to be effective world competitors, but the employees who are discarded are precisely those who are coming under competitive threat from the regimented, cheap labour economies of the four Tigers and their competitors just below them.

Evidence from the USA suggests that the 1960s was the last decade which gave genuine increased prosperity throughout the labour force. Since then, average living standards have stagnated as first the oil price revolution and then the Japanese commercial invasion hit home. Again, there is evidence that working conditions of parts of the labour force are deteriorating. Those left in corporate hierarchies are having to work longer hours with reduced fringe benefits, and rising health care and college education costs are placing the American Dream – of living standards rising in each generation – out of reach of the large, self-designated middle class.

If the working environment has worsened in the USA, which is still relatively highly productive, then West Europe has some tough delayed adjustment round the corner. There is a stronger anti-industrial ethos in parts of Europe than in Japan and the USA, and (in Northern Europe at least) higher levels of social welfare provision. The intensity of education is generally lower in Europe than elsewhere (though German technical education is strong). Annual hours of work are generally significantly lower than in Japan and the USA.

None of this bodes well for Europe as a whole, though improved regional integration through the 1992 process, and the inclusion of EFTA and the former East European economies in a wider economic zone, should continue to provide an economic lift.

None of this is to argue that global standards of living will not continue to increase – on average. It is, though, quite possible that their rise will be partly at the expense of the older industrial powers, which could include the USA and many of the countries in Western Europe. Relative economic decline is nothing new. Britain, for instance, has been in such relative decline for well over 150 years – and there are spectacular cases of countries such as Uruguay and Argentina which in the early 1900s were among the richest countries in the world but which virtually went into free-fall as the result of faulty economic policies that failed to adjust to global market conditions.

As we write, the smooth transition to a post-industrial society capable of providing a steadily rising standard of living to all its members looks increasingly problematic on both sides of the Atlantic. Some sectors of society are sure to adjust to the quickened pace of international competition, and part of their strategy may well be to move away from hardware toward software or systems-integrating activities. There will however be losers. As educational differentials narrow between the older and newer industrial powers, there will be less and less room for poorly-educated 'hewers of wood and drawers of water'. Both brawn and dexterity can be designed into machines – or they can be replicated in an ever-expanding part of the world at a fraction of labour costs found in the older powers. The position of the traditional blue-collar worker, the under-educated, the unintelligent or the lazy in the west looks increasingly bleak. If the lead parts of these economies fail to compete effectively, then the plight of these unfortunates looks even worse.

COSMO-CULTURE: THE DAY OF THE MONGREL?

We are part-way through a period of extraordinary cultural upheaval. Hitherto well-defined national cultures are under challenge from an emerging global culture, which is a mongrel culture taking its language (Standard English) from the Anglo-Americans, its pop idols from the USA, its prestige brands from Europe, its films and television from Hollywood, its employment practices from a meld of Detroit and Osaska, its leisure electronics from Japan, its business ethics from New York and Washington, its sport from a series of television extravaganzas from around the world, its royalty from London and its clothing from Macao and Thailand (though styled in New York and Paris).

Obviously, this is an over-simplification. But we have now gone beyond the stage where it is only the élites of the industrialized world that have a culture in common. Today, anyone who has entered the market economy and (in particular) has access to a radio or television starts imbibing this culture.

There are paradoxes in all this. On the one hand, national cultures have never been more important as 430 million people try to chart a meaningful future after the collapse of the Soviet empire in which they lived. Similarly, fundamentalism is still spreading through the Islamic world, at least partly in a reaction to the materialistic mongrel culture we are describing. Since such nationalism and religious fundamentalism will probably give birth to wars and terrorism which could increasingly involve nuclear, chemical or biological weapons the relevant upsurge of these forces has to be taken extremely seriously.

On the other hand, these searches for a coherent and distinctive local culture are becoming less and less successful. Involvement in the world economy means an involvement with this mongrel culture, and only the most intense core cultures will remain reasonably impervious to change.

The mechanisms for the spreading of this culture are clear. Top government officials, executives, politicians and scientists have increasingly to work in Standard English if they are to be effective. Once that barrier is broken, then the flow of English-language papers and management journals begins. *The Harvard Business Review* and *The Economist* are the new keys to salvation dispensed by the missionaries of the global market to the ruling classes. As imports are opened up, the global marketers appear. Japanese trucks and radios start selling; the Anglo-American oil companies (where allowed) set up their signs; the Coke-versus-Pepsi battle will begin; the Marlboro cowboy will ride into town; the travelling élite will return home with their global brand products (a counterfeit Lacoste sports shirt? A real Rolex watch? The latest Samsonite suitcase?).

Then there is the impact of radio, television and the video-cassette which are breaking down the cultural monopoly that national broadcasting authorities once had. For a number of decades, it was radio which played the dominant cultural role. To the Soviet system, Voice of America and the BBC's World Service were potentially subversive. To the old imperial powers (Britain, France and the USA), the use President Nasser made of Egypt's radio transmitters to advocate pan-Arabism in the 1950s was also deeply subversive, though, in fact, what Nasser was doing was strengthening an Arab sense of cultural and political identity. Later leaders such as the Ayatollah Khomeini in Iran were to strengthen the Islamic content of such messages. An analysis of the rise of Islamic self-confidence cannot be divorced from an analysis of the media through which the message has been passed.

In general, though, the broadcast media have become important agents for the transmission of the mongrel culture. Starting with the American forces radio channels in the aftermath of World War 2, radio became an important force for spreading internationally the impact of US-originated popular music. Television, with its limited broadcasting range, usually remained the captive of the guardians of national culture, though the low acquisition costs and the superior production values of American TV shows made even the most culturally defensive state television authorities receptive to the subversive consumerism of the *Dick van Dyke Show* or *Bonanza*.

The rise of video-cassettes and the spread of satellite and cable-transmitted broadcasting is removing these cultural defences. In large parts of the world, the cultural guardians can no longer dictate what their citizens can or cannot see. So, whenever viewers watch a film on video-cassette from Hollywood (or Bombay or Hong Kong), or satellite news or pop music channel, they are effectively immersing themselves into the mongrel culture – and the job of the cultural guardians becomes that much more difficult.

For good or ill, the diffusion of new culture is overwhelmingly a one-way flow. Obviously, as each country opens up to the mongrel culture it has the opportunity to add a few items to the mix. So, Korea gives the world ginseng; the North Africans add cous-cous to the international variety of foods; the Mexicans add tequila and the Caribbeans reggae music. However, even the Japanese, with a proud culture and a particularly strong economy, have run a significant balance-of-culture deficit as they have emerged into the world. The geographical centre of the mongrel culture will remain somewhere to the east of Hollywood, with the growing importance of Japan slowly pulling it toward the Pacific.

The pervasiveness of this evolving culture will cause serious psychic problems for a number of political centres. If one is British or American, the problems are minimal. The working language is English, and the Anglo-American strands within this new culture remain quite firm. Viewed, however, from Paris or Tokyo, the picture is very different. The Japanese at least will have the psychic satisfaction of knowing that the dynamism of their economy will compensate for some of the cultural depredations which they will otherwise suffer. The position of the French is more serious, for they will have to suffer both relative economic and cultural decline at the same time. The fact that they will be losing ground simultaneously to Germany, Japan and the mongrel culture will be psychologically very difficult to handle.

As one moves to smaller, more fragile cultures the position seemingly becomes more depressing. How can one preserve a national culture, perhaps sustaining a population of not much more than a couple of million people, in the face of all these commercial and technological forces?

In practice, the picture need not be so bleak. The rise of Islamic self-confidence indicates that cultures can gain strength from the very act of rejecting the values of the mongrel culture. As the experience of countries that were unified over a century ago (Germany, Italy, the US) clearly shows, substantial cultural differences can survive against what seem to be overwhelming odds. This is relevant to many of the small nations which are emerging from the Soviet shadow. They will have enough problems of direct political survival to keep the nationalist flame burning bright for some time yet. Historic tensions between Serbs and Croats, or between Estonians and Russians run far too deep to be softened by the lure of new global cultures. People are still willing to die for nations or religions. It matters to them that they are Lithuanians, Kurds, Azeris, Jews, Arabs and so on. The new mongrel culture is superficial in comparison. Who has ever gone to the barricades for the sake of Madonna, Marlboro or Coca-Cola? The internationalist consumer society they represent is a pleasant aspiration, but people are only willing to die for older, more primitive beliefs.

Having said all that, one should not be too dismisive of the emerging global culture. The pop stars and the fast food chains can give the impression that it is a superficial phenomenon which should be treated with a fair amount of contempt, but that would be misleading. First, one must accept that popular culture should not be dismissed purely because it is popular and youth-oriented. Michael Jackson and the Big Mac are both recognized world-wide because they have recognizable strengths in their respective fields and an appeal that transcends cultural boundaries. Nor is this cultural diffusion limited to mass culture – the high culture of the elites is also becoming globalized. Knowledge of painters, film directors and other visually-oriented artists is now spread around the triad world. Thus the Japanese buy Van Goghs; London plays host to a Hokusai exhibition; Italian and Spanish operatic tenors sing to mass arenas on every continent; and the world's leading architects migrate to wherever the money is – primarily Tokyo, Frankfurt and Hong Kong. In literature, there is an international elite of serious authors such as Gunter Grass (German), Vaclev Havel (Czechoslovak), Yukio Mishima (Japanese), Gabriel Garcia-Marquez (Colombian-Mexican), and Wole Soyinka (Nigerian) whose works are regularly translated and published world-wide, showing that there is no Anglo-Saxon monopoly on international recognition.

Our mongrel culture thus exists at many levels and should be accepted for what it is – an amalgam of the best and/or most commercially-driven works or products from around the world, but biased towards the English-speaking world. The geographical weighting of the most important influences at work on it will fluctuate as specific cultures gain or lose artistic and commercial influence. It will, though, always remain a mongrel phenomenon. It will always offer a threat to purists trying to preserve national cultures. To them, it may often appear vulgar and trivial. At heart, though, the mongrel culture is internationalist. The world may be safer as a result.

COPING WITH SUPER-COMPETITION: TECHNOLOGY'S IMPACT ON THE POLITICAL SYSTEM

One theme of this book has been the profound impact that technological change is having on the nature of global competition and corporate structures. Inevitably, this will have implications for governments.

One need for governments is to decide how far they need to go down the sponsored research-consortium route (Esprit in Europe, Sematech in the US, the Fifth Generation project in Japan). This is a question for industrial policy. There are clearly some benefits to such sponsored activities, but there is no evidence that governments have any special insight into how industrial structures will really move over the next couple of decades. What governments have to address is not the task of picking winners, but how they themselves can best adapt to the era of global competition.

The first observation to be made is that government structures have generally responded to the technological revolution in communications and data processing much less radically than companies have been forced to. The latter have been ruthlessly laying off middle ranking managers, closing plants down, transferring production overseas, and generally applying advanced information technology throughout their organizations. There seem to be very few governmental examples of the kind of radical response which has been forced upon, for example, IBM. (Some government departments we have visited in the triad world seem to be only just entering the computer age.)

. . . and yet, there is movement, suggesting that government policies are responding to developments in international communications by an increased institutional fluidity. For instance, although the end of the Cold War explains a lot, there is a sense that building ad hoc international decision-making groups is becoming easier. Witness the relative ease with which the alliance against Iraq's President Saddam was put together: much of the diplomacy was carried out within the United Nations, but the smoothness of the operation tells us a lot about the effectiveness of communications between the UN and the various national capitals. In another case, one can point to the rolling foreign policy representation of the European Community, in which the EC is represented by the country which has just taken on the EC Presidency for its six month term, forming a troika with the country which has just stepped down and the one which will take over next. This is a kind of permanently evolving institution building which the best run companies will appreciate.

Similarly, it must be a sign of health in the world system that Russia's Boris Yeltsin was receiving phone calls from a western prime minister (Britain's John Major) in the middle of the August 1991 coup in the Soviet Union. The ability of the world's leaders to talk to each other on the spur of the moment is one of the most satisfactory aspects of the contemporary diplomatic usage of improved telecommunications facilities.

However, there is a dark side to the technological optimism of much of this book. The same dynamics which ensure that middle ranking countries can be global competitors also make it increasingly easy for them to get access to sensitive technologies (nuclear, chemical, biological) which can be used for war or terrorism against their neighbours or more distant targets.

Most aspects of this problem are frightening. As technological knowledge diffuses, the problems of mastering these technologies get easier. As there are an increasing number of technology-oriented companies in emerging countries, the number of players capable of acquiring the relevant technologies will steadily grow. As technology encourages the miniaturization of industrial processes, the chances of terrorist successes will grow.

This book does not attempt to propose solutions for this problem, but any solutions will have to involve very careful monitoring of sensitive activities in a very wide range of companies – and countries. The global market will need more than Adam Smith's hidden hand to regulate it.

The prospects in this area are depressing; but it is well to be reminded that competition will not be limited to an economic form just because the Cold War is over. It can still come through war and terrorism. Technology is playing into the hands of the new competitors in both forms of competition.

No Hiding Place

There is an old Leslie Bricusse-Anthony Newley Broadway musical called '*Stop the World – I want to get off*'. Today that is just not possible.

In the age of super-competition, there is no way that any government or company can opt for an easy life. Always, somewhere out there in the rest of the world, there will be other companies – sometimes highly automated; sometimes relying on cheap Third World labour – which will be moving ahead.

This message is not aimed solely at the Americans and Europeans. It holds good just as much for the Japanese and for the new competitors who are hitting world markets in their wake.

By not accepting the new competitive realities, both companies and governments can go down ultimately self-destructive blind alleys. The biggest single mistake any one of them can make is to assume that the waves of inter-continental competition which are now hitting all of us are somehow or other the result of unfair practices. They are not.

The reason that competition is now genuinely on a global, inter-continental basis is thanks to the way the electronic revolution is changing competitive parameters throughout the world system. In many cases, it is helping bring new competitors into play. In other manifestations, though, it is also helping the older powers to hang on to their relative positions.

This super-competition will undoubtedly bring pain in its wake. Companies will go bust. Communities will find that their main employers have been driven out of business. Whole nations will find their economies are in apparently unstoppable relative decline.

. . . and we can offer no nice simple solutions.

To reach blindly for protectionist solutions is merely to make the underlying problems worse. The pace of global competitive improvements is not going to slow down because any nation – however large its economy – shuts itself off from the world.

All one can offer, then, is a series of uncomfortable maxims:

For executives:

- Fully understand how the evolution of communications technology is going to affect the way your own particular industry fits into the global market place

- Assess the ways in which the electronic revolution is going to affect the production technology of your industry

- Constantly monitor your competitors (current and potential ones) wherever they may be in the world

- Always have an action-oriented strategy in place to respond to technological and competitive change from wherever it may come

- Think globally: understand your technology: constantly speed your product development: consistently improve your productivity

- Do not, for a single month, rest on your competitive laurels. To stand still, is to fall behind.

For public officials:

- The growing intensity of inter-continental competition is here to stay, and there is nothing any single or group of politicians can do to slow this

- Do not let emotion (particularly racism) blind you to the sources of this trend, which is technologically, not politically driven

- Governments can best help by preparing their citizens for the realities of a super-competitive world – particularly by adequately educating, training and (where necessary) helping to retrain and redeploy them from declining industries to growth-oriented sectors

- Governments can help companies by consistently improving the communications and financial services infrastructure on which world class firms rely. This is why governments which liberalize sectors such as telecommunications, financial services and airlines ahead of the pack will win their economy a competitive advantage

- Policy-makers and civil servants cannot guess the future any better than any other actor in the super-competitive world. Facilitate forward thinking, but don't impose institutional straitjackets

- Xenophobia is a false friend to national politicians in a world of global competition – the 'not invented here' syndrome cripples governments as well as firms

For the average worker or citizen anywhere in the world:

- Life is going to be increasingly tough for the ill-educated, lazy or those resistant to change: factories and offices can get their brute strength or dexterity from machines

- The super-competitive world will still be a rich one, but the wealth will shift towards societies which are adaptable and internationalist in their outlook

- The Global Village will exist, and much of what it provides will be beneficial and even fun. However, an intensification of competition between continents is an inevitable part of this 'Village' life. This will be unpalatable to many – but is inevitable

For everyone – politicians, executives, shop-floor workers, or just plain citizen-consumers:

- In the age of super-competition, there will be absolutely no hiding place: it affects us all, and we all have an important role to play in enhancing competitiveness and exploiting our strengths

- Work to improve your competitiveness, or slide backwards; continuous change and improvement must become a tradition rather than an intermittent and disjointed response to extreme circumstances

- **Super-competition will be a merciless task-master, but a rewarding one**

NOTES AND REFERENCES

Chapter 2
1. *The Observer*, 1 September 1991.
2. *Fortune*, p. 54, 3 June 1991.
3. *International Herald Tribune*, p. 5, 19–20 January 1991.
4. See Yates, J and Benjamin, R I, 'The Past and Present as a Window on the Future', in Scott Morton, M S (ed.) (1991) *The Corporation of the 1990s: Information Technology and Organizational Transformation*, New York: Oxford University Press.
5. Scott Morton, M S, *ibid*.
6. *International Herald Tribune*, p. 14, 14 February 1989.
7. O'Brien, R (1992) *Global Financial Integration: The End of Geography*, London: Royal Institute of International Affairs/Pinter.
8. *Fortune*, p. 58, 3 June 1991; see also Yates, J and Benjamin, R I, *op. cit.*
9. Shevardnadze, E (1991) *The Future Belongs to Freedom*, summarized in *The Observer*, p. 21, 1 September 1991.
10. *Financial Times*, p. 12, 18 January 1991.
11. *Fortune*, p. 38, 17 June 1991.
12. Womack, J P, Jones, D T and Roos, D (1990) *The Machine that Changed the World*, New York: Rawson Associates.
13. *The Economist*, p. 15, 4 April 1992.
14. Womack, J P, *et al*, *op. cit.*
15. See Blackwell, B and Eilon, S (1981) *The Global Challenge of Innovation*, London: Butterworth Heinemann.

Chapter 3
1. Andrews, J (1987) 'Privatization – An Emerging Force', in *1987 Britannica Book of the Year*, Chicago: Encyclopedia Britannica Inc.
2. Gow, I, 'Deregulation, Competition and New Industries in Japanese Telecommunications', in Wilks, S and Wright, M (eds) (1991) *The Promotion and Regulation of Industry in Japan*, Basingstoke: Macmillan.

Chapter 4
1. MAI study, June 1991.
2. De Jonquieres, G. 'Just One Cornetto' *Financial Times*, 28 October 1991.
3. Friedman, A, 'The Ascent of Everest: Coca-Cola's plans for a New Global Sales Assault', in *Financial Times* p. 13, 16 January 1992.
4. *Fortune*, 8 July 1991.
5. *Financial Times*, p. 12, 27 January 1992.
6. Fields, G (1989) *The Japanese Market Culture* (2nd Edition), Tokyo: Japan Times.

Chapter 5
1. Womack, J P, Jones, D L T and Roos, D (1990) *The Machine that Changed the World*, New York: Rawson Associates.
2. *Ibid*, p. 87; *Business Week*, pp. 38–43, 10 February 1992.
3. *Fortune*, 13 January 1992.
4. *Business Week*, p. 38, 16 December 1991.
5. *The Guardian*, p. 25, 27 July 1989; *The European*, p. 19, 7 September 1990.
6. *Fortune*, July 1991.
7. *The Guardian*, p. 11, 11 January 1992.
8. Lynn, M (1991) *The Billion Dollar Battle: Merck v Glaxo*, London: Heinemann.
9. *International Herald Tribune*, p. 11, 8 November 1991.
10. Asher, D A (1991) *Managing Brand Equity*, New York: Free Press, cited in *The Economist*, p. 89, 7 September 1991.
11. *The Economist*, p. 130, 19 October 1991.
12. Porter, M E (1990) *The Competitive Advantage of Nations*, New York: Free Press, pp. 611–15.
13. Umberto Busolati Dell'Orto, Olivetti's Vice President of Corporate Development, cited in *Financial Times*, p. 24, 29 May 1990.
14. Madnick, S E, 'The Information Technology Platform', in Scott Morton, M S (ed.) (1991) *The Corporation of the 1990s*, New York: Oxford University Press, pp. 27–60.

Chapter 6
1. Author's observations and letter from Professor Daniel Jones, June 1992.
2. Servan–Schreiber, J-J (1968) *The American Challenge*, London: Hamish Hamilton.
3. Vogel, E (1979) *Japan as Number One*, Cambridge, Mass.: Harvard University Press.
4. Ouchi, W (1981) *Theory Z*, Reading, Mass.: Addison-Wesley.
5. Kamata, S (1984) *Japan in the Passing Lane*, London: Counterpoint.
6. Rothacher, A (1983) *Economic Diplomacy Between the European Community and Japan 1959–1981*, Aldershot: Gower.
7. *International Herald Tribune*, 16 May 1991.
8. Johnson, C (1982) *MITI and the Japanese Miracle – The Growth of*

Industrial Polity 1923–1975, Stanford: Stanford University Press.

9. Prestowitz, C V (1988) *Trading Places: How America Allowed Japan to Take the Lead*, Tokyo: Charles E Tuttle Co.

10. Van Wolferen, K (1989) *The Enigma of Japanese Power: People and Politics in a Stateless Nation*, London: Macmillan.

11. Abegglen, J C and Stalk Jr, G (1985) *Kaisha: The Japanese Corporation*, New York: Basic Books.

12. Womack, J P, Jones, D T and Roos, D (1990) *The Machine that Changed the World*, New York: Rawson Associates.

13. Peters, T and Waterman, R (1982) *In Search of Excellence*, Harper & Row.

14. *Financial Times*, p. 34, 16 March 1992.

15. Steve Nagourney's work for Shearson Lehman Brothers, cited in *The Economist*, p. 67, 10 August 1991.

16. *The Economist, Ibid.*

Chapter 7

1. This later appeared as Chapter 25 in Reich, R B (1991) *The Work of Nations*, New York: Knopf.

2. Kennedy, P (1987) *The Rise and Fall of the Great Powers*, New York: Random House.

3. Servan-Schreiber, J-J (1968) *The American Challenge*, London: Hamish Hamilton

4. Glickman, N J and Woodward, D P (1989) *The New Competitors: How Foreign Investors are Changing the US Economy*, New York: Basic Books, pp. 265–6.

5. Halberstam, D (1986) *The Reckoning*, New York/Tokyo: Avon Books/Yohan Publications p. 39.

6. Lewis, M (1989) *Liar's Poker: Rising Through the Wreckage on Wall Street*, New York: W W Norton.

7. Julius, D (1990) *Global Companies and Public Policy: The Growing Challenge of Foreign Direct Investment*, London: Royal Institute of International Affairs/Pinter, p. 54.

8. Reich, R B (1991) *The Work of Nations: Preparing ourselves for 21st Century Capitalism*, New York: Alfred A Knopf.

9. Gregory, G (1986) *Japanese Electronics Technology: Enterprise and Innovation (2nd Edition)*, Chichester: John Wiley, p. 80.

10. Horseley, W and Buckley, R (1990) *Nippon: New Superpower: Japan Since 1945*, London: BBC Books, p. 41.

11. Aho, M C and Levinson, M (1988) *After Reagan: Confronting the Changed World Economy*, New York: Council on Foreign - Relations, p. 166.

12. See Choate, Pat (1990) *Agents of Influence: How Japanese Lobbyists are Manipulating Western Political and Economic Systems*, London: Business Books, pp. 7–8.

13. Tolchin M and Tolchin, S (1988) *Buying into America: How Foreign*

Money is Changing the Face of our Nation, New York: Times Books, p. 209.

14. *Ibid.*, pp. 68–70.
15. Glickman, N J and Woodward, D P, *op. cit.*, pp. 210–12.
16. Tolchin, M and Tolchin, S, *op. cit.*, p. 128.
17. Glickman, N J and Woodward, D P, *op. cit.*, pp. 264–6.
18. *Ibid.*, p. 268.
19. Aho, MC and Levinson, M, *op. cit.*, pp. 168–9.
20. Magaziner, M C and Reich, R B (1982) *Minding America's Business: The Decline and Rise of the American Economy*, New York: Harcourt Brace Jovanovich/Law and Business Inc, p. 226.
21. Aho, M C and Levinson, M, *op. cit.*, p. 170.
22. Long, W J (1989) *US Export Control Policy: Executive Antonomy vs Congressional Reform*, New York: Columbia University Press, pp. 15–18.
23. Glickman, N J and Woodward, D P, *op. cit.*, p. 263.
24. Ishihara, S (1991) *The Japan That Can Say 'No'*, New York: Simon & Schuster.
25. *Ibid.*, p. 21.
26. Hodges, M R, 'The Japanese Industrial Presence in America: Same Bed, Different Dreams, in Newland, K (1990) *The International Relations of Japan*, London: Macmillan, pp. 45–70.
27. Glickman, N J and Woodward, D P, *op. cit.*, p. 269.
28. *Financial Times*, p. 20, 12 September 1990.
29. Magaziner, I C and Reich, R B, *op. cit.*, p. 4.
30. Servan-Schreiber, J-J, *op. cit.*, p. 12.
31. *International Herald Tribune*, p. 13, 24 January 1990.
32. Krugman, P (1990) *The Age of Diminished Expectations*, Cambridge, MA: MIT Press, pp. 108–13.
33. Schlosstein, S (1989) *The End of the American Century*, New York: Congdon & Weed, pp. 112–13.
34. Burrough, B and Helyar, J (1990) *Barbarians at the Gate*, London: Jonathan Cape.
35. 'The Future of Banking', in *Business Week*, pp. 36–45, 22 April 1991.
36. Quoted in Schlosstein, S, *op. cit.*, p. 480.

Chapter 8
1. Servan-Schreiber, J-J (1968) *The American Challenge*, London: Hamish Hamilton.
2. Hodges, M R, 'Industrial Policy: Hard Times or Great Expectations?', in Wallace, H. Wallace, W and Webb, C (eds) (1983) *Policy Making in the European Community (2nd Edition)*, New York: John Wiley, pp. 265–93.
3. *Financial Times*, p. 31, 5 July 1989.
4. James, B G (1989) *Trojan Horse: The Ultimate Japanese Challenge to Western Industry*, London: Mercury Books, p. 27.

5. *Fortune*, p. 29, 2 July 1990.
6. Turner, L (1987) *Industrial Collaboration with Japan*, London: Royal Institute of International Affairs/Routledge & Kegan Paul, p. 40.
7. George, S (1985) *Politics and Policy in the European Community*, Oxford: OUP, p. 7.
8. Wallace, H, Wallace, W and Webb, C (eds) (1983) *op. cit.* p. 82.
9. Colchester, N and Buchan, D (1990) *Europe Relaunched: Truths and Illusions on the way to 1992*, London: Hutchinson Business Books, p. 7.
10. Swann, D (1983) *Competition and Industrial Policy in the European Community*, London: Methuen, p. 85.
11. Woolcock, S, Hodges, M and Schreiber, K (1991) *Britain, Germany and 1992: The Limits of Deregulation*, London: RIIA/Pinter, pp. 265–6.
12. *Financial Times*, p. 24, 20 September 1990.
13. *The European*, p. 19, 11 October 1991.

Chapter 9
1. *International Herald Tribune*, p. 4, 16 March 1990.
2. Kennedy, P (1987) *op. cit.*, p. 494.
3. *International Herald Tribune*, p. 9, 28–29 December 1991.
4. Harrison, M. 'Fiat leads drive into East', *The Independent on Sunday* p.6 19 January 1992.

Chapter 10
1. *Fortune*, pp. 32–9, 9 March 1992.
2. Womack, J P, Jones, D T and Roos, D (1990) *The Machine that Changed the World* (New York: Rawson Associates), pp. 262–3.
3. See Robert Wade in *The Economist*, p. 91, 4 April 1992.
4. *International Herald Tribune*, p. 9, 9 March 1992.

Chapter 11
1. *Observer*, 8 September 1991.

Chapter 12
1. *The Economist*, p. 19, 24 April 1992.
2. *The Economist*, p. 103, 13 July 1991.
3. *The Economist*, p. 69, 3 August 1991.
4. *The Economist*, pp. 117–26, 16 November 1991.

Chapter 13
1. McLuhan, M (1968) *War and Peace in the Global Village*;
   Ohmae, K. (1990) *The Borderless World*, London: Collins;
   O'Brien, R. (1992) *Global Financial Integration: The End of Geography*, London: R11A/Pinter;
   Grundwald, J. & Flamm, K. *The Global Factory: Foreign Assembly in International Trade*, Washington DC: Brookings;
   Fukuyama, F. (1992) *The End of History and the Last Man*, London: Hamish Hamilton.

SUGGESTED FURTHER READING

It will be apparent from the end-notes to each chapter which books we have found most useful as source material. The books mentioned below are ones that readers of our book might like to consult for other perspectives on the topics we have covered.

Bartlett, Christopher and Sumantra Ghoshal (1989) *Managing Across Borders: The Transnational Solution*, London: Century Business.
An interesting and influential study of organizational structures in leading multinationals, which advocates a transnational framework based on clear delegation of authority to maintain flexibility and avoid over-complex organization. They stress the need for overall strategic planning to be carried out at the top, but coordination to be as much a product of shared corporate values as of direct supervision.

Contractor, Farok and Lorange, Peter (1988) *Cooperative Strategies in International Business*, Lexington, Mass: Lexington Books.
A standard text, which provides a thorough (if now somewhat dated) analysis of the structure and performance of cooperative ventures between firms. Its examples are drawn not only from Europe, North America and Japan, but also from developing countries.

Czinkota, Michael, Rivoli, Pietra, and Ronkainen, Ilkka (1989) *International Business*, Chicago: Dryden Press.
Another widely-used text, covering most aspects of international business. Although somewhat simplistic in some of its coverage of business-government relations, it contains some valuable mini-cases and is very clear and well-organized. Discusses: (1) IB activity and theory; (2) Trade and financial environment; (3) Business-government relations; (4) Strategic management issues.

Dicken, Peter (1992) *Global Shift: The Internationalization of Economic Activity* *(2nd Edition)* London: Chapman.
Probably the best text on international business written by a non-business school academic (in this case an economic geographer). Discusses the

patterns and processes of globalization, and includes case-studies of industries such as financial services and automobiles. Outlines adjustment problems following globalization and is notable for its clear discussion of economic theories of direct investment.

Drucker, Peter (1989) *The New Realities*, London: Heinemann.
This book by one of the world's leading management experts is a somewhat uneven but consistently interesting discussion of the impact of technology (especially information technology and telecommunications) on the structure of society and ways of governing and doing business. Particularly interesting on the post-cold war global business environment and the need to make ecological matters a priority.

Dunning, John H. (1988) *Explaining International Production*, London: Unwin Hyman.
Professor John Dunning is one of the leading academic experts on the growth of the multinational firm, and this book of essays on the changing characteristics of international production shows him to be a broad-minded economist with a commitment to interdisciplinary research based on wide experience in both studying and advising firms and governments.

Freeman, Christopher, Sharp, Margaret and Walker, William (eds) (1991) *Technology and the Future of Europe: Global Competition and the Environment in the 1990s*, London: Pinter.
A very useful and frequently thought-provoking survey of the issues that the EC will face in the 1990s in industrial development, technology and competitiveness, and the economic and political environment in which it operates.

Julius, DeAnne (1990) *Global Companies and Public Policy: The Growing Challenge of Foreign Direct Investment*, Royal Institute of International Affairs; London: Pinter.
A book that packs a big punch within its 120 or so pages; it challenges many of the existing assumptions of governments about foreign direct investment and makes some original and well-conceived points about necessary policy changes on the part of both home and host governments.

Mytelka, Lynn (ed) (1991) *Strategic Partnerships: States, Firms and International Competition*, London: Pinter.
Discusses the phenomenon of 'strategic alliances', covering inter-firm agreements and government-industry relations in technology in the US, Europe and Japan. Includes chapters on commercial aircraft and tele-communications. Also includes a chapter on linkages established in the context of the EC's ESPRIT collaborative R&D initiative.

Ohmae, Kenichi (1990) *The Borderless World: Power and Strategy in the Interlinked Economy*, London: Collins.

The originator of the concept of the Triad (Europe, North America and Japan) as the key arena in global competition, Ohmae develops his argument that it is now consumers – not governments or even multi-nationals – that are determining business success or failure. Firms must globalize and respond quickly and flexibly to consumer tastes in the different markets of the world economy. Stimulating rather than conclusive.

Ostry, Sylvia (1990) *Governments and Coporations in a Shrinking World*, New York: Council on Foreign Relations Press.
Written from the perspective of an experienced trade negotiator committed to liberalizing trade, it discusses trade and innovation policies of the US, Japan and the EC, and outlines prospects for the international regulatory framework.

Porter, Michael (1990) *The Competitive Advantage of Nations*, London: The Macmillan Press Ltd.
A rather turgid but extremely thorough and influential study exploring the determinants of competitive advantage on the basis of an examination of more than 100 industries, with numerous well-researched case studies. Porter identifies a highly competitive home market as a key factor in ensuring that a country's firms can expand their market share abroad.

Robock, Stefan and Simmonds, Kenneth (1989) *International Business and Multinational Enterprises (4th Edition)*, Homewood, Ill.: Irwin. (5th Edition forthcoming)
The best single international business textbook, particularly strong on the international monetary, trade and regulatory environment and global business strategies.

Strange, Susan and Stopford, John M. with Henley John S. (1991) *Rival States, Rival Firms: Competition for World Market Shares*, Cambridge, UK: Cambridge University Press.
An unusual collaborative effort by a leading international relations expert (Strange) and a business school academic (Stopford), discussing the changing relationships between firms in the world economy, between firms and host governments, and between both host and home governments. It includes valuable case studies on Brazil, Kenya and Malaysia, showing that no single strategy can effectively govern firm-state relationships in all countries or even in one country, but that a mutually beneficial firm-state partnership is possible.

Vernon, Raymond and Wells, Louis (1991) *The Economic Environment of International Business (5th Edition)*, Englewood Cliffs, New Jersey: Prentice Hall.
Two of the main American academic experts on foreign investment provide a valuable survey of the field.

INDEX

Index